CW00481382

# THE BRITISH
# Deer Stalking
## BIBLE

*Peter Carr*

**Author**
Peter Carr
**Design**
Lynne Stephens
**Editor**
Charlie Jacoby
**Sub-editor**
Liz Henry
**Cover photograph**
istockphoto
**Photography**
Unless otherwise stated, the photography is credited to the
remarkable lens of Brian Phipps (Riflephoto.com)

*British Library Cataloguing-in-Publication Data*
A catalogue record for this book is available from the British Library

ISBN 978-0-9549597-1-5

Printed in England by Butler, Tanner & Dennis

Blaze Publishing Ltd
Lawrence House, Morrell Street, Leamington Spa, Warwickshire CV32 5SZ
T: 01926 339808
F: 01926 470400
E: info@blazepublishing.co.uk
W: www.blazepublishing.co.uk

# Contents

# *Introduction*

I have been incredibly fortunate to have spent much of my adult working life in pursuit of British big game in one form or another. I have stalked marauding seals on the spectacular coastline of North Yorkshire; roebucks, water deer and muntjac on England's great estates; wild boar and sika in the northern spruce forests; wild goats on Welsh cliffs and Irish islands and the most majestic of them all, the red stag among Scotland's granite Highland cathedrals and it has all been bloody good fun along the way. If I could go back and change anything it would be to do it all again.

But you too can sample some or all of this sport. It is the right of every person of sound mind to possess a Firearms Certificate (FAC), if you have a good reason to do so. The 'good reason' is the stumbling block that stops most aspiring rifle sportsmen applying. However, good reason can be for sporting pursuits such as deerstalking. All it entails is confirmation of previous and future stalking outings with a professional stalker or outfitter. It's as simple as that.

Successful completion of the DSC level 1 course goes a long way to pacifying your firearms officer. This is not a legal requirement but it will show that you are serious about your sport. The firearms officer has the considerable responsibility of deciding whether to let you loose with a firearm. He or she will assess you during his or her visit to check your security situation - including noting the number of empty wine or beer bottles beside the bin and any bruises on your wife or husband.

Once in possession of your firearms certificate, you become an ambassador for the shooting community. This carries with it grave responsibility. Safety first and good manners second. A chancy shot is the mark of a moron and should never be considered.

Manners is one of my bugbears. A chance encounter with a member of the public as you push your way out of the trees on to a forest ride has all the ingredients of a disaster. They may be trespassing, but you may not be sure of that and even if they have strayed off the public road or footpath you must look at it from their side. A man, no doubt dressed in camo, emerges from the trees with rifle, complete with telescopic sight and a big silencer; this will be something of a shock for the average townie. You must be polite and stop them from panicking. You should point out any error in their direction, show them the right way and wish them good day. If you are suspicious, follow the same tack but immediately report the situation to the authorities when it is safe to do so. Never be drawn into an argument even if it is clear that the trespasser is poaching. Deer are not classed as game in law (nobody knows what wild boar are classed as) and the stalker has no power of arrest in the way the gamekeeper does. Taking action while you have a gun in your hands is folly.

Better to retire from the field and call the police. If the trespasser is armed, events will move quickly and no doubt involve a helicopter and an armed police response unit. I have no desire to be caught up in such a situation. The best place to be is behind police lines not in front of them.

So what to shoot? Britain has a small selection of big game animals and most of them numerous. All six deer species are expanding, as is the wild boar, after being missing from our fauna for more than 300 years and our other more unusual animals, such as the feral goat and Soay sheep have become more available. I have included all the species that can be legally pursued across our isles and Ireland, with the exception of the seal. Hunting seals is an emotive issue. In former times, he was considered a worthy quarry on our coastline, but due to anti hunting propaganda, the shooting of seals has become something of a taboo even within stalking circles.

There is a lesson to be learned from this. Few support the practice of clubbing helpless grey seal pups to death and that is the image the antis have successfully seared into the minds of most of our country's populace, shooters included. The seal is a significant threat to our migratory game fish and other commercial fisheries. The grey seal and the common seal are thriving around our coasts and due to recent legislation that has slipped through (without mention in the sporting press)

negating the 1970 Conservation of Seals Act – which actually contains shooting seasons for both seal species – an individual licence must now be applied for if you want to shoot any seal at all.

The lesson is this: if backdoor bureaucracy has succeeded once then it may happen again. We have a limited number of big game species in Britain and Ireland to pursue in comparison with our continental cousins and we mustn't lose any of them. The game shooter has lost the capercaillie; the wildfowler, the redshank and the curlew (except in Northern Ireland). Oddities may not be the bread and butter of all stalkers, but we should support a fellow hunter's interest.

Furthermore, we must be seen to be managing our quarry in an ethical and sporting manner. The rising deer population has many adverse effects on commercial forestry and agricultural interests. Both professional and amateur stalkers are an integral part of the overall management plan to keep this population in check.

This book is not about deer management. It is about amateur stalking for pleasure. However, we do have a serious job to perform when pursuing our chosen sport and we should attempt as far as possible, to achieve the deer cull targets set out in any management plan, on our particular shooting ground.

This book is not a 'How to' or a 'How not to' kind of publication, but rather is written in the spirit of, 'You can do this too'. All the basic requirements and advice are here to get you into the field. You may learn what to expect and what choice of quarry is available in these isles. This book also includes some of my personal experiences and those of selected colleagues.

Deerstalking and the pursuit of our other sporting species have brought me a lifetime of pleasure. The oft used cliché, 'It's the taking part that counts' is applicable to stalking. Results really aren't everything - indeed failures actually enhance the successes. It will often be hard work, sometimes physically demanding, but it will always be an enjoyable experience nevertheless. Stalking is practised in the wild and wonderful corners of our lands and islands; the stunning locations, coupled with the element of difficulty involved are what make stalking so rewarding. The troubles and woes of daily life are dispelled when we head to the hills or forests in pursuit of sport. This – and the exercise involved – makes stalking a healthy pastime. When we are fortunate enough to grass a beast, the freezer will be stocked with the best free range and leanest meat that Tesco could only dream of.

The object of this book is to inspire new enthusiasts to take up the sport or tempt fellow stalkers to try new species and areas of our varied countryside. Stalking is mostly a solitary sport, unless of course you take Fido into consideration, and all of us – if individual circumstances allow – should aspire to own and work a competent deer dog.

Years from now, when the passage of time has allayed your wanderings and the rifle is gathering dust, there will be a time to reminisce with a fine malt and the photo album upon your lap. Personal memories and photographs will take one back to former times of solitary triumphs and failures. All of these will be re-lived with a familiar fondness, and you will say 'I did that'. ⊙

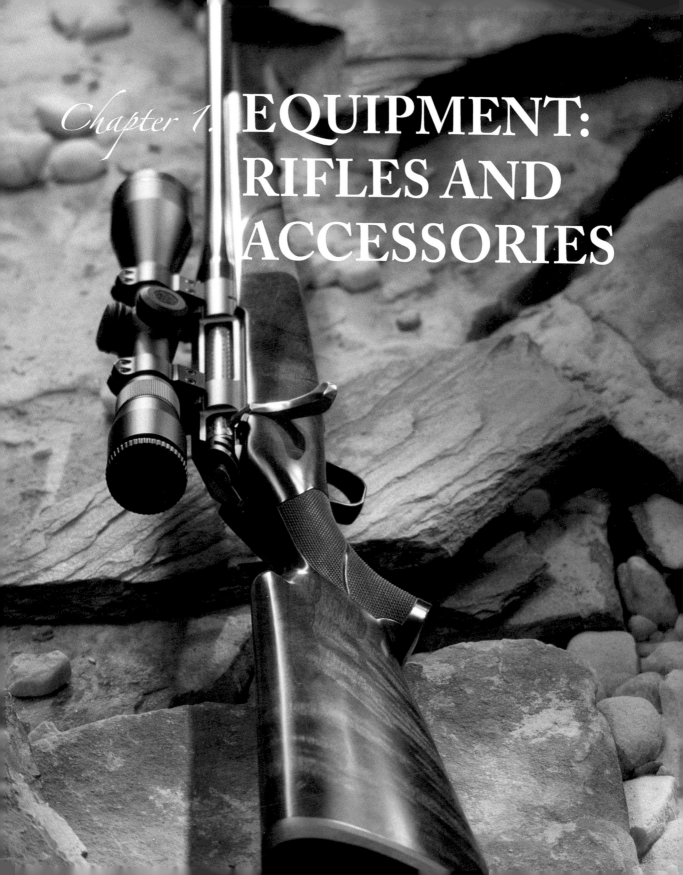

# Chapter 1. EQUIPMENT: RIFLES AND ACCESSORIES

The sportsman who has just acquired his or her FAC will have had in nearly all cases, some degree of stalking experience, as either a guest or at least an observer. Many constabularies advise prospective applicants to pass their DSC Level 1 course which gives any prospective stalker a good grounding in the sport.

Either way, you will soon have to look at the purchase of binoculars, scope, rifle, knife and other essential equipment. Today, there are a myriad options when it comes to stalking equipment. We'll come on to rifles in a minute. Let's look at optics first.

For many years now, I have considered a rangefinder to be a compulsory item to have with me whenever I take one of the rifles out. Having a rangefinder takes the guesswork out of what is one of the hardest but most essential features of shooting - matching range to the known performance of the rifle.

Leupold's new RX series not only gives you the rangefinding facility, but other modes besides. The one that really caught my eye was the ability to calculate the true ballistic range. With its RXIII, Leupold has taken all the guesswork out of the problem by incorporating an inclinometer in the rangefinder. It gives you three true ballistic range readouts: MOA (minutes of angle of elevation for accurate zeroing); 'hold' (number of inches or centimetres to hold over or under the target) and BAS (equivalent horizontal range for your chosen ammunition). This makes the biggest difference on steep ground when taking shots of more than 200 yards. At these sort of distances, when shooting at the 4in kill area of a fox, accurate ranging can make the difference between a clean kill and a miss. Below this range, most centrefires will only be an inch or so out.

For binoculars, I am currrently using Leica Duovid in 8-12x42, because an unscrupulous stalking client decided he liked my Steiners better than his own and liberated them from my Land Rover. The Duovids have however proved excellent and surpass many other makes and models with their flexible switch power feature. Use the lower magnification to spot your subject, then increase the magnification to view greater detail. The Duovid features an automatic diopter compensation, which automatically adjusts when switching powers. Superior lens coatings and high-quality optical glass provide you with exceptional views. That said, I do miss my Steiners. The company has a fantastic range of binoculars available to the stalker.

There are two different types of prism used in binoculars. The first is called the porro prism. First used in 1854 by Ignatio Porro, it is bigger and chunkier and although superior to the roof prism, is being superseded by the sleeker roof prism.

The reason the porro prism is more effective is because the light must change direction only four times. Each change of direction costs around 20 per cent in terms of light quality if lenses aren't treated.

Roof prisms, however require five changes of direction. They also need a mirror – itself made of 72 layers of different material – and are more complex and expensive to produce. They also require a focus lens – a mechanical part – and are therefore inherently less rugged.

*◑ Binos are measured by their magnification, followed by the size of the objective lens in millimetres. So an 8–12x56 offers zoom magnification of 8–12 and a 56mm objective lens*

❂ *Hill stalking is where good glass comes into its own. Buy bigger objective lenses for more light gathering*

So, in a porro system, after four changes of direction, the light quality is 20 per cent of what it was to begin with. The only way to improve the light transmission is for the lenses to undergo a process known as coating.

Lenses are coated in multiple layers of various metals. This helps improve the light transmission – that is, stops any light 'leaking out'. The actual 'recipe' of metal compounds used for each model is a trade secret.

For Steiner's Nighthunter XP binoculars, which are specifically designed to give extremely high light transmission, each side of each lens receives up to 13 different layers of steamed-on metal. To coat the lenses, a carousel is first loaded with lenses and put in the top of an oven. A pot of metal is put in the bottom.

The oven then becomes a vacuum. The lenses slowly rotate as the oven heats up. Once it reaches 3,000°C the container of metal opens and the vapour rises, coating one side of the lens. The metals used depend on which product the lenses are destined for. Some, like the Nighthunters, require many different coatings. The result is improved light transmission.

I would also consider Zeiss's Conquest 56 binoculars. Lightweight and easy to use, the Conquest 8x56 T* and 10x56 T* hunting optics are dust proof and waterproof and are fitted with robust rubber armouring. The prisms feature a phase-correction coating for increased contrast and a four-part lens system gives top optical performance. They come with a high-quality cordura bag, a neoprene carrying strap, an eyepiece cover and a cleaning cloth.

Shepherd's optics give crisp images in everything from bright sunshine to misty conditions. At 1.5lb, Shepherd binos are light enough to carry around all

➲ *Opinion may be divided about which optics manufacturers are in League Division One. In the Premier League of light transmission, however, are Zeiss and Swarovski*

day, and the solid hinge gives added robustness. The unit balances nicely, and has a central focusing wheel with a dioptre adjustment.

The Victory RF binoculars from Zeiss have an operating temperature range of -10°C to +50°C. There's an integrated laser rangefinder and a BIS ballistic program to make calculations easier and rubber armouring protects the binoculars against jolts and shocks. Two models are available - the Victory 8x45 RF and Victory 10x45 RF.

The Frontier ED models offer the user crisp, clear and bright high-resolution viewing. The body, made from magnesium alloy, is strong and stable. All models are nitrogen-purged to avoid fogging and they are sealed to be fully waterproof. The 'open hinge' cut-away design reduces weight. A hard protective case, stay-on lens caps and a comfort neck strap are provided with the binoculars which are available in green and black.

I like Swarovski's EL 10x42 WB. Swarovski's EL binoculars offer low weight, combined with high-contrast, quality images. The large focusing wheel is easy to use when wearing gloves, while the wrap-around grip and thumb rests make light work of long observation periods.

Among the lower orders of binocular manufacturers, Bushnell's flagship binocular line, Elite boasts twist-up eyecups that have four locking positions. The binoculars offer 90% light transmission, BaK-4 roof prisms and a three-phase coating to boost image clarity and contrast. A fully waterproof and fogproof construction ensures the Elite can withstand any shooting conditions.

It is handy to have a pair of compact binos in one's pocket at all times - when you don't you certainly miss them. Hawke's rubber-armoured binoculars have fully coated optics for a brighter, clearer image. They're shockproof and water resistant, and conveniently fold down to pocket size when not in use. The zip-up carry case has a belt loop and wrist strap for easy carrying.

A draw scope is to the hill stalker what a kukri knife is to a Gurkha. But these specialist optics are not for use on the heather-clad hills alone. More and more low-ground stalkers are adding a telescope to their must have equipment list as they have proved invaluable for assessing trophy quality. They may be clunky and lack the nitrogen filling that makes non-draw optics so appealing but they are part of the theatre of stalking. I certainly would not be without mine. I have asked two stalkers, one from the hill and one from the low ground, to share their views on the two main options available to the stalker: the Gray and the Swarovski draw scopes.

Yorkshire roe stalker Gordon Hicks reports: "The new extended Swarovski CTS 85 is the successor model to the CTS 85 which I liked very much indeed. With the many improvements to detail, this telescope once again sets new standards. Particularly striking, however, is the new, more ergonomic design with full rubber outer casing, already a popular feature on other Swarovski telescopes, and the special carrying harness which is simplicity in itself. As expected, this telescope has excellent light transmission, whatever the weather conditions, and a larger field of view than the Gray, although there was little, if any, difference in clarity.

"With a short amount of practice, rapid and precise focusing became second nature using the tube scale for estimating distance.

"This scope has an extremely compact construction, which when collapsed fits comfortably in a jacket pocket, rucksack or between the Freelander's front seats with ease. Plus the integral lens covers and carrying harness are designed for hands-free movement when out stalking. The harness and covers also ensure rapid deployment and protect against moisture and dirt.

"The overall construction is both shock- and sound-proof, due to the rubber armouring. It is also non-reflective and pleasant to handle, even in sub-zero temperatures.

"I use my own Swarovski scope more often from the car to assess heads, and in this situation the Gray is a little too long. However, when actually out stalking, I usually use my own Swarovski placed on the shooting sticks, as they do make an effective bipod. For these reasons I favour the Swarovski to the Gray."

Angus hill stalker Stuart Donald disagrees. "Gray & Company of Inverness is the only maker of premium quality traditional three-draw spotting telescopes left today," he said. "Almost every other spotting telescope available on the market is a sealed unit, using prisms to reflect and magnify the viewed image. Gray telescopes use inline lenses meaning that the overall length is longer, making it much easier to hold steady, especially in a braced position. This makes the Gray much handier to use on the hill than the Swarovski.

"The Swarovski CTS 85 is shorter and heavier than the Gray, with the result that it is difficult to balance when held free in the hands. A good lean is therefore essential; I found a pair of binoculars made a useful bipod. However the Swarovski does have a slightly larger field of view, making target acquisition quicker."

Traditional Gray telescopes are simple in construction, comprising just lenses and anodised alloy tubes. Stuart said, "Clearly there have been no shortcuts in terms of lens quality and overall design, as the viewed image has excellent clarity and is easy to focus. Gray lenses are produced in Germany using the most advanced technology, and immediately incorporate advances in technology. The anodising process means that the tubes are almost unaffected by moisture, and generally resist scratching and everyday wear and tear.

"There are essentially three great benefits to the traditional design of the Gray telescope: light weight, compact size, and simple operation. The Gray is easy and unobtrusive to carry, and after a few hours stalking on the hill, this really does matter. The design encompasses the latest lens and tube manufacturing technology and quality with a surprising degree of simplicity."

It would certainly seem that where you stalk is the biggest factor to consider when buying a traditional telescope. Both Swarovski and Gray optics are manufactured to the highest quality and perform well. If you are a traditionalist then the Gray telescope is probably the one for you – but then not a lot can beat Swarovski optically.

*◑ The modern spotting scope may offer better optics than the old-fashioned 'draw' type, but there is none of the theatre as the stalker sits down and pulls out his scope with a flourish*

My own choice is the CTS 85, which is the successor model to the CT 85 and incorporates many improvements. The Austrian optics company once again sets new standards with this telescope. Particularly striking is the new, more ergonomic design with full rubber outer casing, already a popular feature on other Swarovski telescopes, but including a simple integral carrying harness. I wouldn't be without my drawscope as it gives me a new dimension in quarry identification and trophy assessment.

For rifle scope, the choice is as knotty as for binos. I use the Swarovski z6i 2-12x50 L/SR illuminated rifle scope. It combines everything you need for different hunting situations – this is the all-in-one hunting rifle scope. Swarovski's sophisticated high light-transmission optical system boasts a large field of view with optimum edge-to-edge sharpness, and two reticle choices in 4A-I and TDS-4I. Additionally separate memory locations for day and night settings, guarantee further functionality that automatically switches off the illumination after a set time.

The choice of scopes is incredibly wide and the price variation is too. Firms such as Zeiss, Swarovski and Schmidt & Bender sell at prices from around £2,000 down to not much less than £1,000. I personally think that there is no doubt that where scopes are concerned, you get what you pay for. In the price range outlined above we find excellent build quality, top of the range optics and in most cases after sales back up. However, there are many less expensive brands who offer such products and service to go with them.

The new Victory FL Diavari riflescope line from Zeiss includes a 4-16x50, 6-24x56 and a 6-24x72. According to Zeiss, these scopes are ideal for hunters, technically skilled long-range marksmen and competitive shooters looking for a high-magnification stalking or long-range riflescope with maximum optical performance. The proven and unique FL concept provides maximum reliability for the shot, particularly at high magnification; shooters can recognise even the tiniest details at long range. The extremely compact dimensions and the innovative Bullet Drop Compensator and Rapid-Z long-range shot concepts, enable the Victory FL Diavari riflescopes to meet even the highest demands while delivering a unique visual experience.

Leupold is a make I rather like, producing excellent scopes which are below the price points of those listed earlier. Kahles is one of the oldest European makes and produces optics on a level with Leupold price-wise. IOR and Meopta are also held in high esteem at this price point.

Moving a little further down the price scale opens up an even bigger selection of goodies to look at. I suppose Deben with their Hawke range are one of the best known and although many of their scopes are for air guns, many are eminently suitable for centrefire use. Some of their special reticles are extremely good giving the user pre-determined aiming points at a variety of ranges; I have used one of these for some time now and find them very good indeed.

The Nikon ProStaff 3-9x50 riflescope is fully waterproof, fogproof, and shockproof, and features ¼MOA click adjustments and multicoated lenses. This scope is parallax adjusted for 100 yards and features a 33.8ft at 100 yards set on

↻ *The secret of stalking is walk little, stop lots. That's why binoculars are so useful*

3x and 11.3ft on 9x. It also features the proven 90 per cent light transmission that has made the Nikon ProStaff line so popular when last light is the most important time of the day. The scope is available in matte and retails for around £229.99.

Bushnell has added two new riflescopes with illuminated reticles to the Elite 6500 line. With their 6.5x magnification range, the Elite 6500 riflescopes offer one of the widest zoom ranges in the industry. The new additions include a 1-6.5x24 and a 2.5-16x50. Both feature a brand new illuminated, etched and thin 4A reticle with digital intensity adjustment. The 1-6.5x model is optimised for driven hunting, and the 2.5-16x model is great for still hunting and stalking. Their 30mm tube construction delivers plenty of light and provides more adjustment for windage and elevation. The 2.5-16x50 model features side parallax and focus adjustment (from 10yds/9m to infinity).

The Zos 3-12x56 scope is ideal for centrefire, rimfire and heavy recoiling rifles, as well as air rifles. The scope features a red illuminated acid-etched mil-dot R19 strong reticle for night or low light conditions. The scope's short, 30mm-diameter, one-piece main tube with large objective lenses gives you greater light transmission.

The Burris 3-9x40 with Ballistic Plex Fullfield II scope features extremely rugged 1in aircraft-grade aluminium outer tubes. They offer outstanding optical quality and light transmission, thanks to the multi-coat lenses and positive reticle adjustment, with double spring-force technology – all at a surprisingly affordable price. It is finished in matte black thanks to the Burris hard-coat anodising process

On the subject of stalking clothing, boots are essential if you visit Britain's wild places. Black Islander, in partnership with Diotto of Italy, imports two of the most innovative boots on the UK market today – the 11in No Scratch boot and the 9in Graphite boot. These boots have a number of unique qualities – the all-leather boots are covered with unique man-made waterproof, yet breathable, new concept rubberised fabric which is bonded onto the leather upper and sole, preventing water from entering the boot at the seam. They also feature a Windex waterproof and breathable liner, lightweight, rust-free eyelets, rubber toe and are shod with the time-served Vibram sole.

For a stalking suit, I choose the Deerhunter Game Stalker suit. It is a light and flexible anorak, trouser and cap, perfectly suited for traditional stalking in Realtree AP camouflage. This pattern is especially suited for the autumn and winter, but I find it perfectly acceptable for spring and summer too. The suit comes in the soft, yet durable Deer-Tex stretch membrane material, which is extremely comfortable is wind and waterproof and comes complete with Velcro-adjustable cuffs, knee-length leg zippers and elasticised waistand and plenty of pockets. The snap-pull adjustable hood is kept out of sight and in place when not in use, by two discreet magnets. A hidden zippered neck pocket contains an integral and practical mosquito net facemask. Regardless of where and when you go hunting, you can rest assured that the combination of Realtree AP and manufacturing quality provides the camouflage and reliability that I have come to expect from Deerhunter.

The importance of good clothing cannot be overstated. This was proved recently when two deerstalkers were rescued after spending a freezing January night on the Campsie Fells, north of Glasgow. Conditions were horrendous on the hill, with snow, low cloud and driving winds.

The stalkers, a local man and his shooting client Nick Atkinson from Newcastle, lost their bearings near Dungoil Hill south of Fintry, as weather conditions worsened and darkness fell.

The alarm was raised on a Sunday morning when the men did not return and a full scale search was immediately triggered by Central Scotland Police. As rescue parties from Lomond Mountain Rescue Team, assisted by a local farmer, scoured the area, they were aided in locating the pair by the sound of gunfire.

The two men were eventually found by rescuers and a Royal Navy rescue helicopter and flown to the Southern General Hospital in Glasgow.

Both men were suffering from the effects of the cold after many hours in freezing winds and driving rain, but are expected make a full recovery.

Nick says it was his Deerhunter RAM jacket and trousers that saved his life. "After spending 29 hours on a Scottish fell in temperatures of -10° centigrade

*The author and his beloved Bavarian mountain hound, Jaeger*

and horrendous blizzards, we ended up getting lost and were eventually airlifted to hospital," he says. "But no hypothermia due to Deerhunter clothing!

"I am a loyal Deerhunter equipment user and won't use anything else, from jackets and trousers to gloves."

To the Deerhunter suit, I might add Black Islander Deluxe gaiters. They are exceptional. A lightweight waterproof but breathable soft upper shell is complimented by a hardwearing Cordura lower shell ankle piece that will defy the roughest of heather. A heavy duty front zipper (often overlooked by other manufacturers) enables simplicity of use with Velcro cover flap. Further features are a robust double-riveted large steel lace hook and pop-studded tie top. These gaiters have been my choice for more than a decade.

The small deer stalker needs a roesack. Mine comes from Decoying UK. This is the best roesack available for the price on the market and comes complete with padded back and shoulder straps and big enough for two roe deer or a sika stag if fully extended. When empty, the sides can be folded in and fastened to narrow the profile whilst stalking in dense cover. Inside there's a removable inner sack with its own internal pocket, ideal for knives and other sterile equipment, in strong washable PVC with three external pockets. Made from hard wearing Cordura, this is the roesack of today.

For stalking sticks, the NOBLOCK telescopic bipod shooting sticks by LEKI use only the highest quality aluminum alloy which, through the company's exclusive heat-treating process, reaches an outstanding level of high tensile strength. Shooting sticks are only as good as their adjustment mechanism and NOBLOCK doesn't disappoint in this department. These shooting sticks are exceptionally well designed, tough, stable and reliable.

Casstrom's Wilderness Puuko knife is an exceptional blade and exceedingly good value for money. Crafted in the Finnish part of Lapland, using traditional methods, this is a knife built for a purpose. Laplanders follow the reindeer herds throughout the year living a nomadic lifestyle. They need a utility knife for the evisceration and skinning of reindeer, as a table utensil, to double and this knife is the perfect choice for the deerstalker.

Garlands' roe and fallow deer trays are perfect for filling your boot space safely with shot game. Tough and extremely practical, they offer exceptional value for money. The roe tray measures 100cmx55cmx15cm and the fallow tray measures 100cmx100cmx12cm.

Stalkers go to the UK's midgiest areas. The ThermaCELL is a revolutionary mosquito and midge repellent. Powered by a small butane cartridge providing the heat necessary to operate the device, a mat saturated with Allethrin - a copy of a naturally occurring insecticide found in chrysanthemum flowers - is placed on top of the heated metal grill, which vaporises the repellent allowing it to rise into the air, creating a 225sq/ft mosquito and midge-free-zone in minutes. This device has revolutionised field sport activities in mosquito and midge infested areas. A highly effective alternative to lotions and sprays, I have used the ThermaCELL worldwide and wouldn't be without it.

Now rifles: optics and clothing are far more important to stalkers but there is something about the rifle that excites enormous debate among stalkers.

The Sauer .202 is considered by many to be the epitome of the European bolt-action switch-barrel rifle. I certainly concur with this statement and own two of them. In terms of build, the .202 is a little unusual, in that the stock is in two pieces, the fore-end and the butt. These attach to a full alloy receiver/action which includes integral 1in scope bases, the trigger group and magazine system.

I have Harris bipods, on these rifles. The YGS-BR 6-9 S-series (swivelling) models have a hinged platform allowing the rifle to be tilted to compensate for uneven ground. The legs fold up under the fore-end for carrying in the field, snapping down quickly when required. They are held under tension in either position by coil springs. All models incorporate drilled extensions to mount standard QD sling swivels.

One advantage of the Sauer 202 is that it is easy to switch barrels. I had a Sauer 202 in .300 Win Mag. The switch barrel arrived in .375HH and, even the first time, swapping them took only a few minutes. The barrel is held in place by three bolts clamping it firmly to the chamber, which in theory, allows for

up to 23 calibre changes. A point to note is that magnum calibres can only be changed for another suitable magnum calibre.

It is not the cheapest rifle in the world, but the quality of product is second to none. There is an added advantage: by changing barrels, and possibly bolt and magazine, depending on calibre choice you could have both a fox and deer rifle with the same stock and action. Although you would obviously have to re-zero or buy a set of quick change mounts and an additional scope sighted for each barrel, it would still be cheaper than having to buy two different rifles of this quality.

The action is all steel and the bolt locks into the chamber end of the barrel with six lugs. The bolt handle has 60° of movement, which leaves a lot of room between the bolt head and the scope. I find the Sauer action smooth – so smooth that working it is almost effortless, picking up and ejecting cartridges with ease. The magazine is a single column feed and the standard clip sits flush with the fore-end. The standard magazine holds three or four shells, depending on calibre and is released by pressing a stud just in front of the mag.

The safety lock of the Sauer 202 is an indirect, firing safety lock. It locks the trigger tongue, the trigger stop and the firing pin nut, thus securing all safety-relevant components. The safety button is positioned on top of the stock grip and is easy to reach with the thumb, as is the well-protected unlock button positioned within the trigger guard. To take the safety off, just push up the unlock button with the trigger finger. Simplicity in itself, after five minutes' practice it becomes second nature.

At the same time, the safety bolt is pushed upwards, which releases a red signal ring indicating it is now ready to fire. To make the rifle safe again you simply push the safety bolt down with your thumb. The trigger is precise and light, with no creep, and comes factory set at 3½lb. Pushing it forward half an inch sets the hair trigger, which then only requires 11oz of pressure to fire.

This rifle comes to the shoulder well, and as such is easily manageable and quick to mount. I enjoy shooting the Sauer 202 in .300 Win Mag. It's a nice looking rifle of European origin, and the action is as smooth and silent as any I've handled. The switch barrel may take slightly longer than some other well-known offerings from the continent, but does that really matter? I found the 202 extremely simple to change and the new barrel fitted to the rifle just as precisely as the original. With the many stock and barrel options available you would be hard pressed not to find the rifle/calibre combination that you wanted with this popular offering.

Sauer is not the only rifle make on the market, as more than 90 per cent of stalkers would be quick to point out. There are plenty of others.

Howa Machinery was founded around 1907. The Japanese company has always maintained a great reputation for making good rifles that prove to be accurate straight out of the box and, above all, considerably less expensive than any of their rivals.

One of the many Howa models, the Lightning 1500 has been produced to provide a reliable, accurate, well-finished rifle at a price within the reach of

*Swapping barrels easily on a Sauer 202*

⊍ *The author's
Sauer 202 in .300
Win Mag with
Harris bipod*

most shooters. The Sporter version can be supplied with a heavy varmint barrel or the lighter Sporter version. Barrels can be blued or stainless and many come factory-threaded for a moderator.

Stocks are rubberised and supplied by Hogue, a company well known for quality. These stocks are grippy, and coupled with the stainless barrel it makes an extremely good weather-resistant rifle. The stock itself is built around a fibreglass structure that forms an excellent support for the action. The fore-end is stippled and together with the characteristic rubberised Hogue finish, provides excellent grip in all weathers. The black recoil pad is solid and this, with the sling swivels, finishes-off a practical and useable stock. The pull is comparatively short at 13¾in – this will not be a problem for the average shooter, although taller people may need to lengthen the stock.

Howa designed the stock to be ambidextrous, which, although making it look rather plain, does not detract at all from the overall appearance.

Those shooters who are interested in custom rifles will know that Howa actions, machine-forged from stainless steel, are often used by custom rifle builders – Weatherby's Vanguard rifles are built on Howa actions. The receiver is drilled and tapped for scope bases and there is a large integral recoil lug on the receiver ring that is bedded securely into the stock. The satin finish of the stainless steel gives a pleasing sheen and look to the whole unit.

The magazine is a hinged floor-plate design, and is not detachable; a lever mechanism situated in the forward section of the trigger guard lets the plate drop under spring tension to allow access to the magazine.

The 7in twin-lugged bolt, cams into the action when the bolt is closed, ensuring excellent positive support. The ejector is a plunger type, and as the claw extractor engages primary extraction, the sprung loaded unit within the bolt body forcibly ejects the spent case. The whole extraction and ejection system works efficiently.

The safety operation is performed by way of a simple sliding knurled lever. This is accessed from the right-hand side of the action tang. In the forward position the rifle is ready to fire. A reasonably quiet rearward roller action back to safe locks the trigger and sear, but still allows you to operate the bolt and safely unload the rifle, should you wish.

The trigger itself is excellent, set at no more than 2lb, it is light, responsive and totally predictable, and it does aid in shrinking those groups down-range. I would choose to leave the factory settings well alone, but you can adjust if you feel competent to do so. You need to remove the stock to gain access to the adjusting screws.

Accuracy is reasonably good. Howa guarantees 1.25in groups at 100 yards, but again, as in most cases, seeking the best round for the rifle and possibly going down the home loading route should close these groups down. In fact, home loaders have already documented instances where the factory guarantee figure has been more than halved.

Tucked away in Cornwall, not far from Liskeard, is the headquarters of RUAG Ammotec UK. Probably best-known as suppliers of top quality ammunition such as Norma, RWS, and Rottweil, it also supplies a wide range of other shooting accessories well known to the shooting world. Possibly the most famous of these is Perazzi shotguns, followed closely by Lightforce, Bettinsoli, Nightforce and the list goes on. So it comes as no surprise to learn that this progressive organisation also has on offer a couple of rifles of undoubted quality.

The firm of Roessler have brought out two interesting rifles known as the Titan 3 and the Titan 6. The Titan 6 (so called for its six-lug system) runs with the bigger stuff – the range of calibres stretches from .243 up to .300 with 16 options in between.

Distributed by RUAG under the RWS brand name, the Titan is made by the Roessler family in Austria, a country long known for quality firearms.

It is a modern bolt-action rifle based on a long history of top quality European workmanship. In my opinion some of the best rifles ever made have come from continental Europe where they have been used for big game hunting for decades. Always innovative and practical, you get the feeling that European rifles are made by folk who really know what shooting is all about.

One of the unusual features of the Titan is that it offers the opportunity to switch barrels. This has practical implications, particularly today when adding rifles can bring your collection under scrutiny from the local constabulary. Another feature is that many of these changes can be carried out without the need to change the bolt face which, if upgrading, will of course entail a substantial saving in outlay.

Another service offered is the Titan configurator chart. This can be looked up online at www.jadg-shop.at. The prospective buyer can choose from a number of options, ranging from the purely cosmetic to the highly practical. There are for instance, six choices of stock and seven choices of barrel supplied by makers such as Heym and Merkel.

The heart of any switch-barrel system has to be the receiver and this is where the Titan claims a difference. Machined from a solid block of aircraft-grade aluminium, it has a cylindrical cross section except for the integral recoil lug machined under the receiver ring. A flat on the bottom houses the trigger group, tang and safety catch, all of which are attached to the receiver by screws. The receiver ring and bridge are drilled and tapped to accept Weaver-type bases. The surfaces have a black anodised finish that matches the nicely prepared blue/black barrels.

As a matter of note the barrels come with no iron sights, which in these days of almost compulsory scope sights, makes perfect sense. Another benefit is they are supplied ready screw-cut for moderator fitting. The barrels come in two lengths: 56cm for standard calibres and 61cm for magnums.

Interestingly, the inside of the receiver is devoid of any grooves or channels. The bolt is guided along its path by the trigger sear protruding into the receiver and engaging with a groove machined into the base of the bolt.

The bolt fit is excellent, producing minimal side movement. This system also allows the bolt to be quickly removed by depressing the trigger which frees the bolt allowing it to slide out. The bolt is of one-piece construction with no protrusions. The locking lugs are machined into the bolt body and when the bolt is closed, these engage in corresponding shoulders located in the rear of the barrel itself. The provides a secure and stress free lock-up. The bolt handle is large and certainly affords a good grip.

The tang-mounted safety is three positional and is situated sensibly on top of the pistol grip. Pushing the slide forward reveals a red dot and the rifle is ready to be fired; bring it back to the centre position and the trigger is safe but the bolt can be opened; and in the rearmost mode the safety locks both bolt and trigger. This is in my opinion one of the best safety systems to be produced on a rifle in a long time.

To change a barrel is simplicity itself. The recoil lug under the receiver is split lengthwise - to change, undo the two transverse Allen screws, slip out the barrel and put the new one in. The fit is a firm push fit – a slot on the barrel shank engages with a pin in the receiver ring to ensure a perfect location.

The magazine is made of steel, with a plastic base and is the same size for all calibres, a filler block being used to take up unwanted space. On depressing two side-mounted plungers simultaneously, the magazine drops out easily.

Scoped up and fitted with a moderator, overall weight adds up to about 9lb. In the field, accuracy should be around half an inch at 100 yards – more than good enough for foxes out to a couple of hundred yards, if not more.

With the range of choices available you can mix and match a rifle to suit your own requirements. I'm not saying this would be a better option than a custom-built piece but it's a good way to at least personalise your rifle.

*❍ A note shows that this Tikka T3's barrel is freefloating*

In the Tikka range, the introduction of the T3 made all earlier Tikka models obsolete. Eyebrows, initially raised when this happened, soon lowered again because the T3 has proved to be an excellent rifle in all its many guises. These take the form of an entry model (the Lite), right up to the Tactical model - with several others in a variety of finishes and calibres in between. Popular as a deer rifle, it is the rifle of choice for the Forestry Commission.

All models of the T3 use the same magazine size, so its construction requires a filler block at the rear, allowing all cartridge lengths to work. The construction of the magazine is polymer. I have to say I am not a great fan, much preferring a metal construction, but the polymer model is nothing if not functional and there are absolutely no feed problems.

The T3 has an adjustable single-stage trigger unit that breaks at a definite 4lb. If adjustment should be necessary, access to the adjustment screw can be made by removing the stock. This weight of trigger pull would be on the heavy side for most shooters and so some adjustment should be beneficial. There is a set trigger option available.

The trigger blade is slim and grooved and there is enough space between it and the trigger-guard for a gloved hand to operate freely. The safety catch is positioned to the right of the bolt shroud and is within comfortable reach of the thumb. It is straightforward to use: forward means the rifle is ready to be fired; back and the rifle is safe, with both bolt and trigger locked.

With its T3 series, Tikka has produced an all-out winner, offering something for everyone, at sensible prices and in a wide choice of finishes and calibres. The maker's biggest head-scratch will be how to produce something even better in the future.

I suspect that virtually every rifle enthusiast will have heard of the legendary Remington 700 – it's a rifle with probably more history attached to it than any other:

It all started with the introduction of the Model 721/722 line of firearms in 1948. They soon caught on due to their build strength and durability. More importantly, they were accurate straight out of the box – something new in those days. When the improved, even more accurate Model 700 was released in 1962, it simply revolutionised the American rifle market.

Few sportsmen all those years ago would have believed that nearly 50 years later the 700 would still be going strong. Today, the Model 700 is still known for its accuracy and its timeless aesthetics, not to mention its continued usage in the hands of the US Marine Corps.

Remington has produced some 50 different variations from classic wood to modern synthetics. Calibres are many and varied, ranging from the .17 Remington up to safari calibres like the .375 and .458. The same basic rifle can be found in the hands of both rabbiters and professional hunters in Africa. With manufacturing figures heading towards four million, it is a classic that's showing every sign of continuing its success.

Why is it then that this particular rifle has caught on as well as it has? Much has to do with the subtle changes Remington has brought in over the years.

Modern Remington 700s come in many guises, not least synthetic or laminated stock versions, as well as a stainless steel, fluted-barrel variety and tactical rifles. Yet the original timeless appeal is still there.

There is another factor too. The action, designed by Mike Walker, is often described as the world's strongest bolt-action. Its strength stems from the receiver, which starts life as a solid piece of round bar stock, and is milled into shape to resist distortions. The bolt is substantial in construction and the lock-up is achieved via a pair of opposing locking lugs. The bolt face is recessed to cover the rear portion of the cartridge and there is a plunger-style ejector with space for the extractor within the bolt face. Though small, it cleanly removes a spent round from the chamber.

Counter-boring the bolt face to fit snugly into the back of the barrel enhances the strong, rigid lock-up characteristics of the system and the lock-time is good. Firing pin travel is approximately 0.3in, helping to achieve maximum accuracy.

The detachable one-piece trigger unit does need some tweaking. Although the trigger breaks cleanly enough, the pull is heavy, as is the case with many American rifles. There are custom-built units on the market that will solve this problem and advice can be obtained from many of the professional gunsmiths, such as Mike Norris and Chris Bowers. After all these years the Model 700 remains a benchmark firearm – long may this continue.

Ammunition is loaded through the top of the receiver as the magazine is a blind box system, there is no hinged floor plate attached to the trigger guard. As there are less cut-outs in this system, the stock is that much stronger. The barrel is not free floated but is bedded near the front of the barrel channel in the stock; bedding of the action comes in the form of pillar columns to the stock screw recesses to stop material compression and the recoil lugs' rear face is bedded against an alloy block.

As far as accuracy goes, this rifle will print sub-1in groups at 100 yards and devotees of home-loading their own ammunition will be able to improve on this.

I have always liked Heym rifles, stemming back to the first time I saw a deer shot – the rifle was a Heym. Since then I have owned a couple of my own and always been impressed by them. The latest offering, the Heym SR21 Classic, is a great-value rifle that's accurate, reliable and beautifully crafted.

Heym is one of the top German manufacturers associated with high-quality, desirable stalking rifles, but for some reason their products have never really caught on over here. I'm not sure why, as they really are extremely well-made, accurate and beautifully finished.

From a handling point of view, the Heym SR21's classic lines and stock make it a joy to shoot. The long fore-end affords a good grip and the length of pull makes for a comfortable hold. There are several stock options with various grades of walnut available, obviously costing more than the standard production model. For those who like continental styling, a hog's back stock is an option. The Classic model's walnut has straight-grained figuring, albeit a little light in colour for my taste, and is nicely finished with a rubbed oil surface. The stock measures 14½in and has well-cut chequering on both fore-end and pistol-grip. The pistol-grip cap has an insert that can be changed to suit personal taste.

The engineering, as one would expect from a German manufacturer, is first class; the action is 8¾in long – more than adequate for bedding purposes. The top of the action is drilled and tapped for scope bases. Reeves, the importers of Heym rifles, has adapted sets of Leupold mounts to fit the SR21 perfectly and allow for a wide range of sizes. The bolt is quite long and has six four-inch straight flutes to reduce friction and weight; it is of one-piece construction and has three locking lugs. The lower lug lifts up a cartridge from the magazine while the lug positioned at 10 o'clock has a sprung extractor claw, the third lug incorporating a plunger-type extractor button. There is a recess behind the lugs, each of which are angled for an extremely smooth pick-up, typical of this manufacturer's attention to detail. A sprung plunger at the base of the shroud prevents the cocking piece from moving until the bolt is fully closed, so you need to overcome the slight pressure consciously as you close the bolt.

The barrel is a slender sporter profile with a muzzle diameter of 0.555in, and is threaded for a moderator at the factory so you can guarantee that it is well cut and concentric to the bore. The 22¾in length is right on a sporting arm – not too long but long enough to achieve good ballistics.

To the rear of the bolt shaft is the prominent bolt shroud that houses the safety and cocking piece. The safety is a wing-type model which operates as a lever on top of the shroud and this has a three-position function.

Forward (red dot) and the rifle can be fired; fully rearward (large white dot) and the bolt and trigger are locked; and in a halfway position (small white dot) the trigger is safe and the bolt can be operated if you need to remove a cartridge from the barrel's chamber for safety reasons.

The trigger has a crisp, single-stage pull of 3½lb and little creep. It also has the option pushing the trigger blade forward to operate the 'set' mode and reduce the trigger pull weight to a hair's breadth.

The trigger is adjustable via an Allen screw through the front of the guard. It is nice to find a metal magazine - this is a straight-feed system and houses three rounds. The mag is detachable by means of a large, external push-operated button recessed into the right underside of the stock.

A firm push and the magazine pops out under pressure from a wire plunger, like the Sauer rifle method. It is worth a mention that a replacement magazine costs over £100 to replace – so don't lose it!

The Heym SR21 is available in many models, from short-barreled Keiler to upgraded Concord models with superior wood and more ornate engraving. When you look at what is available on the market at the same price, I cannot understand why Heym is not more popular in this country. These are excellent, accurate rifles and, as I've found from my own experience, a joy to use.

I'd heard rumours from the RPA stable about a prototype .308 with a short barrel. There is certainly more stock than barrel, making the balance quite different to most rifles. Yet at the same time, it feels just right. Even after fitting the Ase Utra Jet Z compact suppressor the gun doesn't seem muzzle-heavy – unusual for most sporting centrefires. In fact, the balance reminds me of lighter Anschutz carbines in .22LR and .17HMR, so the concept isn't new – it's just a concept rarely seen in a rifle destined for the deer stalking market.

Visually, it looks exactly the same as the RPA Thumbhole Hunter, but with a short 16in threaded barrel. It is available with an equally hardy and hard-wearing general purpose stock. Add an average-length suppressor and the barrel length will be approximately 20-22in long – the same length as most sporting barrels. As with all RPAs, accuracy is not compromised, so the four-lugged Quadlock bolt system, coupled with its two-stage trigger assembly (set at 0.8lb), makes for a smooth and simple action. This is not a particularly light rifle, weighing in at 8.4lb, but remember that it is highly accurate, with a guaranteed accuracy of 0.5MOA (min ½in group at 100 yards) when using average-quality ammo. To guarantee this, light actions and thinner barrels cannot be used if several shots are taken in short succession. You may argue that a woodland stalker, other than when zeroing in, will never have the need to take multi-shot sessions, but for an extra 1-1.5lb, you could have one of the most accurate sporting rifles on the market.

T/C stands for Thompson/Center. This company is popular with sport hunters throughout the United States. Indeed, the Contender Carbines made by T/C have become an industry standard across the pond. It was still a surprise to many in the industry however, when T/C launched a bolt-action rifle named the Icon into an already-crowded marketplace. No doubt the closing of Winchester's New Haven plant encouraged the company to make this bold move.

Paul Mauser developed his 1898 action 110 years ago and hosts of talented people and arms companies have reworked, refined and augmented that design. That said, T/C has produced a truly new design of centrefire rifle with detachable magazine, combining the best elements of several rifles to make an excellent contemporary stalker.

The handsome walnut stock has clean, classic lines, a relatively open grip and 20-lpi borderless chequering. For a rifle in this price bracket the walnut is surprisingly high quality. Apparently T/C has 600 walnut blanks in stock from its old days in the wood trade, which would suggest that if this rifle takes your fancy, you should buy one while stocks last (literally) – when this walnut supply is exhausted, it could well have an upwards effect on price.

The rifle's well-figured and red hued walnut stock has a smooth oiled finish. Generous panels on grip and fore-end feature neatly-cut chequering. Equally, the Icon Weather Shield medium action comes with composite stock and stainless barrel, with a choice of black or Realtree camo finish.

A black rubber pad complements the butt. There is no fore-end tip, grip cap or palm-swell. The comb is straight, with a pull length of 14in. Overall the stock

has clean, classic lines, giving it an agreeable conservative look. A relatively open grip and fore-end welcomed my hands; it shouldered well and pointed effortlessly.

A one-piece, CNC-machined receiver action sits in a single-piece aluminium bedding block via three integral recoil lugs, giving strong, solid bedding. T/C's own 24in, medium-contour barrel is button-rifled and comes screw-cut for a moderator in ½in UNF.

The Icon comes with integral Weaver-style bases built into the bridge of the receiver. There are, of course, many rings on the UK market that fit this type of mounting system.

The full-diameter bolt has three front-locking lugs and a sleek, sloping rear shroud – reminding me of a Sauer – which slides smoothly in the action rails. With each Icon, T/C supplies a polymer 'doughnut' for disassembling the bolt. It sounds awkward but it's actually a quick process. The spoon-style bolt handle, part of the bolt assembly's primary parts, is easily removed – as it is not integral and can be exchanged for an optional round-knob, knurled or butter knife version.

The Icon's bolt stop is a slender lever at the traditional spot on the left receiver wall. It pivots from the front so you can hold the rifle and operate it conveniently with one hand. It is designed so the rearward flung bolt force bears on the rear of the stop in the receiver wall, and not on the pivot pin.

Like the bolt, the forged receiver shows some muscle and the long tang is a deliberate feature: it minimises bolt wiggle at full extension. The jewelled bolt (not on all models) has a low lift of 60°, further enhancing its effortless simplicity in use. The stock is secured to the action by three stout guard screws, one into each lug.

A removable box magazine holds three short action rounds and tapers at the top to feed cartridges in a straight stack system. This straight-up feed is smooth and reliable and is obviously influenced by Tikka.

The trigger, designed by T/C expressly for this rifle, is easily adjustable from 2½-6lb by reaching through the tang with the supplied Allen wrench, without having to disassemble the rifle. Dry firing, I found the trigger wonderfully manageable at a crisp and consistent 3lb. A two-position thumb safety works smoothly and quietly, disengaging sear from trigger.

I added a Zeiss 2.5x50 Victory scope and a T8 moderator to the rifle. After zeroing the rifle without a problem, I achieved a ½in group off the bench. I was going to use the Icon for stag stalking on the hill and checked zero at 200 yards on arrival at the keeper's house. In windy conditions I still achieved an acceptable 2in grouping.

This rifle was a real pleasure to shoot. Fit and finish were first-class, as was the handling. The trigger was a joy and, fitted with the superb Zeiss Victory scope and T8 mod, it was as good a set-up as it gets. T/C has taken a considered approach and the Icon is brilliantly conceived.

Bill Ruger is a well known modern gun designer whose achievements include among others the single shot No.1 lever action carbine, the Mini

*T/C's Icon rifle*

14 and a whole range of handguns. All are or were extremely successful and manufactured in large numbers by the company he founded, Sturm Ruger & Co in Southport, Connecticut. But don't be fooled by the homespun 'one man and his gun' marketing spiel from Ruger. The firm is listed on one of the New York stock exchanges and its business is about producing rifles in large numbers.

The most popular rifle that the company produces is the highly modernised Mauser-type, turnbolt centrefire, known as the model M77. The original M77 was introduced in 1968 and came in only one grade, but with a choice of a number of popular calibres. The Hawkeye is the latest addition to the successful M77 design.

I tested this rifle along with a number of others all of which, including the Ruger, would have found a place in my gun cabinet. This goes to show that most factory-manufactured hunting rifles are up to what it says on the box.

The M77 Hawkeye is fitted with Ruger's new LC6 trigger (standing for 'light and crisp'). It is not a bad trigger at all and it has no obvious take-up so I can happily agree with the crisp description. However it had a heavy trigger, with a pull weight of about 4lb 11oz. The LC6 is certainly not terrible by any means, but in my opinion is slightly too heavy to be used for deer stalking, or for that matter for vermin control.

The Ruger is pleasing to the eye and the stock has the best grade of walnut that you can expect of a rifle in this price range. It exhibits a wonderful distinctive grain and the red rubber butt pad, fitted to 'absorb the most punishing recoil' from any calibre, looks stylish. I am unsure about the Ruger's matte blue metal finish. It is nicely done, but the maker's standard polished blue has been excellent and in my opinion is much more attractive.

The action is the well-known KM77 MKII variant. This is an investment cast, controlled feed action with a nicely turned bolt handle for good scope clearance.

The Hawkeye has an internal, staggered cartridge, steel, box magazine similar to the Mauser 98 with a hinged floor-plate. The floor-plate release and trigger guard are nicely done. There is no attempt to free-float the barrel; it maintains essentially full wood contact all the way from the tip of the fore-end to the action.

At first when I cast my eye over this rifle, the nice wood and integral rings that were supplied by the manufacturer are easy to work with, I thought that the Ruger was well on its way to winning the comparison. When I started shooting the Hawkeye it proved to be a comfortable pointable rifle, that handled well indeed. However with the Hawkeye's sluggish heavy trigger, I felt a little less comfortable loosing off the rounds. This is a minor complaint that could of course be easily rectified. Due to this slight shortfall, I did not consider that it was top of the league in the accuracy department, making on average 2⅛in groups at 100 yards – I was using .270 Winchester, 100-grain Super X ammunition. Whilst I was more than pleased with these results, I did get slightly tighter groups with other rifles that I tested and this was definitely down to the heavy trigger.

Wilhelm and Paul Mauser were two brothers from a large family who were living through hard times during the 1850s and 60s. Through hard work, technical skills and business acumen they founded the Mauser weapons factory, which even today enjoys worldwide fame and whose name is synonymous with firearm quality.

The brothers began work as children, as did their father, in the royal weapons factory in Oberndorf-am-Neckar in Germany. In 1963, Mauser acquired the production rights to a sports rifle with a short bolt, developed by the renowned shooting and rifle dealer, Walter Gehmann. This bolt action rifle was introduced in 1965 as the Mauser Model 66.

In 1995-1996 The Mauser Company was taken over by the Rheinmetall Group. The gun-producing section of the company then became Mauser-Werke Oberndorf Waffensysteme Gmbh.

At this time the Mauser Model 96 was introduced as the new hunting rifle with a straight-pull action.

In 2000, Mauser Jagdwaffen GmbH and its European sister companies, JP Sauer & Sohn, Blaser, and Swiss Arms were unified by the German investors Michael Lüke and Thomas Ortmeier under the SIGARMS name. 2003 saw the introduction of the M03 bolt-action sporter. This is a rifle with numerous innovations, the likes of which have not been seen at Mauser since the legendary Model 98 and the Mauser 66. The Mauser action was of course originally designed for the military but was soon adopted by sporting enthusiasts because of the reputation it gained as a reliable and accurate infantry weapon.

*Detail of a Tikka T3 rifle*

Many makers of quality custom rifles still use the Mauser action as a template on which to build their own firearm.

The main feature of the M03 is its capacity to swap barrels and calibres easily. There has been an increasing trend across the trade to provide suitable switch-barrel rifles in Germany. This is facilitated by the use of a full, steel inner chassis that combines the receiver and barrel mounting bar in the fore-end; the barrel is secured by two fixed studs under the chamber enabling the barrels to be swapped quickly by use of a key. The bolt has interchangeable heads that can be used on different calibre cartridges while the magazine comes in one size but will accommodate a range of ammunition by using a packer filling internally.

The M03 has a large heavy bolt that does nothing to detract from the wholesome feel of this rifle; in fact if anything it has been engineered in a way and with such interesting features that it is a pure pleasure to use. The receiver allows easy access in the event of a jammed cartridge and can be singly loaded if required. Due to its length, it is able to take calibres from .222 up to .375 inclusive.

The one-piece scope mount and scope must be removed before taking off the barrel, but the quick release design allows it to be removed and replaced easily and without detriment to accuracy or loss of zero.

The classically designed stock comes in a high quality walnut on the standard model and with a beautiful, deeply grained richly coloured variant on the deluxe version. Its style allows for ideal eye to optic alignment. The rifle comes in either satin black, weather resistant non glare or deluxe silver nitrated finish, along with a pleasing piece of engraving.

I tested a .308 standard M03 and found it to be an absolute delight to use, partly due to the single set trigger being crisp and not unduly heavy and maybe also because of the robust feel when handling. Being slightly on the heavy side at 7¾lb, recoil was minimal.

The Steyr arms factory was founded in the Austrian city of the same name back in 1864, and at first, manufactured military weapons. Not long after setting up production, the company turned its attention to sporting rifles. Two men were responsible for the most famous rifle that this company turned out – they were firearms designers Ferdinand von Mannlicher and Otto Schoenauer. Mannlicher was renowned for the many military actions that he designed, but it was Schoenauer's rotary magazine that became better known. The name Mannlicher Schoenauer became synonymous with a stylish turnbolt repeating rifle that housed a rotary magazine and sported a short barrel and slim fore-end.

When the rifle went out of production in the late 1960s, it was replaced by one of more modern design, the now familiar Steyr Mannlicher.

The revolutionary bolt action design of the Safe Bolt System (SBS) must represent the next generation of Steyr precision rifles, and should be a trendsetter for future bolt action rifles. The action that is the focal point of the Steyr SBS has a totally rigid, high-strength, steel receiver which houses its unique bolt. Boasting four locking lugs, the SBS bolt is stronger than strictly necessary and has a rotation of only 60°, which is all that is needed for it to be unlocked.

Grooves in the bolt body guarantee reliable function under adverse conditions, and the bolt field strips in seconds without tools. The chamber has been safeguarded against unexpected excessive pressures - up to 120,000psi, with conventional proofing using loads that produce up to 70,000psi.

Steyr's high quality cold-hammer-forged match grade barrel is screwed into the receiver. The SBS's special smooth trigger comes set at just over 3lb from the factory. Even with the safety in the fire position, no amount of slamming the butt on the floor will make the SBS fire. The receiver is drilled and tapped to accept the same scope bases as the Browning A-Bolt, a feature probably designed to appeal to the American market. The receiver is also a closed top design; this makes it difficult to manually load a cartridge into the chamber through the ejection port.

While some people are concerned that no mechanical device can be 100 per cent safe, and that by its nature, firearms safety must be taken seriously, ultimately the responsibility for the safety of a firearm rests with the person who handles it. However, Steyr has incorporated safety design features into the SBS that dramatically improve safe handling and usage. The SBS roller tang safety has three positions: fire, load/unload and safe. The logic cannot be faulted; when the safety is forward, bullets can go forward (fire), and when rolled back, bullets stay back (safe). In the middle (loading position), rounds can be loaded or removed from the chamber, but the SBS cannot fire. What's more, this Steyr's safe position is unique.

In the rear, safe, position a white dot is visible – the rifle cannot be fired and the bolt is locked, but this is only one component of the safety feature. As an added measure of caution, the bolt handle may also be pushed down about 1/8in to a double lock-safe position where the firing pin is shifted out of alignment. When the safety catch is moved off safe, the bolt handle moves back up to its normal position.

The synthetic composite stock is ergonomically designed, with a flat bottom forearm that rests naturally on a branch or shooting rail. Although it is synthetic the stock feels natural and seems to focus the recoil down and away from the face. It fits the rear hand beautifully, and has a slight palm swell.

The Steyr Mannlicher SBS Prohunter comes in a variety of versions and calibres including .243Win, .25-06, .270Win, 6.5x55, 7x64, 7mm-08, .308Win, .30-06, 7mm Rem Mag and .300WM. Using Hornady's 7mm Heavy Magnum factory loaded 139-grain cartridges, I managed to shoot some tight groups; with the average within a 1¼in circle.

This really is an excellent hunting rifle that has numerous desirable engineering features, including the two-position magazine, adjustable length of pull, easy-to-use rotary tang safety, and Millet flush-mount swing swivels. The ProHunter has a high degree of intrinsic accuracy and a quality, rotary cold-hammer-forged barrel that is superior to most of its contemporaries. I have been an enthusiastic collector of the old Mannlicher Schoenauers for years but the Steyr Mannlicher SBS ProHunter is a fantastic reason for me to move into the 21st Century.

At the end of WWI, several army officers took control of a Czech firearms plant and began making rifles based on both Mannlicher and Mauser designs. Named the Ceskoslovenska Zbrojovka AS (Czechoslovakian Arms Factory Ltd), commonly known as CZ, in 1924, the company made military rifles before majoring on bolt-action sporting firearms after WWII. These gained an excellent reputation with hunters worldwide.

For several years during the Cold War, the export of arms from Soviet Bloc countries to the West was restricted. Only when international relations improved did we begin to see CZ firearms for sale in the UK. It was the big ZKK-602 action that created a near-cult following, especially in the US. Here was a true magnum action, designed and built for big cartridges, not a standard action opened up. For anyone considering an African safari, the 602 was a serious contender when choosing a rifle.

The current CZ 550 is almost identical to the ZKK-602, with a few minor changes – and by changes I really mean improvements.

The receivers of both models are made of forged and machined steel. As nearly 40 years of production have shown, the quality of steel used and overall workmanship is high. In design and operation, the action is based largely on the classic Mauser 98.

CZ rifles provide controlled round feeding, with a large external claw extractor and fixed mechanical ejection. The slot on the bolt face for the ejector is below the left locking lug. This arrangement is better than that of Mauser 98 actions in which the left locking lug is split to accommodate the ejector.

Original Mauser 98 actions have an internal collar in the front receiver ring. When a Mauser barrel is properly fitted, the end of the barrel tightens up against this collar and at the same time the barrel shoulder tightens against the front of the receiver. When the bolt is closed, the nose of the bolt fits inside the collar, flat against the end of the chamber, with the cartridge enclosed in barrel steel right up to its extraction groove. The right side of the collar is slotted for the extractor. Looking into the receiver, the collar looks like the letter 'C'.

Some Mauser derivatives have been made with the collar slotted on both sides, in order to make it easier to broach the locking lug raceways in the receiver. While this system has proven satisfactory, most Mauser enthusiasts feel the collar should be left as Mauser designed it. The CZ actions retain the C-ring design. The receiver also has built in bases for scope rings.

The first difference I noticed between the current 550 and my 602 was the safety catch. The 602's safety lever operates by pushing forward for safe and back to fire, whereas the opposite is true of the 550. The two-position safety locks both sear and bolt. Another change is in the shape of the cocking piece. The 550's cocking piece is more streamlined in appearance.

Bolt disassembly is easy. Depressing a small button on the left side of the cocking piece allows the firing pin to be easily removed for inspection or cleaning.

Metal finish on the 550 is highly polished and finished in a handsome satin blue. Overall, the 550 action appears to be better finished than its predecessor. For some reason, the bolt operation of the 550 was noticeably smoother than the 602 and operated fluidly and reliably.

A complaint I have heard about the 602, is cracking of the stock in the tang area from the effects of recoil. The 550 adds a heavy stock reinforcing screw in this area that should end such complaints, although I have to say I have never suffered any such cracking on my own 602. Chequering, finish, and overall appearance of the 550's stock is however considerably better than the older 602.

CZ barrels are cold-hammer-forged and have a good reputation for accuracy. Scope rings are well made of machined steel. The rear ring fits a notch in the rear base to prevent movement and the quality, fit and strength of these rings is excellent. I believe however they are only available as high mounts from CZ, presumably because they think that all of their customers will be hunting in low light conditions and so will be using scopes with large object lenses. I should say that the rifle that I tested was not fitted with optics and I used express sights when I test-fired it on the range.

The stock on the 550 that I tested was of quality Turkish walnut and the 18 lines-per-inch chequering on pistol grip and forearm is hand-cut. It's maybe not up to custom standards with a few overruns and flattened diamonds but it's pretty good by factory standards.

The trigger on the 550 is a single-set design. The rifle can be fired simply by pulling the trigger, as with any other rifle. Alternatively, pushing the trigger forward sets it for a much lighter break. Unset, the trigger on the test rifle broke at 3lb 12oz, with some creep. Set, it broke cleanly at 12oz. The trigger mechanism is adjustable and appears to be simple, safe and reliable.

On the range this rifle was a real pleasure. At around 9lb 6oz, it is no lightweight rifle but it is nicely balanced and it handles well. It proved to be completely reliable, with cartridges feeding smoothly from the double-stack magazine. Mauser actions are designed to feed from the magazine. When firing single shots on the range, proper procedure is to load the cartridge into the magazine, so that as the bolt is closed the cartridge rim can slide behind the

*The CZ 550
American*

extractor claw. However, on the CZ rifles the extractor claw is bevelled and relieved. In an emergency situation, a single cartridge may simply be dropped into the chamber and the bolt slapped shut. The extractor will snap over the cartridge rim. This procedure does stress the extractor however and should be avoided when time permits. Apart from the slight creep on the trigger, there was nothing else that I could find to criticise.

I tested the rifle chambered in .375H&H using open sights and shooting a series of three rounds at a time, managed to average 2¼in groups with Federal 270-grain softpoints.

Savage Arms has gained a reputation for producing accurate, no-nonsense rifles. I was initially drawn to their Weather Warrior series by a chance look at a Savage Arms catalogue that said about its Model 16:

'…Savage offers the Weather Warrior, a rifle tough enough for any conditions. It starts with a stainless steel action and barrel for maximum corrosion resistance. The barrelled action is dual pillar bedded into a synthetic stock impervious to moisture. Savage's revolutionary AccuTrigger lets you safely set pull weight just the way you want it. This diverse line includes left-hand models in both short and long actions.'

This interested me, because conditions can get fairly tough when you find yourself belly crawling through a Scottish peat bog, towing a prized rifle along with you and hoping that this final stage of a prolonged stalk hasn't done any irreversible damage to your pride and joy. How, I wondered, would the Model 16 stand up to Savage's claim about its invincibility?

Notable features include a three-position tang mounted safety; smooth bolt knob, and black synthetic magazine follower. The AccuTrigger is adjustable from about 2.5 to 6 pounds on this model.

The rifle that I tested came with its trigger set close to the maximum setting. I lowered the pull weight to a clean 2.5lb, using the supplied AccuTrigger adjustment tool.

The Savage AccuTrigger is a breakthrough for which Savage Arms deserves all the credit they have received. The AccuTrigger is simply the best trigger assembly available on a mass produced rifle.

The lightweight, black synthetic stock is well shaped in the modern classic style. The fluted comb is high and straight, intended for use with a telescopic sight. It is finished with a point chequering pattern that helps break up the blandness of the synthetic stock and improves the grip. The black plastic pistol grip cap bears a Savage logo and the butt pad is black rubber. Studs for detachable sling swivels are included.

Like most moulded plastic stocks, this one has slightly too much flexibility which make it easy to twist or bend the forearm so that it touches the barrel on either side by applying a moderate amount of lateral pressure. This I felt, might change the point of impact under certain conditions, but, for the most part, isn't problematic.

The Savage 110 action, coupled with the extremely accurate headspacing allowed by the Savage barrel attachment system, has long been noted for superior accuracy. The barrel is free-floating for its entire length. As with all Savage 110 actions, to remove the bolt the operator must simultaneously pull the trigger and press down on the cocking indicator/bolt release at the right rear of the action.

Something that I noticed on the range was how easily the bolt chambered cartridges from the magazine. There was little resistance and the process was extremely smooth. I suspect that the synthetic follower has something to do with this. All groups that were made consisted of three shots and with the Winchester ammunition I consistently contained them all within a 1¼in circle at 100 yards. The Hornady ammunition was better, with the largest group measuring 1⅛in and the smallest just ¾in, showing that Savage rifles live up to their motto 'The Definition of Accuracy'. I am certain that this rifle will find favour with many stalkers, especially those on the hill – professional and amateur alike.

Mercury Rifles' products are a recent addition to the mid-price rifle market. Hailing from Italy, the first model to be made available is the 870. Available in standard wood, luxury seasoned walnut or synthetic, Mercury's rifles are built for regular hunting, making them the perfect rifle for the professional or regular stalker.

These rifles are easy to handle and are reliable. The combination of Italian and German engineering with specifications set for the demanding UK market, results in a gun that is exceptionally accurate. During recent tests by one sporting writer, the groups were so tight at 100 yards that they could be regarded as single hole. This places the gun above most of its rivals at a similar price point. The British Deer Society, who recently took delivery of two from distributor Reeves UK, has been delighted with them and the groups achieved during their stringent testing.

The 870 is obviously a practical rifle, built for reliability in the field, but with a surprisingly good finish – the stock in synthetic has a reassuring feel to it without the 'emptiness' that makes some synthetic stocks feel weak. The quality of wood used in the entry level 870 Standard is much better than average, but it is the 870 Luxury that surprises with a beautiful piece of old walnut that gleams with internal colour.

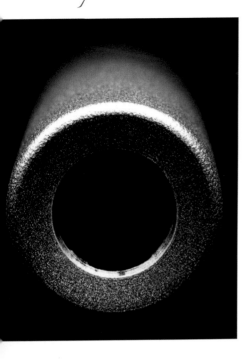

*The crown of a Sako 85*

Mercury's rifles are perfect for the stalker who wants an attractive rifle with a long lifespan. The .22in free-floated barrel boasts cold-hammered steel, giving improved accuracy and durability and screw-cut UNF threaded as standard with an invisible join screw cap. The action is cut from a single block of chromium-nickel steel and is smooth, quiet and clean; the single set trigger is crisp, responsive and reassuring. Trigger release was consistent at 3½lb, but using the set trigger this was dead on at 1lb. Set triggers are not for everyone but I have always liked them and once familiar with their use, do help with accuracy. The safety catch is a toggle type lever to the right of the bolt shroud. In the back position, a white dot appears to show the rifle is on safe, locking both trigger and the bolt. Pushing it forward reveals a red dot indicating the rifle is ready to fire. The bolt locks into the action via twin-opposed front-locking lugs and there is a small claw extractor and plunger type ejector. There is capacity for four .308 cartridges on the model tested, housed in the steel-hinged floorplate.

What initially impressed me with this rifle was its fine balance (without the moderator) and its soild feel, even though I was handling the synthetic stock version. There is no doubt that this will be a serious contender in the mid-range price bracket. Using some Remmy scope mounts begged from a colleague, I coupled a Schmidt & Bender scope to the rifle and after initial bore sighting, punched a clover leaf through the target paper. After a couple of scope adjustments I was repeating this through the bull at 100 yards, not bad from an out-of-the-box rifle. Indeed I recently heard from a keeper who purchased a Mercury 870 and bettered this when he zeroed a one-hole group at 100 yards.

This is a well thought-out rifle that wants to spend time in the field, not the cabinet. Synthetic, standard wood and deluxe wood models are available, starting at £640 for the standard wooden stock, but for those who like high-quality walnut, the deluxe version is extremely good value at only £740. This rifle is a serious contender for an extremely accurate work horse, at an honest price.

If you want the next-best thing to a custom rifle, the Sako is probably it. Once you have recharged your bank account, the popular Sako action makes the rifle nearly as customisable as the Remi 700. And now that the Sako 85 has taken over from the good but slightly annoying Sako 75 (who will miss the Key Concept system of locking the rifle and then losing the key?), its place in deerstalkers' hearts – thanks to its ability to put bullets in the hearts and lungs of deer – is now assured.

The name Sako is an acronym for Suojeluskuntain Ase ja Konepaja Oy (Civil Guard Gun and Machine Works Ltd), a Finnish firearms manufacturer formed in 1927. Since then a few organisational changes have taken place, and in 1987 the state-owned company Valmet and Sako merged to form Sako-Valmet, with 50 per cent of the company falling under the ownership of Nokia and 50 per cent under the ownership of Valmet. After considerable organisational shifts in 2000, Beretta made a substantial investment in Sako and it now effectively controls the company.

The Sako name is associated with quality, accuracy and reasonably priced products and it also produces the lower-priced range of Tikka rifles.

The Sako 85 Hunter rifle has a series of actions: extra short, short, short magnum, medium and long. The actions offer traditional Sako features such as action sizes matched to cartridges, mechanical ejection and integral tapered scope mount rails. Additionally, on the Model 85 there is a controlled feed mechanism order to ensure reliable cartridge feed to the chamber. The magazine is detachable and the rifle can also be directly loaded through the ejection port.

A single-stage trigger pull is adjustable from 2lb to 4lb, and a single-set trigger is available as an additional option. The safety catch has a mechanism that allows loading and unloading of the rifle with safety engaged. The oil-finished, walnut stock is of a classic design with a strong, extended recoil lug incorporated in the fore-end. Open sights with post bead are adjustable for windage and elevation, while integral rails for the scope mounts are fitted to the receiver.

The Sako 85 action includes a front-locking bolt with three lugs that cocks on opening. The bolt lugs are integral with the bolt body and rotation is through 70°. The biggest change in the 85 action compared to its predecessor, the Model 75, is what Sako advertise as 'controlled cartridge feeding'. Other benefits, according to the company, include controlled-round feeding, silk-smooth bolt-travel movement, adjustable trigger and Total Control magazine-latch technology.

The receiver is of a machined steel, flat bottomed design and the ejection port is well enough proportioned to allow cartridges to be single loaded directly into the chamber a desirable feature on a hunting rifle.

The back of the bolt is shrouded and an extension at the end of the striker bearing a red dot protrudes from beneath this shroud when the striker is cocked. The bolt release is located at the left rear of the action and pressing the rear of the release simply and easily removes the bolt.

When you have removed the bolt it is important not to turn the shroud unless you intend to disassemble it with just a slight rotation of the shroud, the bolt tends to spring apart and unfortunately it comes apart far more easily

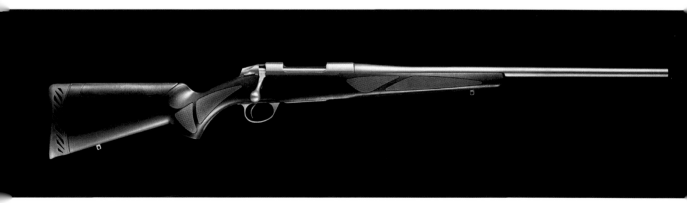

◕ *The best place to get to know your rifle is on the range*

than it goes back together. However, when you want to take the bolt apart for cleaning, it is easy to do so without the use of tools.

The safety catch is a two-position slider that is put in the forward position (fire) and is located at the right and to the rear of the receiver, just behind the bolt handle. In its rearward position the safety locks the bolt closed, but this feature can be overridden by depressing a small metal button immediately in front of the safety. Pressing this button allows the bolt to be operated with the safety on; a good system that sounds a bit odd but works well – it may help prevent accidental bolt opening caused by snagging in the field.

The extractor is a claw mounted at the front of the bolt, while the ejector is located at the rear of the receiver and is spring loaded. The rate at which the bolt is pulled back determines how forcefully the case is ejected, in the same way as the Mauser 98 type fixed ejector. Both the extractor and ejector work well.

The Sako 85 feeds cartridges from a removable, staggered-row box magazine. The magazine latch is in front of the flush-fitting magazine and must be pushed back to release it – an irritating process. Failure to push the magazine up renders the latch immoveable. On the plus side, it is possible to load it through the ejection port with the magazine still in place.

I am not sure that the controlled feed action works particularly well on the Sako 85. The extractor is much smaller than the full-length extractors on a Mauser 98, and takes a smaller bite on the case rim. If you close the Sako's bolt about halfway, until you hear the next cartridge in the magazine click up, and then pull the bolt back and try to close it again, it will jam the rifle by attempting to double feed. In that situation, a controlled feed action should hold onto the first cartridge until the bolt is completely withdrawn and it is ejected. If the bolt is run forward while still holding the first cartridge the extractor should keep it in place and guide it into the chamber. This would stop the bolt from attempting to pick-up the second cartridge from the magazine, thereby preventing a jam. The Sako's extractor only seems to take a strong hold on the cartridge at the end of its journey to the chamber, by which time it'll be a bit late.

One benefit of Sako's extractor is that it will easily override the rim of a cartridge fed directly into the chamber, like any other push feed action, and its receiver-mounted ejector lets a reloader deposit fired brass neatly to hand by opening the bolt slowly.

Most users will appreciate that the Sako 85 operates smoothly and feeds reliably. Its action is noticeably smoother than some other rifles in its class, although in my opinion it is not quite as smooth as a Steyr Mannlicher, or a Mauser M03. It just goes to show that there is no such thing as a perfect hunting rifle – each design has its own strengths and weaknesses.

The cold-hammer-forged, free-floating barrel sports a target-type crown, but I believe that it may be more susceptible to damage in the field than a conventional hunting crown.

Sako rifles come with a 100-yard, 1in accuracy guarantee. I'm pleased to say that when I took mine to the range, it didn't disappoint – there aren't many other manufacturers who guarantee that.

Gun making ran in John Moses Browning's family. Just before his father died he handed the family business over to John, who, despite having no funds or experience with machine tools, transformed the small gun store into a thriving workshop that employed seven people.

After struggling through the early years, one of John, and his brother Matt's, inventions caught the eye of the managing director of Winchester. He travelled to 'The Wild West' to meet the brothers and they struck a deal between the two companies. Winchester became the first in a list of manufacturers licensed to use Browning inventions and make their firearms.

In 1897, the Belgium Company, Fabrique Nationale obtained a licence to produce the 7.65 Browning pistol that incorporated a novel locking mechanism. This began an uninterrupted alliance between the arms factory in Belgium and the Mormon inventor from Utah. The culmination of John Browning's personal inventiveness was in designing the Auto-5 semi-automatic shotgun, which was a tremendous commercial success. It prompted his first visit to the FN Factory in Herstal, Belgium. He died of a heart attack in 1926 on his 61st visit to the Flemish factory just as his prototype B25 was completed. His body was taken back to the US for burial with full military honours.

The Browning X-Bolt rifle was introduced in 2008 to huge interest at the Safari Club International's annual convention. With that in mind, I was more than happy to get the opportunity to test the latest addition to Browning's range – I picked up the Hunter model. It came with a walnut stock wearing a synthetic satin finish, while its barrel and action had a low-lustre blue finish. The gun also boasts a bolt action push feed that cocks on opening and uses a new, detachable magazine system.

As detachable magazine systems go, the X-Bolt is extremely good, possibly one of the best that I have ever used. The magazine body is made of a high-impact polymer, which is less likely to be damaged than a steel magazine, they also seem to feed more smoothly than steel magazines. This one holds four rounds in a sort of rotary system that feeds cartridges into the chamber in a straight line and is exceptionally easy to load. The magazine fits easily into the rifle and it doesn't matter if you stick the front or the back of the magazine in first, or whether you insert it level - it just clicks securely into place.

The magazine feed is reliable and the rifle can be single loaded by inserting a cartridge directly into the chamber or by simply dropping a cartridge into the loading port on top of the empty magazine and closing the bolt. It is a reliable push-feed action.

The one-piece bottom iron and trigger guard is made from an alloy, the finish of which is a perfect match for the matte blue action. The trigger guard bow itself has a squared shape at the front, and it allows adequate space for gloved fingers.

The steel X-Bolt receiver has three wide facets on top that are more or less the shape of the bolt body it contains. It uses a separate recoil lug fitted between the barrel and receiver. A convenient bolt release is located at the left rear of the receiver, which is pressed in to remove the bolt. The top of the receiver is drilled and tapped to accept X-Bolt scope bases.

*⋒ The Sako 85 with magazine detached. Some people love detachable magazines, others consider them too easily dropped*

The bolt assembly uses a steel bolt body, a separate bolt-head double-pinned into place at the front, a bolt handle assembly on a collar that is pinned in place at the rear and a shroud that is pinned in place at the back. The bolt head uses three locking lugs at the front of the bolt, which ride in grooves in the receiver as the bolt is withdrawn to minimize slop; it requires only a 60° bolt rotation to open or close. When the bolt is pulled the entire way back, wobble is noticeably less than with a conventional Mauser 98 type action.

The A-Bolt's familiar bolt shroud and rotating bolt head are gone. The whole X-Bolt rotates when the handle is lifted, as per a conventional bolt action. The body is polished and left in the white and the blued bolt handle terminates in the distinct, angled and flattened ball made popular by the A-Bolt, which is arguably the best shaped and most comfortable bolt knob on the market. The X-Bolt extractor is a small Sako-type at the front of the recessed bolt face, and the ejector is a plunger type. The shroud, which appears to be made of aluminium and is pinned in place at the rear of the bolt, is streamlined and designed to keep powder gasses from a blown primer or a ruptured case, out of the shooter's face.

The new trigger is set at the factory with about a 4lb pull, which is clean and without creep. Adjusting the pull weight is a simple procedure that just entails removing the stock by undoing two bolts, and turning the trigger adjustment screw to its optimum position. As conventional (non-AccuTrigger) hunting rifle triggers go today, it is about as good as it gets.

The two-position, tang-mounted safety is smooth, positive and quiet; it locks the bolt closed when applied. The slider's rear position is safe, and forward is fire. An unusual feature is a small, square button at the root of the bolt handle that pops up when the safety is switched on. Depressing this button allows the bolt to be opened with the safety on, allowing you to remove an unfired cartridge from the chamber.

The barrelled action is glass-bedded in the stock. The X-bolt barrel is free-floating and the muzzle is finished with a target crown. It seems that it is a current manufacturer trend to put target crowns on hunting rifles, for some reason.

The X-Bolt Hunter stock differs considerably from the previous A-Bolt Hunter stock; it has no cap on the pistol grip, which does have a slight palm swelling for comfort. The comb is deeply fluted and high enough to position the eye correctly behind a telescopic sight. The fore-end incorporates a wide, downward, slanting finger groove, which seemingly serves no practical purpose except to reduce the fore-end's chequering coverage, and therefore presumably making it slightly cheaper to produce. Browning should be congratulated for using genuine hand-chequering on this medium priced rifle. In my opinion the chequering patterns on both the pistol grip and the fore-end do not blend well with the outline of the stock.

The bottom iron for the new detachable box magazine system extends laterally all the way across the bottom of the stock and well-up both sides – an unusual arrangement. The barrel is free-floated in the fore-end channel and overall the inletting of the barrelled action into the stock is about average for today's factory-built rifles.

The butt terminates in a soft, rounded and contoured, 1in thick recoil pad. Detachable sling swivels are provided. Aesthetically, the stock leaves something to be desired – essentially it needs to be cleaned-up and made more elegant.

The weight, balance and overall handling of the basic X-Bolt Hunter are good and there is always the Medallion version if you want a fancier upgrade. The Medallion is functionally identical to the Hunter, but features better wood with a rosewood fore-end tip and pistol grip cap, glossy stock finish and a high-polished, lustre-blued barrelled action – it's pretty.

The X-Bolt Hunter that I tried was fitted with a Schmidt & Bender, Zenith 1.1-4x24 scope along with the impressive flash dot reticle – an ideal scope for hunting in Africa or driven boar shooting, although maybe not a first choice for deer stalking in Scotland. When I tested this rifle on the range, I used Federal Low-Recoil 170-grain FP ammunition at 100 yards. In three-shot bursts, the smallest group I managed was 1in and the largest was 1½in. The X-bolt will eclipse the popularity of the A-bolt and is certain to become a winner with deer stalking enthusiasts.

The Blaser R93 is a unique rifle, and while at first glance it might look like a traditional bolt-action, it actually employs a patented straight-pull bolt with radial locking system.

Using a pivoting short-throw bolt handle, the bolt slides straight forward and back to feed and eject ammunition. It's simple and wickedly fast. The Blaser R93 was designed as a modular system. This means the bolt can be changed from right-pull to left-pull in seconds, and barrels can be exchanged quickly and easily. This makes the R93 versatile indeed – invest in one action and stock and you can shoot a multitude of chamberings. Factory barrels in 28 different calibres are offered. The barrel can be switched easily in under two minutes, with a simple T-handle wrench.

I have tried the Blaser R93 Luxus in .300 Win Mag and I immediately felt comfortable with the rifle. It came to the shoulder well and pointed easily, making target acquisition a dream. This well balanced rifle was perfect for both driven boar and big game hunting. The R93 has proved popular with UK hunters

for deer stalking in the smaller calibres; indeed many Forestry Commission rangers use the synthetic stock version as their personal workhorse for deer management.

Being German built, it is obvious that the initial concept of this rifle was aimed at the wild boar market for German driven hunting. The attributes required for this kind of fast shooting are the same requirements as for dangerous game hunting, when the shooting can be fast and often life threatening. In this kind of situation, rapid reloading, reliability and accuracy are essential and in these three fields the R93 is not lacking.

The first thing I noticed, cosmetics aside (this rifle's stock was of the finest Turkish walnut), was the bolt; there is no bolt throw as the bolt is a straight-pull action, designed to pull directly back in one motion. Not only does this give the user a lower clearance for a scope, but it also has the advantage of speed and ease of use in critical situations.

Another fundamental feature I noticed right away was the cocking mechanism. Rather than having a normal safety, which can fail, the Blaser R93 has an actual cocking mechanism. Located on the tang, this is as far as I am aware, a unique feature to the R93. Instead of serving as a simple safety, it actually cocks the rifle. To de-cock it, the cocking piece is simply pushed upward and forward at the same time. When the rifle is not cocked, it is completely safe, as there is no tension on the firing pin. To open the bolt without cocking it, you simply push it forward until you feel resistance while pulling the bolt.

German manufacturers favour switch barrel rifles and this is a great feature of the R93, making it extremely versatile. Blaser have been leaders in the field of switch barrels and the R93 is probably the fastest switch barrel around. Blaser claim that a barrel can be changed in less than a minute; I got it down to just under two minutes, but I am fingers and thumbs at the best of times.

There are obviously tremendous advantages in the ability to change calibre on the same stock and receiver, not least economy, as one would only need initially to buy the one rifle. Take this .300 Win Mag for example - you can turn it into a .243 by simply changing the barrel, magazine and bolt-head. The entire operation can easily be done by oneself with the supplied assembly keys.

The R93 can also be taken apart for travel with a few simple twists of the supplied assembly key. Once you reach your hunting destination, you can reassemble it in seconds and it's still dead-on accurate. This has its obvious advantages for airline travel when hunting abroad.

The system really is a marvel in modern modular engineering. The action is precisely formed and incorporates steel orienting hubs, so it comes together exactly the same each time. The barrel bolts in with two captive Allen-head screws in the stock so you don't lose them. The magazine fits in a mortise precision formed for it. Then, providing you have the magazine in correctly, the bolt slides in from the rear but not like an ordinary conventional bolt. Because the Blaser is a straight-pull design and, when out of the rifle, the bolt is squarish and slightly ungainly looking, with two long steel rails protruding forward from the bottom portion of the bolt. Those two rails line up with and slide forward into two grooves incorporated into the stock. As the bolt slams home, the bolt handle itself rotates slightly forward and locks, activating the multiple locking lugs around the bolt body.

To remove the bolt, depress the right side of the magazine, push in the bolt catch located on the top right of the action and slide it out. Another unique feature is that bolts are available in right or left hand and are, as one would expect, easily swapped over.

All Blaser rifles enjoy an enviable reputation for accuracy. One of the things that make them so accurate is that the barrels and chambers are cold-hammer-forged at the same time. Many other makers hammer-forge the barrels, then ream the chambers. By using specific tools for each chambering and doing it all at once, Blaser's production staff is able to hold the tight tolerances necessary for supreme accuracy.

The R93's unique scope-mounting system is a saddle-type mount that fits securely into dovetails in the barrel. Apparently it returns to zero reliably and holds its zero well; and because the scope mounts on the barrel instead of the receiver, you don't have to switch scopes when you change calibres. Numerous calibres are available up to the .416 Remington Magnum plus different gunstocks, from the Offroad to the Safari.

On the range, I was immediately impressed with the trigger. It was light enough, sitting at exactly 2lbs, and one of the best factory single stage triggers I have ever used. It was comfortable and an easy natural squeeze, helping to keep your shot on target. After coupling a Kahles Helia 1.5-6x42 scope to the R93 and initial laser bore sighting I was soon producing sub ¾in groups at 100 yards, using Lapua's 185-grain Mega ammunition.

As a driven boar-hunting rifle the R93 is as perfect a tool as one could wish for. The straight-pull action takes a little time to get used to, but once mastered it becomes second nature.

Many African PH's have been slow, however, to take up the R93 Safari. The R93 will, without a shadow of a doubt, get-off three shots faster than any

standard bolt-action or double rifle but reloading of the magazine afterwards is somewhat slower. Blaser have responded consummately to this criticism by launching the new R8. The R8 magazine and trigger system can be quickly disengaged from the rifle and replaced by a second magazine-cum-trigger unit in seconds; yet another feature unique to Blaser. Of course this means buying a secondary magazine-cum-trigger unit, but in a dangerous game situation, another filled clip of ammo in your bush shorts could be the difference between life and death.

Merkel has been a well-known name in shotgunning circles for some time, but in recent years the German manufacturer has become famous for producing the world's most affordable classic double rifle – not to mention drillings, and the firm's popular single-shot rifle. Yet in the KR1, Merkel has created a thoroughly modern rifle along classic lines, which has the potential to eclipse the Blaser R93 straight-pull – a rifle that has proved popular on both sides of the North Sea and English Channel.

The Merkel KR1 is different from traditional bolt-actions – in fact, it's different from any bolt-action on the market today. It is actually a turn-bolt action with forward locking lugs, but the resemblance to the classic Mauser action stops there, as the bolt only has a short uplift. The body of the bolt actually acts as a shroud that encases and protects the entire receiver. This is what makes the Merkel system stand out; like the Blaser R93 straight-pull it allows for speedy bolt manipulation, but still has that added feeling of security on lock-up, as it is still a true turn-bolt – unlike the Blaser. This design also allows for a short return, and offers better protection from dust and debris than almost any other action available on a modern hunting rifle.

The three-position safety is of the tang shotgun-style; when you place your thumb on the locking lever, it automatically depresses, avoiding the possibility of accidental operation. When set on safe, either cocked or uncocked, the bolt remains securely locked.

The KR1 comes complete with a single set-trigger as standard. The trigger breaks with a predictable single-stage pull at 3lb. The set trigger, achieved by pushing it forward, releases at 2lb (on the test rifle, at least). The set trigger is a little too far forward, which could be a problem for some smaller-fingered people; but the trigger guard is large and accepts a gloved digit easily.

Other standard features include good quality iron sights and a quick-detachable one-piece saddle scope mount. The supplied scope mount attaches positively and gives a sense of rigidity in the system; the clamping movement is engaged by rotating two levers forward to lock the mount – an integral pop-out bar indicates when they are tight enough.

The KR1 is a switch-barrel rifle, which is the current vogue for many German rifle makers (Sauer, Blaser, Mauser, and so on); standard barrels come in 20 or 22in, magnum in 22 or 24in. Barrels chambered to cartridges of like case-head diameter can be swapped by removing the bolt assembly and two hex-head screws, the rear one under the hinged floor plate, the second a couple of inches forward in the bottom metal. To go from standard (.30-06) case-head

diameters up to belted magnums, a locking bolt head with the appropriate bolt-face diameter and the proper detachable magazine are required.

After a few attempts, I soon became familiar with the procedure and could change the barrel in a matter of no more than two minutes. The saddle scope mount is mounted on the barrel as there is no receiver in the traditional sense again similar to the rifle's closest rival, the Blaser R93 - hence the barrel scope mounting system. Therefore with a scope and mount for each barrel, one can switch calibres back and forth, even in field conditions, with complete confidence in the rifle maintaining its zero.

The walnut stock on the test rifle was close-grained, good quality and richly coloured, and capped with a thin recoil pad. Merkel has opted for a traditional Germanic look on this modern gun, and it works well – the finished result is extremely pleasing on the eye.

When shouldered, the KR1 pointed well and the hogs-back stock profile without a cheek-piece had an adequate length of pull which fitted me perfectly. A Bavarian cheekpiece is available on higher grades, and a Monte Carlo cheekpiece comes as standard on the safari version. Chequering adorns both the pistol grip and fore-end, enabling firm and positive mounting. The rifle handles brilliantly and comes up smoothly with the scope but, at least for me, it also comes up well with the iron sights, which I favour for both driven boar, and up close on dangerous game. The KR1 is a really remarkable hunting rifle that is a clear contender to the popular Blaser R93 straight-pull alternative. The test rifle that I used was right-handed, but left-handed models (both locking housing and stock) are also available for true south-paws like me.

In the field, the action was extremely slick and fast; it seemed quieter in operation than the straight-pull action of the Blaser R93, but does that really matter? I didn't get the chance to shoot a boar with the rifle, but on the running boar target on the range I found the KR1 a real joy to use. It may also have a place for some dangerous game hunting, although the top end calibre is limited to .375 – a little light for elephant and buffalo. However, this fast-handling offering from Merkel would certainly be up to adequacy for both big cat and bear hunting.

Looking for the ideal deer stalking calibres for the UK, with their uses for the occasional travelling sportsman? A one-rifle choice for UK deer would be the .243 Winchester. For all UK species and the occasional safari or boar/moose hunt I would probably choose a 6.5x55 Swedish or .30-06 Springfield. That said, the .300 Win Mag is suitable for all UK, European and US game, plus a perfect choice for all African antelope. For the regular travelling hunter, I consider this calibre to be the perfect one-rifle choice, as it is suitable for everything but the big five, although it could be considered a little on the large side for smaller deer species. You may encounter difficulties obtaining a variation of this calibre for UK deer, but there are a number of firearms certificate (FAC) holders who do possess a rifle in this calibre for British cervids.

Many and varied are the views on which is the best centrefire moderator. One thing is certain: arguments will rage on for as long as people use moderators.

*⌒ Shooter demonstrating Blaser's legendary straight-pull action*

*Sporting Rifle* magazine has conducted in-depth tests using sophisticated sound measuring equipment to come up with tables showing decibel levels and proclaiming one make or another to be quieter than others. Yet when actually in use in the field it is extraordinarily difficult to tell the difference with the human ear, if possible at all. As an example I have a Wildcat moderator on one of my rifles. In one of the tests I read it showed well down the list, but I really like it and have no reason to change what is a efficient unit.

Peter Jackson of Jackson rifles is one of the leading retailers of moderators in the country offering BR, ASE Utra and Sak models – all good and retailed by a man always ready to share his knowledge freely. Then there is the PES range distributed through JMS Arms; and JLS stalker silencers also have their followers.

A moderator that has seen a lot of favourable press is the A-Tec, an over-barrel design, which gives good sound reduction according to its users.

Gerry Lapwood's Husher moderators are unusual in that they have no internal baffles and can have extra chambers added to improve efficiency. UK Custom Shop produces the Wildcat range; nicely made in stainless steel,

➲ *The unusual-looking Merkel KR1*

↻ *Muntjac are now a sought-after quarry in England*

they are strippable and lightweight. Finally one should mention the LEI, a good example of a muzzle-mounted moderator, and aluminium-cased with stainless baffles.

So where does this leave us? Basically the choice comes down to two types, muzzle mounted and over-the-barrel versions. Both have benefits and disadvantages, relating to price, user-friendliness, ease of maintenance and longevity. The benefits have to be weighed against variations in length, weight, price and materials used.

What really doesn't help someone choosing a moderator for the first time is that you can't just take out a selection and try them. All you can do is to read the test reports on as many as you can and find one in your price range.

One thing you can rely upon, however, is that they will all do the job well enough. Using a moderator not only cuts down disturbance to others, it protects your hearing. In the field, the use of a moderator diffuses the sound so that the quarry cannot usually detect the source – particularly useful when out after foxes.

Whichever one you decide upon, always remove the moderator when returning home after shooting. Some advocate a quick spray with something like WD40 for the models that do not come apart, whereas those that can be dismantled should be given a regular clean. ⊙

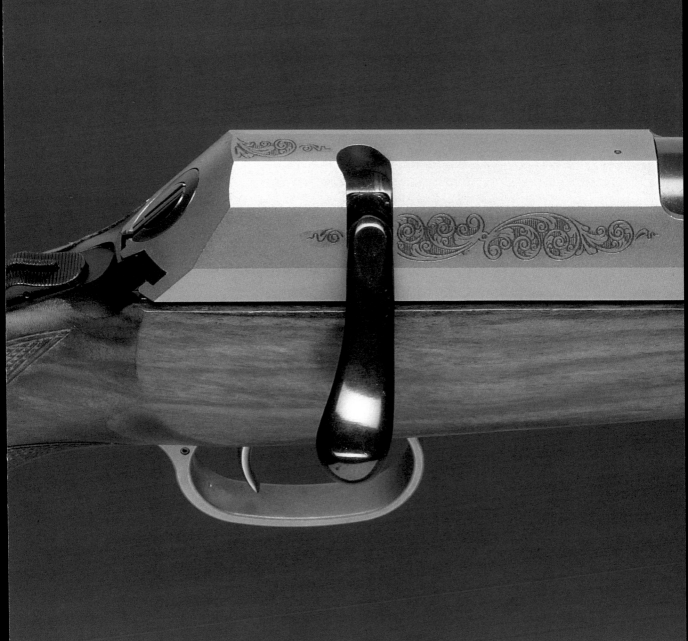

*The author's roesack*

# POPULAR CALIBRES

⊙ **.243 Winchester**

*Introduced by Winchester in 1955 for its Model 70 bolt action and Model 88 lever action rifles, after necking the case down from the .308 Win, it is an ideal and successful calibre for most deer and foxes, with the 80-grain option for foxing and the 100-grain bullet for deer. I would feel under-gunned on a big woodland stag or wild goat.*

⊙ **.270 Winchester**

*Introduced in 1925, based on the .30-06, it is necked down to take a .277 bullet. Loaded with the 130-grain bullet and with a muzzle velocity of 3,100fps, it is adequate for all UK deer and wild goat. For boar and moose the 150-grain bullet should be used.*

⊙ **.308 Winchester**

*Introduced as a sporting cartridge in 1952, it is simply the 7.62x51 NATO round. Almost every make of high-power sporting rifle offers the option of a .308. In power, it is almost the equal of the .30-06, delivering about 100fps less than its larger counterpart for any given bullet size. An ideal round for all UK species of deer.*

⊙ **.30-06 Springfield**

*A US military cartridge born of the .30-03 by using a more streamlined bullet. Suitable for all UK and most European species – woods bison, or wiscent, are the only exception. This calibre is extremely popular in the US and is suited to most game there except bison and large bear. Also an excellent choice for all African antelope (except giraffe) or dangerous game.*

⊙ **.300 Winchester Magnum**

*Introduced in 1963, it is similar to the .300 Weatherby Magnum, and like other cartridges in this class, recoil becomes an important consideration for some hunters. A popular African round and suitable for all antelope but not dangerous game, though some do favour it for leopard.*

⊙ **.300 Winchester Short Magnum**

*The WSMs represent the start of a new era in cartridge design. The .300WSM was introduced in 2000 and absolutely duplicated .300 Winchester Magnum velocities, but using 10 per cent less powder.*

⊙ **6.5x55 Swedish Mauser**

*Adopted by both Norway and Sweden as official military ammunition in 1894, this calibre is popular partly due to its low level of recoil. An excellent cartridge for deer when using a 140-grain bullet.*

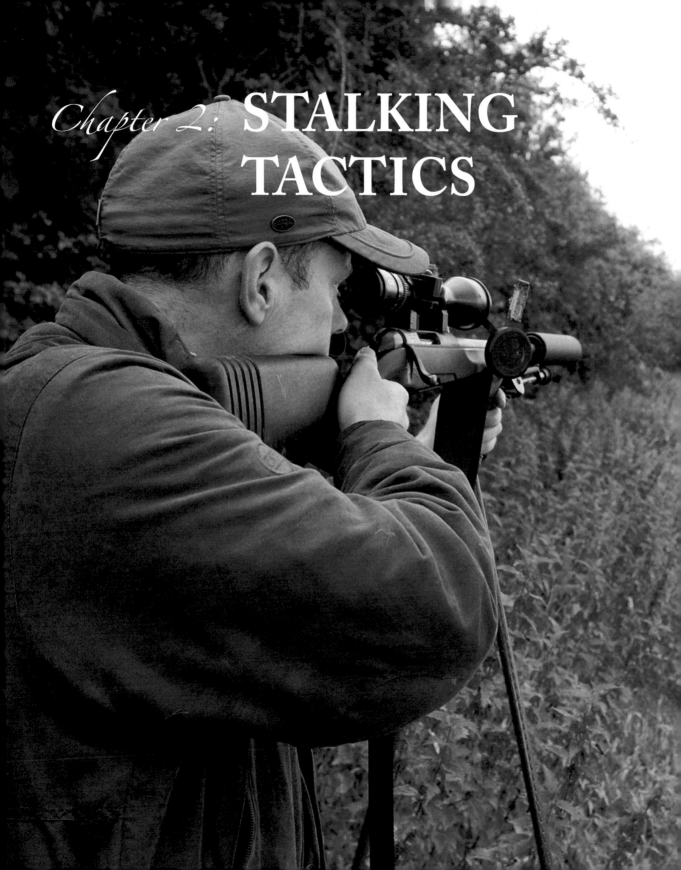

*Chapter 2:* **STALKING TACTICS**

*↻ A stalker leads a
garron across a burn*

The stalking of big game in Britain and Ireland can be broken down into two disciplines: hill stalking and woodland stalking. The latter can be further broken down into high-seat hunting or ambush tactics, and foot stalking or seek-and-stalk tactics. Unfortunately, the nitty-gritty of scopes, ballistics and fieldcraft is far, far more complicated.

Hill stalking is fairly simple. The stalking of deer on the hill has its roots in the Victorian era of the big game shots and the annual trip north to have a go at the red stags. The sport and traditions have changed little this past Century and I for one love being on the high tops in pursuit of these animals. Most of us will be guests, invited or paying. Few will own our own deer forest (using the term in the Scottish sense and not as in woodland), so we will rely on our estate stalker to guide us to a suitable stag.

I have seldom found the Scottish stalker to be anything but dedicated to his job. The best word of advice that I can give is look after your man, especially if you are planning on a return visit. Your stalking guide is the secret to the day's success. He will be knowledgeable about his forest, its history, its beasts and he will know the fickle conditions of his ground. Stories shared over lunchtime when enjoying your well-earned packed lunch, are all part of the day and you will learn much from him. Your man may be resplendent in his estate tweed, as

will the ghillie leading the pony or minding the Argo. He will show his concern for the deer on his forest and – make no mistake – you are a guest in his domain, paying or not.

When it comes to shooting your stag, he will quite rightly be choosy. The majestic monarch of the glen that you think would be perfect above your fireplace may well be in his prime and your stalker will want to leave him to serve the hinds. The stalker knows best and he will want you to take a 'shootable stag' - that is one with unsuitable antlers or an old beast past his prime. This is not trophy shooting in the sense that you are attempting to take the best head: it is quite the contrary. The trophy you will eventually hang on your wall will have been won by plenty of exertion, with a dash of determination. It will be a head culled from the herd to benefit it as a whole and you will have become a part of a longstanding tradition.

Tip your man well and he will look after you; upset him and you will no doubt get the full hill stalking experience and be walked off your feet via every Munro hill in the forest.

All free-chase hunting comes down to a degree of luck – better described as a chance of circumstance. However the hunter can increase his or her chances by fieldcraft and the distillation of advice from others, and seldom more so than with woodland stalking.

There may come a time when you acquire your own stalking lease or permission and you will be on your own. There may be a cull plan to adhere to or you may be required to make up your own management plan. Either way, you have plenty of choices to make.

The use of a well placed high-seat in an area obviously frequented by deer vastly improves the chances of success for the stalker. Advantages of high-seats are threefold: first of all, safety as always should be the first consideration and from an elevated position the bullet will obviously be aimed towards the ground. Secondly, high-seats allow a group of stalkers to hunt a particular area at the same time, thereby increasing the success rate and thirdly, ambushing the deer lessens the chance of disturbing and alerting the quarry.

Many will say that high-seat shooting is lazy, boring or indeed both, but I think it is the complete opposite. Not only does it take a great deal of effort to find a suitable site and place a high-seat, but also, there is so much in nature to observe that I never find the wait boring. What I do find hard to deal with is anticipation. The grass is always greener on the other side of the fence. I am absolutely terrible at sitting in one place for an extended period. I have a tendency into talking myself into believing I would be better off on foot and this is not always so. I have learned to be disciplined and results have followed but I have never been bored or felt lazy when waiting in ambush.

The siting of high seats is down to the particular area and its own set of variables, but the prevailing wind must be the second consideration after safety. Trial and error will show you the best places and that is when the portable or semi-portable lean-to type seat comes into its own. Signs of regular deer activity are always a good guide. Look for ride junctions or positions covering a food source. Once you have proved a place, then that is the time to replace the lean-to with a more permanent structure – but don't forget about crop rotation. A favoured field of turnips or harvested beet will probably not be re-sown with the same crop for five years.

Obviously the placement of a high-seat should not in an way be close to a bridleway or footpath and, where woods are accessible to the public, suitable 'keep off' warning signs should be fixed to the ladder.

Foot stalking in woodland or on farmland never fails to give me a buzz. You must locate the game and stalk into a suitable shooting position for the shot. It sounds easy but, in practice it is not.

Wind direction is the key to everything. Even on days when it seems there is none there usually is. A cigarette lighter is a good indication of wind direction in your actual location, but not so good at indicating eddies and currents a little further away. The powder bottle is better; a container of kids' bubbles probably the best. It really does show what a light breeze is doing.

You must always work into the wind. Remember that, especially on days of light wind, the direction may often be variable and one must be prepared to alter the plan. Never push a bad position.

Concentration is the key to success when foot stalking. Without it, your chances of success are virtually nil. Two steps forward, one step back, progress must be slow and spy often. There is just as much chance of bagging your buck at 30 yards as there is at 150. Look for movement or colour. Anyone can spot a deer in the open, but the flick of an ear or a patch of red coat that catches the observant hunter's eye increases the chances of success. There is a natural tendency to tackle

your stalking ground the same way each visit. Obviously, if the wind is in a different quarter, then you may well change the usual plan. However, try to vary the route taken and indeed the time as deer are quick to realise what's going on if you repeat the exercise identically on each occasion. I learned this the hard way whenI had to reduce roe numbers that had invaded a particular area of fenced forestry in a short period of time. I hit the woods every morning and evening at a similar time. Success rates plummeted after a week of hard hunting and I changed my time in the woods from 11am until 3pm. Results went up again and enabled me to take the required number of animals in a fortnight of intensive stalking. However too much pressure will force any deer population into nocturnal feeding habits, so be aware.

Tactics are the key to woodland stalking success. I was fortunate in falling in with Robin Horsfall, an ex-SAS sniper who was part of the team that stormed the Iranian embassy. Robin taught me that there are many skills a sniper learns that are relevant to the stalker and I was amazed at how much of his knowledge made sense in the field. The first true military snipers were countrymen and gamekeepers who developed their skills during WWI.

The word 'sniper' is often misunderstood and usually misused. In the media, any shooter with a rifle is called a 'sniper' and small arms fire is incorrectly referred to as 'sniper fire'. This creates dramatic images and often sensationalises unskilled gunmen. The title of sniper is tarnished by sensationalism such as this and bears little semblance to the real professionals who are the epitome of infantry fieldcraft and marksmanship. A man who uses a rifle is quite sensibly named a 'rifleman'; whether he is a good or bad shooter he carries a rifle. If a rifleman is gifted or trains hard he can become a good shot. Good shooting is marksmanship so subsequently he earns the title of 'marksman'. The skills of marksmanship are extensive and are among the many skills that a successful sniper will learn. To achieve any standard as a marksman, a rifleman must be able to:

• Adjust his fire by accurately reading the range to the target to within 10 per cent of the actual distance
• Read the wind and its effect on the fall of shot
• Read the light and its effect on the fall of shot
• Read the topography and its effect on the shot
• Aim off for the movement of any given target
• Control his breathing and subsequent trigger operation.

All this for just one shot - but as any good hunter knows, the first shot is the best shot and often the only one that counts. Many people think that a sniper has to be able to hit his target from more than 1,000 metres. Some can, but from that distance, he is only really utilising his marksmanship skills: at that range, his other skills are almost irrelevant. A military sniper, just like a stalker, must close to within at least 250 metres of his target. The sniper needs to then identify and kill with one shot, and withdraw while remaining unseen. When being tested during training, a sniper fires one shot and then a man known as a walker, stands within ten feet of him while he takes a second shot. If at this point

a trained observer cannot see him, the walker then moves to where the sniper is hidden and places one hand on the sniper's head or barrel. If the observer still cannot see him, he passes the test - provided he can see the observer through his sights, and his wind and range settings are correct. This is not too different from the skills required by a deerstalker to complete a successful hunt.

In addition to the aforementioned skills, a sniper must become proficient in camouflage and concealment. This is not simply a case of wearing camouflage clothing and hoping not to be seen. Anyone walking across a typical piece of rural England could not fail to notice that even over a short distance, the land and foliage can change considerably. A sniper has to change his dress to suit the land as he moves through it. This he achieves with a camouflaged ghillie suit that has extra elastic strips stitched into it for additional natural material; as the ground changes, the sniper updates the look of his suit to blend with the environment. Just like stalking game animals, this requires patience and skill to get things right the first time.

Robin always lined the inside of the arms and legs of his ghillie suit with orthopaedic felt. It was adhesive on one side and had 2cm of soft felt as a lining. When crawling through gorse bushes or over broken stone, this cushioned lining saved his skin in the true literal sense. When waiting with the rifle at the shoulder the elbow was also protected from becoming too painful.

A sniper uses the cover that the land offers to make his movement easier. Hedgerows, high undergrowth and woodland offer obvious cover, but few stalkers are aware that the relief of the land can also offer enough cover to make a person invisible while standing, without having anything between himself and his target.

Just as a man is clearly silhouetted on the horizon, conversely he becomes less visible as he moves off the horizon. If he moves in the natural shadows he is harder to see and if his dress matches the foliage behind and around him, he can disappear from view entirely. I have often sat in front of a bush in full camouflage with my weapon held in a firing position, without being visible from the front. This can be handy for a hunter who requires a good field of fire, an unimpeded view and a comfortable firing position.

A sniper also has to be an expert map reader. To move into close-range of an enemy, it is important to be able to know what is beyond the next valley, when the woodland comes to an end or if there is an obstacle that cannot be crossed, such as a river. The stalker should always try to know where he is in relation to the game, how he will stalk the game and what terrain he will encounter on his hunt. He must also, of course, know the way back.

An appreciation of the relief of the land can be most helpful. Ground that is invisible to the enemy or game is known as 'dead ground'. A man may walk rather than crawl in these areas, moving more quickly and thereby saving energy.

A sniper has to be a good observer. He must be able to look through the foliage and spot what doesn't fit. Anyone can see a deer in the open but animals have evolved to stay alive. Those with the best camouflage live longer. To see game before they see you when stalking takes practice and above all, patience.

*⟲ Steve Sweeting*
*in more traditional*
*Realtree camo*

Stalkers who talk aren't stalking, they are conversing; stalkers who rush aren't stalking, they are walking; and hunters who shoot and miss are usually impatient.

A sniper must be able to combine all his skills in order to be successful. He must study the terrain and figure out where his target is most likely to be. He must plan his route so that he can close in as easily and effectively as possible. He must remain invisible by the effective use of camouflage and the ground he must cover. He must find a good firing position and constantly check the changing weather for its effect on his windage and elevation. He must be alert, still and watchful until the opportunity to shoot arises. Then, as the anticipation of a kill causes the adrenaline to surge, he must control his heartbeat, slow his breath and wait for the target to offer a clear lethal shot. Exhale, squeeze the trigger smoothly and follow the shot through to the target. Reload quickly for the second target or fade away and disappear.

The British Army and Royal Marines have two ranks of sniper. The first rank is 'sniper'; the highest rank is 'sniper marksman'. Most of the skills mentioned are relevant to good and efficient hunting with a sport rifle. When serving within the regiment, kit was important to Robin in his job – and should be important to any stalker. Robin's main sniper weapon was a Tikka Finlander .223 bolt-action rifle, a folding front bipod and hollow point, match-filled ammunition.

⊃ *Expanding
ammunition*

The Tikka is still a top sporting rifle today. There is no shortage of choice for expanding ammunition these days, for example Nosler Partition, Power Points, Barnes Triple Shock and Swift A-Frame, to name but a few. If you are a reasonably good shot and the best group you can achieve at 100 metres is 10cm, better quality ammo will often halve that group if you find the best ammo to suit your rifle; I am a Norma fan, I don't have time to reload and Norma has never let me down in the mulititude of rifles that I have used in the past.

Most important of all to a stalker are optics. In Robin's job, he used an adjustable X3-12 scope. Whatever magnification, size of objective lens or even brand of scope you use, you should strive to mount it as close to the barrel as possible. The usual comment you hear a shooter make is 'you can barely get a fag paper between them.'

This gap isn't really what it's all about though. The more significant measurement, from a ballistics point of view, is the 'height above the bore'. This is the measurement from the centre of the bore to the centre of your objective lens. The default figure usually quoted in ballistics tables is 1.5in. There are a number of 'non-ballistics' reasons why low is good. The least important of these to shooting is looks: a rifle with a high mounted scope simply looks odd. I won't dismiss this totally. You need to like your rifle to shoot to your best with it. More important is how the rifle feels. A rifle with a big heavy scope mounted high up is going to feel top heavy, wanting to twist in your hand.

Worse still is a scope which is so high that your cheek is not on the stock when your eye is properly aligned. This encourages inconsistency of head position and makes acquiring a target in the scope slower, as you cannot just naturally mount the rifle to the shoulder and immediately see through the scope. Rifle manufacturers take this into account and fit stocks with high combs but, if you fit a big enough scope, you can still have problems. On the continent, a high scope position is popular among boar shooters, but they tend to use 'see-through' scope mounts so that when the rifle is mounted in a hurry it can be pointed like a shotgun by looking through the holes in the mounts.

Obviously changing the height of your scope cannot change the actual performance of your rifle and the trajectory of any given round. What it does affect is what we call the path: where the bullet is in relation to the line of sight. I think we need a bit a revision here. We need to remember the bullet starts off underneath the scope and, when fired, immediately starts to drop. However, relative to the line of sight, it goes up and crosses the line of sight. After some distance the bullet drops and crosses the line of sight again, this is where the rifle is zeroed. After this it is under the line of sight.

If the rifle in question was a .243Win, firing 100-grain bullets, zeroed at 100 yards with a scope height of 1.5in the bullet would first cross the line of sight at 68 yards reaching at most 0.06in above it before dropping back under it at 100 yards. With iron sights, the bullet first crosses the line of sight at 46 yards and rises 0.17in above it.

I am telling you this to show you I understand the theory – and you may be one of those people fascinated by maths. What generally works in the stalker's

favour is that a deer's heart is a relatively big target compared to the head of a pin we all like to hit on the range. Stick to your sub-one MOA desires but think about increasing your averages in the field with a slightly less rigorous approach.

If only bullets, like light, travelled in a straight line. What we see through a riflescope comes straight at us from its source. The bullet we send back, however, describes a curve as it passes from the rifle muzzle up through the line of sight, to the top of its arc, and back down through the line of sight. As it travels onwards, it loses its battle with gravity faster and faster.

If you are the kind of shooter who likes to zero at the range you hope to shoot at, then further down-range your bullet will be a long way off target. To take an example, imagine a roebuck at 100 yards. With your scope zeroed at 100 yards, you aim at its heart and – bang – it's dead. If your roebuck is 200 yards away, you will need to aim high and that's when knowing the exact range becomes crucial. At 300 yards, if you don't aim high (depending on your bullet and cartridge), you risk hitting it in the leg. And the further the range, the harder it is to judge.

Take the same deer, only this time you have a rifle zeroed at 200 yards. That means that, 200 yards away, you will hit it bang on. At 100 yards, with no compensation, you will hit it high but still in the heart area. Popular stalking calibres such as .243, .270, and .308 zeroed at 200 yards shoot at least 8in low at 300. But they are still in the heart at 250.

It's down to 'point blank'. The meaning of this phrase depends on who's saying it. If it's a newsreader saying 'shot at point blank range', then the dead bloke was a few feet from the end of the barrel. To a rifle shooter, point blank means the distance up to which you do not have to bother about aiming high because the bullet will not hit low enough to worry about.

You make your own decisions about your optimum point blanks, depending on the size of your target, how far away you expect to shoot it and how high your bullet goes. If you have a medium-sized red deer, you want to hit it either in or next to the heart in about a 4in-diameter circle. So the 'optimum point blank zero' is the zero where your rifle will shoot less than 2in either high or low to the maximum possible distance. If your zero is too close to your rifle, then the bullet will hit lower than 2in sooner after that zero. If the zero is too far, then the bullet will have to go above your 2in amount high at some point. When you have the optimal zero the bullet rises to as near as possible to 2in above line of sight, meaning the bullet will be close to the line of sight over the greatest distance.

The good news is that the point blank is optimum – not perfect. Don't strive for a point blank Nirvana because chances are you won't find it. No calibre will allow you to aim at a deer's heart and be at point blank from 0-300 yards.

For the most popular stalking and foxing calibres this theory would lead to a zero of nearer 180 than 100 yards. However, many people feel this is too far and they may never need the 200-yard-plus benefits it would bring. The compromise they use is to zero slightly high at 100 yards to make the rifle shoot near the point of aim from 0-200 yards.

*⋒ A stalker's ammo pouch*

When you hit a deer with a bullet, the knocking-down power it delivers is properly called hydrostatic or hydraulic shock. Just like the hydraulics in a car, it's all about the transfer of power through liquid.

Damage is caused in several ways: there is the physical damage of the bullet expanding on the way through the animal and becoming a bigger object by the time it comes out or stops. The damage caused by a bullet slicing through an animal is technically called the 'permanent wound track'. Then there are the 'secondary missiles' caused by the bullet striking and splintering bone and sending it off in different directions through the tissue, each of them a little bullet on its own. And there is cavitation, which is where the bullet piles up tissue in front of it, making a hole up to 30 times its own size.

This should be an argument for large calibres but the Government recently allowed smaller .22 centrefire calibres for some muntjac and Chinese water deer in England. Deer laws in England have been different to those in force in Scotland for many years. Lots of people expected this recent round of changes made to the law to even things out – but no. From a ballistics point of view there is nothing to suggest that a roe in Scotland requires less weight of bullet and less energy to kill it.

I know people who used to use .22 Hornet and even .22LR for killing deer. We wouldn't dream of it now. You can kill a deer with a .22LR but you would have to hit it in just the right spot. Shoot a deer with a .243, .270, .308 and especially a .375H&H (it's on the list of approved deer calibres) and all you have to do is put a shot in the heart-lung area, which is a much bigger target. But if you look at the damage a .220 Swift, 223 or .22-250 does to a fox and think what that would equate to on a muntjac, I think even without resorting to ballistics tables you can say they would do the job.

For the two small deer found in England, minimum calibre is now .220, with muzzle energy not less than 1,000ft/lb and minimum 50-grain bullet. Scotland does not specify a calibre for roe but says that the bullet must weigh at least 50 grains, have a minimum muzzle velocity of 2,450fps and a minimum ME of 1,000ft/lb.

The classic scene the books describe is a roebuck standing in a woodland clearing, perfectly positioned sideways-on, standing still and conveniently 100 yards away. Life isn't always like this. Deer and other wild animals don't just jump out and stand sideways-on when they see a bloke with a rifle. While you are looking down your scope at them, they wander about, sometimes facing you, sometimes half facing away and other angles in between.

I rely heavily on patience. When stalking any animal, I get myself into a good spot and wait long enough to be offered the chance to shoot.

Sometimes waiting isn't an option though, such as with a wounded beast or for stalkers under pressure to meet a cull. So how do you shoot an animal not presenting the classic side-on shot? If you are shooting at foxes, squirrels and rabbits, you are probably wondering why we are even giving this a thought. Hit it in the front end – head, neck or chest – and it will die no matter what angle you are firing from. To quote Matt Brammer's father, a renowned shooting instructor: "Shoot it in the head and its arse dies, but it don't work the other way around."

With a deer, there is a much larger area where a hit won't result in a clean kill and the length of the bullet track inside the animal being that much longer means you have to start considering the animal as a three-dimensional object, not a 2D paper silhouette. You need to imagine the path the bullet will take through the animal, not just the point on its side you want to aim at.

To help you imagine this, try drawing the view looking down on a deer, then draw lines from different angles passing through the heart. You will see, for example, that from behind the animal you need to start aiming somewhere near the back of its ribcage, not at the usual spot just behind the shoulder, which would (in this case) miss the heart completely and smash a lot of bones in its front end.

All of this is presuming your shot is good in the first place. If you miss and shoot the animal in the heel it doesn't matter where you are firing from, the result will be the same: a wounded beast and a long follow-up. ☉

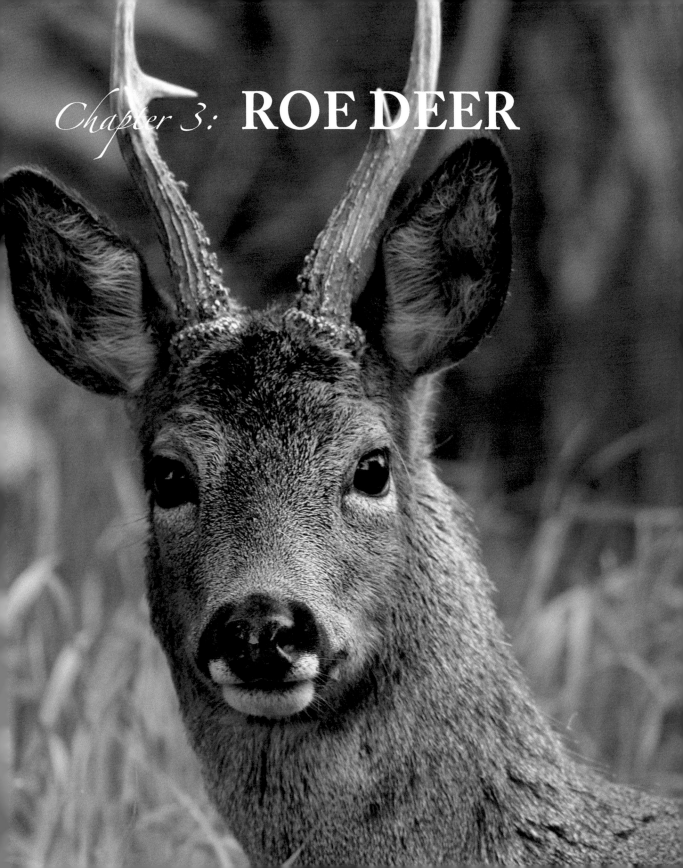

*Chapter 3:* **ROE DEER**

The roe deer (*Capreolus capreolus*) is common today throughout Scotland and England, except for parts of the Midlands. But the indigenous English population all but died out in the 19th Century. Forest clearance and persecution in the early 1800s led to the extinction of roe deer in nearly all of England, with just a few left in the Lake District. Even in Scotland this species was at one time only found in the Highlands and a few southern areas of Scotland. However, in the Victorian era there were reintroductions in the south of England from continental stock, that have since prospered beyond all expectation and this introduced population is expanding northwards at a rapid rate.

Modern forestry and farming have suited the roe deer. The indigenous northern population has and is still spreading steadily southwards with roe now starting to become established in the Midlands, the last tract of England yet to be colonised by roe other than Kent. The Midlands is without doubt, where both the northern and southern populations will certainly coincide in the immediate future.

It is commonly believed that the roe was completely absent in the south of England at the turn of the 19th Century but this may not be quite true. A remnant population may have actually survived at Cannock Chase in the West Midlands. The Normans introduced some roe from northern counties to Staffordshire but these were thought to have gone by the turn of the 20th Century. It appears that they did not and the roe have slowly populated the surrounding area in more recent times, and will shortly be joined by both British

populations as they colonise the Midlands. It is also worth noting that the roe of Petworth Park Estate in West Sussex were never extinct and the present population evolved from animals contained within the park wall.

There were further introductions to the Petworth area and also to Milton Abbas, Dorset, in the early 1800s. Thetford is the stronghold of the species in the east of England. This thriving population owes its establishment to William Dalziel MacKenzie who released a number of German roe imported from Württemberg onto his Santon Downham Estate in 1884. Another notable release was in the Lake District in 1913, when a Mr Alan Curwen, the owner of the Belle Isle Estate on Windermere, released six pairs of roe imported from Austria in an attempt to 'improve' his native stock.

Scottish roe are thought to be mostly native stock, although the south-west population was mainly achieved by introduction. The Marquis of Bute introduced roe to his Culzean Estate in Ayrshire at the beginning of the 19th Century. Finding conditions favourable, these roe quickly spread eastwards.

Wales has recently seen the return of the roe deer where it has been extinct for centuries. In the mid-1980s the species pushed across the English border into Wales in the Mortimer Forest area. Roe now occupy much of the territory from the English border, west towards the Cardigan area, stopping just short of the coast, and as far north as Bangor. It is possible that some of the roe in Bangor descended from a small number of German roe introduced to the Vaynol Estate deer park by Mr G Assheton Smith in 1874. These survived up until WWII and it is thought that none actually escaped – but if deer are good at anything it is escaping from enclosures. Kimmel Manor deer park in Denbighshire also contained roe at some stage in recent history but little is known about where they were from or what became of them.

In Ireland roe deer have a brief but illustrious history. The species was never indigenous to the country but a few were liberated at Lissadell, County Sligo, in the early 1870s by Sir Henry Gore-Booth and appeared initially to do quite well. Some of these bucks produced enormous multi-point heads. These roe originated from Duplin Castle in Perthshire (an area that produces quality trophies today). These roe survied for half a Century and a few spread into County Mayo but were never numerous. After the area was planted with forestry the deer damage was not tolerated and the species was shot out of Ireland completely. In 1910 the then Duke of Bedford introduced a few of the largest of the three roe subspecies, the Siberian roe (*Caprelous caprelous pygargus*). These animals appeared to have become established but, immediately after WWII, they numbered no more than three or four individuals. Most of the missing animals – no doubt due to rationing – ended up illicitly in the locals' kitchens.

Roe deer are elegant, with a bounding gait when alarmed, and bucks are slightly larger than does standing 30in (76cm) at the shoulder and weighing up to 55lb (25kg). They are short-lived, with bucks rarely exceeding five years, and does living perhaps six or seven.

Winter pelage is a grey-brown, often with one or two white chin bands

*Definitely one to cull, this buck*

called gorgets. Bucks shed their antlers annually in the autumn and early winter. In the absence of antlers in late autumn, the sexes are distinguished by the rump patch. Does have a triangular white caudal patch, with an obvious anal tush. Bucks on the other hand have a less obvious and kidney-shaped rump patch and no evidence of a tush. The moult begins in the spring, with the winter coat being shed from March through into May. Roe often look ragged at this time. The coat has a moth-eaten appearance until finally shed, leaving a rich, reddish-brown summer pelage.

Often seen in family groups of buck, doe and followers during the winter, roe deer sometimes herd up in hard weather to take advantage of a particular food source. In April the yearlings are cast out and the buck becomes more solitary, spending much of his time marking and patrolling his territory.

Roe deer are active 24 hours a day, though can turn nocturnal if frequently disturbed. Peak activity is at dawn and dusk. Long periods are spent lying in cover ruminating between feeds. The deer favour woodland and forest, but may occupy fields and hedgerows in high-density areas, such as the Wiltshire downs. Bucks are often solitary but sometimes stay loosely connected to the doe and her follower or followers. In winter during harsh conditions, roe deer may come together to form small groups.

Only the bucks sport antlers, which grow in winter and are shed in the autumn. A typical head has three points per antler, a brow top and back point, normally less than 10in (25cm) long. However some impressive and multi-pointed trophy heads are regularly taken in Wiltshire, Somerset, Sussex and Hampshire. Scotland also has its medal producing counties, mainly Fife and Perthshire. During winter, when the antlers are growing, they are covered in velvet which dries and becomes irritable in spring as the antler becomes hard. Bucks clean their antlers by fraying on suitable saplings, rubbing both velvet and bark away causing serious damage to the tree. The further north you go, the later the roebucks become clean, but most mature animals are in hard horn by late April or early May, apart from the youngest of bucks.

Malformed heads appear more common in this species than other British deer. All antler growth is related to the male hormone and if this is lost or interrupted antlers continue to grow but not harden. A perruque head is the usual result of uncontrolled antler growth. Perruque bucks are eventually sentenced to a long and lingering death as the head becomes flyblown or the antler mass grows over the eyes.

Mossed heads occur when the hormone is halted temporarily and the exaggerated antler hardens as the hormone returns. A coalesced head is where the antlers become fused during growth due to the pedicles being extremely close together on the skull. These unusual heads are highly sought after by continental sportsmen and command high prices as trophies.

Roe are mainly woodland deer, but they are an adaptable species and their rise in numbers has led them to colonise more open areas such as open heather hill where they are referred to, not surprisingly, as hill roe. Modern agricultural ground seems to favour them as well, especially if there are thick hedges, copses

*The author with German client Count Erbach and two good roebuck*

and small areas of woodland. The current practice of autumn-sown cereal crops no doubt helps this and other deer species through the lean winter months. Roe will not tolerate sheep on the ground and will desert pastures where they have been previously seen when sheep are allowed to graze. The same can be said for cereal fields that roe are frequenting; when sprayed, the roe will seek their fodder elsewhere. Roe are turning up everywhere these days - on golf courses and graveyards. The roe deer is primarily active during the twilight and can be seen throughout the day in undisturbed areas, but will turn nocturnal through constant disturbance.

Roe are selective browsers, actively seeking different food types, dependent on the season. They eat herbs, fungi, hawthorn tips, brambles, fruit, clover, heather, cereals, bilberry and coniferous tree shoots, especially larch. This species comes into conflict with farmers and foresters when the bucks mark their territories (and to remove antler velvet) in the spring and during summer when rutting by fraying saplings with their antlers and, to a lesser extent, by browsing on tree shoots and commercial crops.

The rut occurs mid-July to mid-August. Shortly prior to the rut, bucks become aggressive, maintaining exclusive territories containing one or more does. Fights between bucks can result in serious injury or even death, the winner taking over the loser's territory and attendant doe. Does maintain loose territories, often overlapping with other does. If unaccompanied, or if her

➲ *Roe will eat grass – but you will not find them in the same fields as sheep*

attendant buck has been shot, a doe will seek a buck and return with him to her home range.

Bucks usually mate with several does. Courtship involves chasing between the buck and doe for some time until the doe is ready to stand. During the rut the doe makes a high-pitched, piping call to attract a suitor. Although mating occurs in August, the fertilised egg does not implant and begin to grow until January. This delayed implantation is thought to be an adaptation to avoid giving birth during the harsh northern winters. The gestation period is nine months; four months of non-embryonic growth followed by five months of foetal growth. In late May or early June one or two kids are born (occasionally three). Mortality is high and foxes heavily prey upon kids. Though weaned by the onset of winter the kids are still heavily dependent on the doe and first winter mortality is also high through starvation or adverse weather conditions.

When alarmed, bucks and does give a short staccato bark, which is often repeated. Bucks, inquisitive during the rut, will give a similar but less harsh guttural challenge bark.

Roe are a wonderful animal to stalk. Many are shot from high-seats and foot stalking but the most exciting way to grass a roebuck is by calling them during the rut. Stalking roebucks during the July/August rut can be frustrating as a lot of activity is apparent but the bucks are too busy chasing does. This is spectacular to watch but frustrating as approaching them at this time is difficult. It is therefore better to call one to the rifle during this time. Calling roebucks is not particularly difficult and with a little practice most stalkers will be able to produce the right notes.

I learnt this particular aspect of stalking from an audio tape entitled *Roe Calling* by Richard Prior and, once I believed that I was making the right notes, I took to the fields and perfected the technique there. Fortunately I grassed a buck on my first attempt, which gives some credence to the tape's worth, and there is nothing like success to create confidence in one's own ability.

The rut, of course, must be current to stand the chance of calling up a buck, so after 10 July be vigilant for rutting activity. Once you have seen roe chasing in your area it is time to try the call. Weather conditions play an important part in roe calling. A hot, humid, oppressive day that threatens thunder is perfect, but rutting will take place as long as it is warm – even in rain if it isn't too hard. Cold, inhospitable and bitter weather is a waste of time. After breakfast through to mid-evening I have found is the best time. Early mornings have proved hit and miss, no doubt due to night time rutting activity – the amorous but exhausted deer decide to lay up during the first hours after dawn. Generally from the end of July into the first week of August the rut is full on.

If you know an area that is holding a buck, find a good position, near some cover, that will give him the confidence to approach but has a good view and a clear shooting zone. The wind must obviously be taken into account but do not overlook your rear position as a buck could just as well approach from behind.

I cannot over-emphasise the use of effective camouflage. Gloves are a necessity, as is a wide-peaked hat – your face and hands will stand out

enormously to an inquisitive buck. Make no mistake: the buck will uncannily home in on your position.

You must be in a comfortable position and well hidden. Ensure your rifle is easily accessible as events may unfold fast. Let the area settle down. You may even get a territorial buck coming in to investigate, thinking that you are a possible usurper, if he heard the sound of your arrival but failed to scent you.

There are three types of calls to imitate; the first is a kid in distress. By replicating this call you could draw in a doe that may have a buck in attendance. Call number two is the doe in heat call, which I have had the most success with, and the third call is known as the terror call. This call imitates a hard-pressed doe being forced to stand by an aroused buck. If used correctly it can produce rapid results and I have had bucks literally racing to my position.

The choice of calling aids is a difficult one. Most commercially made calls do work and will come pre-tuned. Our continental cousins are masters of the art and I am fortunate to have a handmade terror call that is great to use. The most popular call is the Buttolo bulb call that can be kept in the pocket and used one-handed with practice. All three of these deer calls can be imitated with the Buttolo. The Hubertus cherry wood call has also proved popular and can be self-tuned using the attached tuning dial to get the right sound. With this call you can either make the kid-in-distress or the in-heat doe sound. Faulhaber manufactures a neat little box set of three calls that include the kid, doe in heat and terror call. They take a bit of practice, especially the terror call, but I have had great results with this set in the past.

The kid distress call is a series of high-pitched peeps, roughly in time with the kid's imagined breathing. I try half a dozen or more peeps and then wait five minutes before repeating the operation. Often a doe will come without a buck, and you must wait for her to depart the scene before moving on as we do not want to unnecessarily educate the deer to our hard-learned ruse.

After half an hour or so with no result I usually try the doe in heat call. A lone doe will look for a buck making a receptive two-tone squeak. You must vary this call in intensity for more realism, because a doe going about her beat looking for love will be raising and lowering her head as she walks and calls. Try your call for a few repetitions – maybe 10 or 12 – and wait, as the buck may take some time to come to you. After 10 minutes or so try another series of calls; repeat this for 45 minutes to an hour. Do not be disheartened if nothing happens: often as not, the buck will already have a doe with him and she will be trying her damnedest to stop him running to you. Remember, the doe dominates the rut and she is in charge of rutting activity, so it may prove difficult to get the buck to leave the jealous doe.

If this is the case then the next call to try is the terror call. This call is difficult for a territorial buck to ignore – it will really wind him up as he believes an interloper has invaded his territory. Be ready: the response to this call can often be spectacular, but get it wrong and you won't see a thing.

When roe mate, they run around in circles and figures of eight, thus making the worn down trods known as roe-rings. If you come across one of these sites it

*⋒ Deer damage to a sapling*

is often worth waiting a while to let the woods settle down and then trying the terror call. The resident buck has obviously got a doe with him so the other calls will probably not elicit a response as consistently as the terror call will.

Some bucks may be extremely cautious – especially if they expect another buck to be in the area, which of course they would if you are using the terror call – so watch out from behind. Sometimes, especially if his blood is up, the buck may ignore your scent completely and come rushing in. That's the joy of roe calling: no two days are alike.

In the early 1990s I was fortunate to fall in with Stuart Donald. He was old school and taught me a great deal about hill stalking and the red deer that were close to his heart. But his talents weren't limited to Highland red deer, as he was – and remains – the most knowledgeable roe stalker that I had ever met. It was Stuart that first taught me how to call up roebucks, with first the Buttolo call and then the Hubertus cherry wood call. And as head keeper on Glen Moy estate, part of the Earl of Airlie's vast acreage, he presided over one of the best deer forests and grouse moors in the Angus Glens. I listened intently to his instructions, initially on the operation of the Buttolo call, but actually being shown how to work the bulb is the quickest and most successful way to become a proficient caller. I was soon delivering the required 'fiep' at the right pitch that emulated a distressed roe kid calling for the doe. These calling lessons took place at his house, nestled below the aptly named Donald's Hill in the heather-clad Angus glens. Stuart was a hard taskmaster who wasn't short of a curse if I got it wrong – but the smell of a peat fire and a rapidly dwindling bottle of single malt still remain sharp in my memory, as does Stuart's wife Aileen who must surely have been driven half crazy by my noisy efforts.

I remember the joy I felt when I first lifted a doe in the long heather, followed by a buck on my first attempts with the Buttolo under Stuart's direction. This was on a weekend that still remains the best two days roe stalking I have ever experienced.

It was late July in the mid-1990s when we left the keeper's house in the small hours. We headed out in the 110 Land Rover, parallel to the Moy Burn, driving past the shoot bothy perched below the Shank Hill that lies in the shadow of a higher peak, the Dog Hillock. It was on the Shank that I enjoyed afternoons walking up rabbits over Stuart's springer spaniel, Misty, and on the high ridge of the Dog that I'd stood in February, driving mountain hares. Sadly, the hares are now a shadow of their former number, probably due to climate change. Stuart cut the engine as the Land Rover rolled quietly to a halt beside the West Glen bridge, below the twin peaks of Finnbracks and Manywee.

As we set off, I struggled to keep up with the Scottish superman as he strode out up the steep West Glen road until about half-way up the face of Manywee. He halted beside an outcrop that shielded us from view but would give us a good sight of the hill's face.

Trying not to look out of breath I peered through the binoculars. "Out of breath are ye?", mocked Stuart as he deployed his three-draw Gray's telescope to scan the Glen below us. "Just a tad", said I. "Aye, it's a fair pull upwards for a young loon like yer sel" he continued. Then, becoming all-serious he calmly directed my gaze towards a doe lying in the heather. "Ya ken yon white rock below the big peat hag, just below there is a roe doe". I pointed the binos in the required direction and found the white rock, but couldn't see the doe. "Ya ken the doe Peter?" "Yep", I lied. "Good, because there's twa of them, she has a wee buckie tending her", said Stuart.

I carefully slid my 6.5x55 Browning A-bolt out of the canvas gunslip and deployed the bipod. Lying prone next to Stuart I cupped the Buttolo and gave the four fiep squeaks at five-second intervals, suppressing the two holes on the bulb.

The result was instantaneous. The doe rose and cantered towards us with the buck following on. I fitted to the rifle and picked the buck up in the scope as the two deer closed fast. Stuart carefully exchanged the telescope for his Zeiss binoculars and let out a low whistle. The two deer instantly halted which was what I needed. I ran the crosshairs up the front near leg of the buck and settled mid-shoulder and paused a breath before squeezing off a 169-grain Norma soft point. The buck was killed instantly, its legs kicking involuntarily. Quickly, the doe realised this wasn't a great place to be and bolted off over the adjacent ridge.

"Aye, now you've shot him you'd best go git him", instructed a smiling Stuart. I soon realised my folly in going out on the hill wearing Le Chameau wellingtons,

a mistake I have not since repeated. By the time I had retrieved, gralloched and carried back that buck, my feet were both blistered and cooked.

Next day we again parked alongside the West Glen bridge, but this time would follow the West Moy Burn below the tops of Finnbracks. The early morning was a real pleasure to be on the hill; the 'gadow, gadow, gadow' calls of the cock grouse were a delight. A midsummer sun rose above Glen Ogle in a duck-egg blue sky. The heather-clad hill threatened to burst into a purple carpet within the next few days. Flushing a ring ouzel, it flew on ahead for a few yards before alighting and flicking his white bib towards us in an agitated fashion before flying on again to a repeat performance. I found the going easier now that I had swapped my wellingtons for hill boots, complete with Black Islander gaiters.

We wouldn't be needing the call today as we rounded a bend in the burn and put up a roe kid. The kid ran on and began 'fieping' in his own language. Slowly lowering ourselves to the prone position both a buck and a doe appeared from nowhere. The doe was on our side of the burn and the buck was on the opposite bank, as was the kid.

I then witnessed roe behaviour that I have never seen since. The doe, obviously concerned about her offspring, stretched her neck forwards and puckered her lips to make a sound like a toddler pretending to drive a car: 'Brrrrmmm'. Her kid skipped up the burn away from us; it knew we were there and was alert. The doe trotted alongside, up the waterway. We waded into the burn half-crouched, and moved on in pursuit – but the buck saw us. He began prancing slowly forward, raising his front legs high in an exaggerated fashion. The doe then caught his attention again and he too skipped after the kid. This game of cat and mouse carried on for a good two hours with the concerned doe calling in this unusual fashion until finally the buck jumped over the burn.

We came to rest on a small bump of turf and I unslipped the rifle as Stuart whispered: "You'll nae be quick enough, but mind the wee calfie as he's crossed the burn twa." Sure enough, the young roe was between me and the buck, who was now hot on the tail of the doe amid obvious foreplay. Stuart let out a low whistle, which caused the buck to spin round and face us head on. The only presentable shot was at the base of the neck and I took it, flipping the buck over in spectacular fashion.

We waited until the doe and kid were out of sight before approaching my second trophy. When I made as if to gralloch the beast, Stuart berated: "Nae, nae, nae – we'll be here half the afternoon going on your performance yesterday, move over and watch and learn." Stuart deftly eviscerated the buck in a professional fashion that would equal Doctor Quincy's best autopsy.

That second deer carried a poor, spindly head. Neither of the bucks that I'd shot that weekend were impressive by trophy standards – hill roe seldom are – but to me both were perfect. These two might be the least impressive heads in my collection, but the spindly-headed roe remains without doubt my personal favourite – and the pursuit of these two bucks still remains among my best stalking memories.

◐ *A buck and a doe who clearly know the photographer is there*

It was the hunt for big roe heads that drew me to Wiltshire. My friend and colleague, Jost Arnold had returned to the UK from Germany to hunt quality roebucks, as they have become something of a rarity in the fatherland. The German roe are doing well as a population but the trophy quality has fallen dramatically in the last two decades. In the UK we have been slow to accept the roebuck as the respectable game quarry that he really is. It wasn't so long ago that he was shot on shotgun drives, snared and considered vermin. Thankfully, things have changed and the graceful roe has been elevated to the status that he deserves. On the continent, he has been a highly sought-after trophy for hundreds of years and this has had its influence on the trophy quality today. The big bucks have been repeatedly shot out and have not been given the opportunity to pass on their genes to the next generation, therefore only the inferior bucks have been able to breed, resulting in the situation we have today. This is a lesson from which we can all learn. Managing roe is just that – management.

On this particular day, Jost and I were in Wiltshire near the village of Great Bedwyn, hunting with my friend and colleague Del Waters. Del had done his recceing well and he had two medal quality bucks that he wanted culling. One had been displaced and was licking his wounds and residing in an old overgrown orchard in the centre of the estate. The second buck was the one that had ousted the first. Both were old animals that Del was familiar with and their time had come.

After checking into the pub we were soon on our way to check zero. A ½in group later, Jost and I followed Del down an overgrown ditch towards the orchard and that date with number one buck.

Now Del was as happy as a pig in the proverbial, slopping through the mud and slime in his wellingtons. Jost and I, however, were less than happy, as our ankle boots proved utterly inadequate for amphibious stalking. The further we went, the deeper the goo. Overhanging briars and rambling rose thorns did their best to add to the discomfort, as did a squadron of early season mosquitoes, whose bites raised welts that gave us the look of smallpox.

After three parts of an hour, our African Queen experience was over and we crawled quietly from the ditch into the leeward corner of the overgrown orchard. Thankfully the breeze was fresh enough to disperse the mozzies and begin to dry our lower legs. Del confirmed he was pleased with our ditch manoeuvre with a thumbs up, happy that we had entered the orchard unobserved and that we still held the advantage.

Making ourselves quietly comfortable against some long-fallen crack willow, the wait began. I soon began to doze in the late evening sun as the blackbirds started their sundown kak-kak chants. Jost slowly raised his binos to a muntjac doe that ambled across the rows of gnarled fruit trees.

Zippering up my fleece, the sun began to dip below the Downs to our west. I was starting to feel the wet cold in my sodden boots when a roebuck appeared as if from nowhere on the glade before us. Del was already glassing the buck and slowly began shaking his head. "It's not the buck we want boyos", he said in his southern Welsh drawl. The buck trotted purposefully forward to some apple tree whips that were growing up from a mature apple's root suckers and began to thrash them like my old headmaster once did to me for, as I recall, having a ferret in class.

The buck suddenly stopped and stiffened, staring down the glade. After a few moments he broke into a trot. Immediately, another buck stood up and bolted through the hedge into a field of winter wheat.

"That's our buck", whispered Del, as he belly-crawled past us to the orchard's hedge. Jost and I followed suit.

The buck was parallel to us, he had our scent and began to move away. He was limping badly and had quite obviously been having a bad time of it. Jost chambered a round into the Blaser 6.5x55. The buck that was still in the orchard had now seen us and let out an alarmed bark. This actually worked for us as the battered buck stopped at 120 yards and looked back. Jost had picked him up in the 2.5-7x56 Schmidt & Bender scope. It was all he needed to let loose the 140-grain Federal bullet that smashed the buck's shoulder, destroying its heart and lungs, putting an end to its suffering for good.

Pumping Jost's hand I said "waidmannsheil" and Jost replied with the customary "waidmannsdank". Del was extremely pleased. The buck was old and distressed but he carried a heavy, even trophy that would surely make a CIC bronze medal.

The following morning found us driving the green lanes looking for the second of our roe duo. We had passed up on a number of bucks on the estate, looking for the right beast.

Del certainly knew his deer. After the fourth circuit of the selected area he killed the Subaru's engine. Without a word he signalled for us to get out quietly.

*Roe deer are masters at hiding out in thick cover*

We quickly moved the 100 yards it would take to find the gap in the hedge and on to the stubble field to our left. Adjacent to the stubble field was a steep bank cutting and at the far end was the buck browsing on some stunted hawthorns. Back to belly crawling and discomfort, as small stinging nettles found their way through my jacket and trousers to torture me with those vicious stings that come back to haunt you when you wash later, as the water sets off the reaction once again. Nettles aside, we soon reached a rise in the ground giving us a good position for the shot.

Del glassed the beast, who was still browsing away unconcerned and confirmed that it was indeed 'our boyo'. Jost, in kneeling position, raised the rifle in an experienced manner, picking up the buck's front leg in the scope and running the cross hairs up to the shoulder. He halted his breathing and squeezed off the round that found its mark. All done in the fluid manner of an experienced hunter, the buck catapulted forward and kicked its last. Walking forward together we were a happy group of stalkers that morning. The buck was a real belter, once again a heavy trophy, but this one had wide antlers, almost like a Siberian roe. A second CIC bronze medal. Both Jost and Del were overjoyed and well they deserved to be. Two outings, two great stalks, two perfect shots and two wonderful trophies. It doesn't come much better than that.

One of the best-kept secrets in UK roe stalking is my own home area of East Yorkshire, where the chalky Wolds produce good-sized heads. I had invited two pals there to shoot a roe buck apiece during the rut. Both Tommie Hynes and Meehal Grint were former clients of mine who I had become firm friends with over the years. Tommie regularly invited me to Ireland to hunt wild goats and I would often hunt with Meehal here in England.

The bucks had been chasing hard and the weather was on our side. I was quietly confident that we would be able to grass two bucks without too much difficulty, leaving an evening free for a bit of partying. Alas, I could hardly have been more wrong.

Roe buck hunting during the rut is rather anti-social, to say the least. You must grab what sleep you can given the appalling lack of daylight hours, which usually amounts to three hours tops. And while mealtimes are disruptive at best, it is really the post-hunt festivities that suffer most; normally an important part of any hunt, during the rut they are virtually non-existent. This hunt was no exception.

Meehal worked for Kings Seeds, the game-cover seed manufacturer. He was keen to see how a trial strip sown a couple of years ago to create a diversionary feeding area for deer was doing, as it contained chicory. This bushy, blue-headed herb is an important ingredient of Kings' own deer lawn mix. The results were actually quite impressive, with this tract of land proving particularly attractive to the deer. The roe especially seemed to hold the chicory in high esteem.

The first season after planting chicory it just looks like a light-green dandelion plant that roe can't get enough of. When the plant bolts, though, it reaches 4ft or so and produces beautiful blue flowers, and while deer enjoy the leaves at all stages of growth they much prefer the flowers at the budding

*The author and Wes Stanton with a buck shot at Balmoral*

stage. Chicory is a perennial plant that grows back from the rootstock if dismembered or eaten and is practically hassle-free, especially if planted with the special deer lawn-mix that Kings offer (the legume content provides self-sufficient nitrogen). Height can be managed by topping in areas of low deer density, but in higher-density areas you can count on the deer to keep it in check.

Anyway, I was keen to get a buck under our belt but the first two outings had been fruitless. The good weather had deserted us, replaced by a fresh north-westerly breeze and overcast skies that didn't help my roe calling one bit. I had guided Tommie on the first stalks and left Meehal in the high-seats, but on the second day I left Tommie in a lofty perch overlooking a wide, grassed ride. With Tommie ensconced in his eyrie we headed into the wind toward the willow plantation and the chicory, where I hoped I could put one of King's finest on to a shootable buck.

Things started to come together as we cautiously crawled under the hawthorn hedge to spy toward the chicory crop. There was a ride cut through the crop and, spying down it, we could see the backsides of two roe. One was obviously a doe as its tush could be clearly seen below its triangular white rump patch. The other was a big-bodied animal whose kidney-shaped bum patch confirmed he was a buck. Together we crawled towards the flowering chicory, which was the objective of the roe's attentions.

Reaching the crop we silently rose above the tall, blue flowers and the unwelcome thistles that had invaded the mix. Both the buck and the doe were feeding contentedly on the tasty new buds and leaves. I could see his antlers and was happy to take him from where we were, but unfortunately he was still backside on to us and we were way too close at about 30 yards or so. I nudged Meehal to be ready to shoot. He half mounted the .243 Tikka T3 as I gave the softest peep on the Hubertus cherry wood call. Both buck and doe snapped their heads round to face us. The Swarovski reticle centred on the buck's neck as Meehal squeezed off a 100-grain Federal soft-point that downed the buck cleanly. Silently we waited for the confused doe to move back off into the willows before I quickly gralloched the buck where he lay. After a hasty photo shoot we headed back to the vehicle. It couldn't have gone better for either of us.

Unfortunately for the likeable Irishman, though, he'd been struck with Murphy's Law. Not long after we had left Tommie, the neighbouring farmer had pulled up just over the boundary and deployed a bird-scarer to disperse the blue carpet of pigeons that had descended on his swathed rape. The gas-gun had effectively obliterated any chance of Tommie taking a deer that session. True, deer soon get used to gas-guns, but that titbit certainly didn't help much on this occasion.

The following morning Tommie struck out again, this time because of a dog walker that had gotten an A-road mixed up with a green lane. Top gun Meehal Grint however had been overlooking a small plantation adjacent to a field of spring barley from a boundary seat. He was just packing his rucksack ahead of the pre-arranged pick-up time when a buck arose from the barley and sauntered across the conservation headland, toward the plantation. He failed to get there though, instead becoming Meehal's second buck as he fell to the Tikka T3, a perfectly-placed shot killing him instantly as he nosed through the hawthorn.

That evening would be Tommie's last chance, so pulling out all the stops I put him in a high-seat that simply couldn't fail. The wind was perfect and I knew of a buck that regularly passed this high-seat on a well-used deer trod. As I passed his rifle up to him I wished him luck, before heading off to place Meehal in another seat, giving me the evening free for a few hours of photography on the farm.

It proved to be an uneventful evening for Meehal and I, and we headed off in the Land Rover with fingers crossed that Tommie had grassed a buck. I was admittedly dubious, as Meehal had not heard a shot; from his position and with the wind being in the right quarter he should have heard it if Tommie had fired. There was still a good half-hour of shooting light left though, so, with defiant optimism, we pulled to a stop half way down the green lane that led to Tommie's position.

Soon after, I spied a buck chasing a doe from the plantation where Tommie was deployed. The buck pursued the doe in and out of the hawthorn hedge that

ran parallel to the green lane, heading in our direction. I was in a dilemma: this was Tommie's buck for sure, but time was against us and there was no sensible way to try and get it back towards Tommie.

Fortunately Meehal made the decision for me, suggesting I try the call; either the buck would come in or perhaps the doe would head back into the plantation, hopefully taking the buck with her and past Tommie. There was some sense in his suggestion. Sometimes an in-season doe will try hard to keep a buck with her: it is then that the terror call is best put to use.

I half hoped that a few peeps imitating a standing doe would send the lovesick duo back into the young trees though. Winding the window down I blew four peeps that got an instant result. The buck left his current beau who was playing hard to get and galloped directly towards us. Meehal slid out of the passenger seat and dropped to one knee. At 20 yards the buck was still speeding in and I had to cough to stop him. For the third time in as many outings the Tikka T3 made a moderated thufft as it spat out yet another Federal soft-point towards the buck's vitals. A satisfying thrump saw the buck leap forward in an adrenalin-fuelled death rush to finally roll over with legs wind-milling wildly before slowing to a stop as his life left him. Meehal had claimed three bucks, employing some impressive shooting, but my conscience began to bother me.

Poor old Tommie had come a long way for a roe buck and I had failed him. But though it was with a heavy heart I picked the Irishman up from his high-seat, I needn't have worried. He was happy for Meehal and christened him 'golden gonads' as he pumped his hand with genuine congratulations. Tommie politely requested a photograph with the buck, his buck, that Meehal had grassed and I was more than happy to oblige this perfect gentleman of Galway.

After eviscerating the buck and a quick clean up we unanimously decided to descend on the local Chinese restaurant, despite looking like three displaced mercenaries. The fun-filled evening ended a great hunt for Meehal, and Tommie – ever the natural comic – was no less willing to make us laugh than before. And even if he was secretly disappointed then he hid it well.

We have much to learn about roe deer from continental Europe. Count Erbach is one of Europe's leading roe stalkers. His family has a rich hunting heritage and he is a direct descendant from a long line of hunting Earls who can trace their roots right back to the crusades. Indeed, the Count and his father, the present Earl of Erbach, have the largest single collection of roe buck trophies worldwide in their Bavarian Castle. The castle collection is a treasure trove of hunting paraphernalia, trophies and sporting firearms. But it is the roe trophies, which have been added to by the family for more than 150 years, that form the most significant part of the museum display.

The Count regularly hunts roe buck in both England and Sweden. He likes the way we stalk and manage the roe in our isles and has hunted with me, and I with him in Bavaria, for more than a decade. It is never a case of guiding him, as he has to be the most experienced hunter I have ever had the pleasure to hunt with. To put things into perspective, he shoots more than 200 head of hoofed game each year, plus a respectable tally of other dangerous game.

I generally find the bucks and then leave him to it, following on behind to ensure no boundaries are inadvertently crossed as duty of care demands. The count is a true sportsman and is only interested in harvesting old roe bucks. He participates in both locating and evaluating bucks with his Zeiss spotting scope.

We were hunting in late April with Wiltshire Deer Services, which cover a large slice of the county and some parts of Somerset. Meeting up with Robert, who was our rep and guide, in the growing dawn, we soon left the tarmac behind and weaved our way to the top of an escarpment. It wasn't long before the growing daylight revealed a huge buck below us, eagerly browsing away on the new hawthorn buds. I carefully assessed the buck in my Swarovski spotting scope and it was immediately clear that this trophy-quality buck was an old beast. His carriage alone indicated his age, and it was confirmed by a big, thick, heavy neck and greying face.

Leaving the vehicle behind, we took a wide detour to get the right side of the wind and began to stalk into the buck. This was some roe buck – we could see he was exceptional with the naked eye at a good 300 yards. Using the undulating topography we made good use of dead ground but suffered some hairy moments cresting the occasional rise that required a belly crawl. However, that wasn't our only concern as we closed on the buck. A pair of lapwings took great exception to our trespass into their territory. The two plovers put up a right merry dance, dive-bombing and scolding us with their mournful alarm call. There was little doubt that there was a nest somewhere nearby and we wouldn't be spared their attentions until we moved out of their personal space.

Meanwhile, the buck was still happily browsing away, oblivious to the din the lapwings where making. A large stretch of open pasture lay before us and our present position was fast becoming untenable. Quickly sliding forward, and avoiding a number of cowpats, Count Erbach took the initiative, deployed the Harris bipod and Blaser R93 rifle. The range was close on 200 yards, I decided, as the buck filled my binoculars. I heard the conscious exhalation as the Count stalled his breath half a second before the gun spat a 100-grain Norma soft-point. The muzzle crack was instantly followed by a satisfying thump as the bullet struck flesh and bone. Rearing up momentarily, the buck burst into an adrenalin-fuelled death dash before rolling over and kicking wildly until his legs steadily wind-milled to a stop as life left him. Giving the animal the customary 10 minutes, the count made the rifle safe and we approached his prize. "A top trophy for sure," he remarked enthusiastically. The trophy was found later to weigh 670 grams.

Over three more outings, Count Erbach added four more bucks to his tally, before we then moved on to Somerset for his final two stalks. The morning outing was a wet and windy affair and the only buck we saw was a heavy head in velvet that actually bounded across the road as we drove around spying in the inclement conditions. All mature bucks look to be carrying heavy heads when still in velvet, but we were close and he was enormous.

We departed in the early afternoon and decided to target the jay-walking buck, as he was sure to become a road casualty if the morning's behaviour was anything to go by. I am not a fan of shooting bucks in velvet, though don't get me wrong – I have seen many heads cleaned and coloured by a competent taxidermist that could easily be mistaken for naturally-coloured antlers. This road was a busy one at rush hour and it seemed a sensible plan to shoot this particular specimen if we could.

The Count and I sat between the roots of an old and decaying elm, waiting near the roadside plantation for the buck to make an appearance. As far as textbook stalking goes, coming events couldn't have been any easier. Just as the area settled down after our arrival, the buck skipped onto the scene and stood broadside at 60 yards, surveying his territory. Count Erbach shouldered the rifle, ran up the buck's front leg and settled the Swarovski reticle on the killing triangle, then sent a Norma soft-point into the roe's vitals. The shot had been good and, though still in velvet, it was another great head for the castle collection – it later weighed out at 520 grams. ⊙

## ROE DEER FACTS

### ⊙ Open Season

*England & Wales*
*Bucks      1 April - 31 October*
*Does        1 November - 31 March*

*Scotland*
*Bucks      1 April - 20 October*
*Does        21 October - 31 March*

### ⊙ Rifle & Ammunition

*England and Wales requires a minimum calibre of .240 with a muzzle energy of not less than 1,700ft/lb*
*Scotland specifies no minimum calibre but requires a minimum of 50gn bullet, a minimum muzzle velocity of 2,450fps and a minimum muzzle energy of 1,000ft/lb*

### ⊙ Outfitters

*Cervus UK, contact Owen Beardsmore 01283 711878 or 07968 829540*
*www.cervus-uk.co.uk*

*Mike Dickinson 01538 308697 or 07721 671746*
*michaeldickinson@btopenworld.com*

*Steve Sweeting 07792 874511 or 07768 268410*
*carminnowsestate@msn.com*

*Others can be found in* Sporting Rifle *magazine  www.sporting-rifle.com*

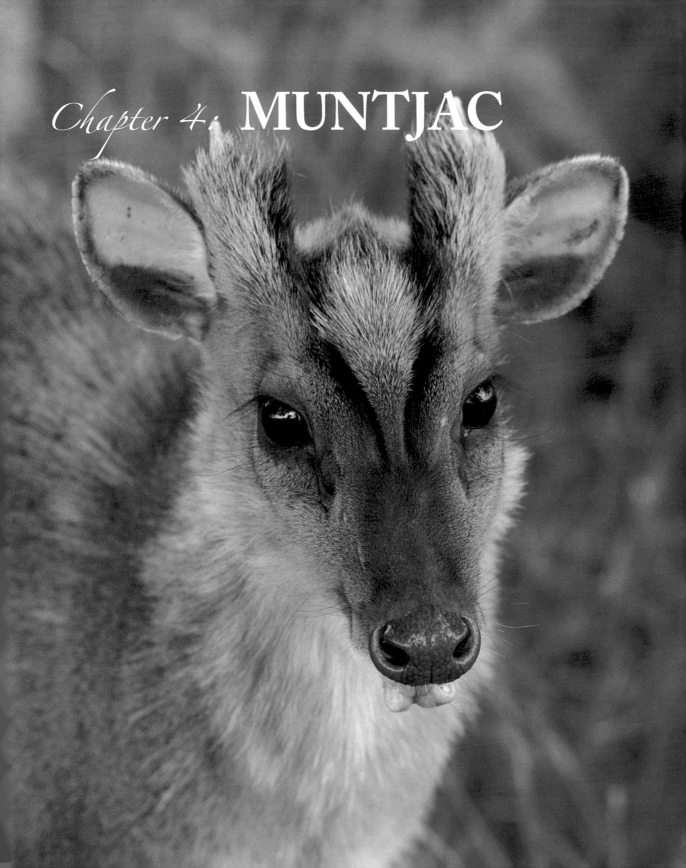

Chapter 4: MUNTJAC

Muntjac (*Muntiacus reevesi*) are the UK's smallest deer. Despite the species only being first introduced to Woburn Park by the 11th Duke of Bedford in the 1890s, it is now believed to be the UK's most numerous deer species. Its expansion has been halted at the Humber estuary in a line roughly drawn east to west from Hull to Manchester. At the source of the Humber, where a number of rivers converge, there is a mass of urbanisation with a number of major industrial towns centred around Leeds. This effective urban barrier peters out along the M62 into a vast track of open moorland that the muntjac are reluctant to cross before urbanisation once again becomes apparent at Manchester and its surrounding towns.

Up to now this has been an effective barrier, however a number of small localised populations have recently sprung up north of this line. Personally I have great misgivings about this, as I believe this aggressive little deer could oust the native roe from certain areas. There can be no doubt at least that it will compete for bramble browse, as the leaves of the blackberry are important for both species.

There can also be little doubt that these isolated populations have been deliberately introduced. The 11th Duke of Bedford usually shoulders the blame for the introduction and subsequent establishment of this species in the English countryside. In fairness, his grace cannot be expected to shoulder all the blame as the muntjac is an escapist by nature and, without doubt, a number of other collections provided escapees to form the nucleus of the wild population we have today. Since their initial introduction to Woburn, releases and escapes from nearby Whipsnade, plus other collections in Northamptonshire and Warwickshire have all led to the establishment of this species in the wild.

An interesting story was related to me by an old Woburn resident, who said that some squaddie during the war years left the Woburn Park gates open and a number of the deer escaped to freedom as a consequence. How many I do not know but this must have happened more than once.

Game shooting estates have, without a shadow of doubt, been a major factor in the expansion of England's muntjac population. Managed game coverts offer thick cover for shelter and security and obviously a regular supply of quality high-energy food during the lean months of the year. Predation of fawns by foxes will also of course be minimal on a well run estate staffed by diligent keepers.

Outside England, further deliberate movement and release have all contributed to the rapid spread of this species that is also currently invading Wales. The species is not yet present in Scotland although isolated muntjac sightings have occurred in various locations along the English side of the border. Recent reports of road casualties in Ireland suggest that this deer has been transported across the Irish Sea to be deliberately released.

Muntjac are a small, stocky little deer. They are a sleek, russet-brown in summer pelage, darkening to grey-brown in winter. Bucks have long pedicles extending to facial ridges, carry short antlers up to 4in (10cm), and exhibit visible upper canines. Both sexes have large facial glands below the eyes but

these are much more pronounced in bucks. The muntjac's haunches are higher than its withers, giving the deer a hunched look. The tail, wide and white on the underside, is held erect when disturbed. Mature bucks weigh up to 35lb (16kg) and stand up to 20in (50cm) at the shoulder. The species has a long life, with bucks making it up to 16 years and does up to 19 years.

The muntjac's habitat is varied with deciduous, mixed or coniferous forests holding them, preferably with a diverse understorey. They tend to be creatures of dense cover and favour in particular a thick bramble understorey. But they are adaptable and so long as there is sufficient cover and forage, muntjac will attempt to colonise any area. They are now a common sight on arable farmland containing woods or copse within its boundaries. Railway embankments, gardens and allotments all can and do support muntjac. When the animal is flushed its tail is raised, showing a distinctive white underside as it departs at a rapid rate of knots.

Muntjac are generally solitary or found in pairs (doe with kid, or buck with doe), though pair bonding does not occur. Bucks defend small, exclusive territories against other bucks while does territories overlap with one another and with several bucks.

In contrast to all other species of deer in Britain, muntjac do not have a defined breeding season. Instead, they breed all year round, the does being able to conceive again within days of giving birth.

Bucks may fight for access to does but remain unusually tolerant of subordinate males within the vicinity. Muntjac are capable of procreation at eight months and breed all year round. After a gestation period of seven months, the doe gives birth to a single kid and is ready to mate again within a few days.

These deer are selective feeders and active – many a stalker has viewed a muntjac through the scope waiting for it to pause, only to find that no shot presents itself. They take a varied diet according to region and availability, including herbs, brambles, ivy, fruit, flower buds and coppice shoots. In high-density areas this may result in the prevention of coppice regeneration and the loss of some plants of conservation importance, such as primroses and cowslips. The muntjac has also been blamed for the loss of nesting sites of rare birds such as the nightingale.

They make a short, sharp dog-like bark often repeated for many minutes (up to an hour), hence the muntjac's other name of 'barking deer'. A muntjac in mortal danger may scream, and maternal does and kids squeak. There is no fixed season for rutting.

The shooting of heavily pregnant does is recommended, in areas where numbers must be controlled. Thought-provoking this may be but it is a much better practice than orphaning fawns by accidentally shooting a lactating doe, as this deer breeds all year round.

The muntjac is fast-becoming a sought-after trophy species with both continental American and British stalkers. High-seats are the best option for shooting this species, as they never seem to stand still for longer than a few seconds and generally eat on the hoof. If one does foot-stalk into a muntjac, it

*Jost Arnold and a medal muntjac*

○ *When still and in*
*cover, muntjac are*
*almost invisible*

is often a case of playing catch-up but is exciting nevertheless.

Bucks can be called all year round but it is essential not to overdo it as once a buck finds out it is a human on the other end of the call and not a receptive female it can take a season or more before he will fall for the call again.

The Buttalo or Fauhaber doe-in-heat calls work well but my particular favourite for calling muntjac is the Hubertus cherry wood call. It is essential to pick a good position where the buck cannot sneak up on you, and make minimal movements, preferably just the eyes.

Let the area settle down and repeat the call as often as needed. Muntjac are not as fussy as roe and sometimes they will come charging in and at others they will be ultra cautious but are intrigued by the call enough to bring them into shot. However beware of animals that come in at the gallop to your calling efforts, as these are more often than not mature does that have left a fawn in cover.

I recall taking three Flemish guests muntjac stalking in Suffolk. We arose early on this particular February morning, with headaches owing to an intense flirtation with Miss Stella Artois the previous night. Englishman Chris Beadle had joined the group and he sat beside me in the Subaru at 5.30am chuckling at the groaning Belgians squeezed into the Forester's rear. My fingers were still numb from de-icing the windscreen as I eased the vehicle out of the pub car park, heading for the wood.

The frosted road glistened in the headlights ahead, its beauty belying the hazardous surface. I was relieved to leave the asphalt ice-rink behind and

◌ *Muntjac are always on the move*

persuade the Subaru onto gravel through a gateway into Howe Wood. Pulling up at the first high-seat, I watched Tom climb into position and passed up his rifle. Snaking on through the wood, I dropped off Derek at the next seat and then Rudi before we returned to renegotiate the tarmac for the half-mile drive to Green Wood.

Pulling gingerly into the lay-by and cutting the engine, Chris and I dismounted, our exhaled breath condensing into mist-clouds. Chris unzipped the Tikka .243 from its slip, pocketed the clip and slung the empty rifle over his shoulder. I was glad of the red-lensed pen light I'd brought, its red beam giving enough illumination to light our way yet not promote our presence.

The going was rather more difficult than I'd first imagined. Numerous rain-filled tractor ruts had frozen over, making it like walking on light bulbs. Even with care, it was impossible to avoid the ice-trap and its knock-on effect of scattering roosting wood pigeons above. This completely gave us away to the other woodland inhabitants.

We reached the high-seat and climbed up behind Chris, feeling amateurish and not in the best of humour. Chris clicked four rounds into the clip, loaded the rifle, applied the safety and settled back for the wait. A muntjac nearby began barking his warning, spreading the news that there was danger in the wood.

My humour became blacker still as the wait began. Our undignified entry had made the woodland deathly quiet. The pitch-black gave way to indigo, then mauve as the sky brightened from the east. A rifle report from Howe Wood promised success and rekindled our interest.

This was the second day of the hunt. The Belgians had so far shot nine muntjac bucks in two outings. The 'keeper, Geoff Garrod, had also shot a medal-head buck on the boundary and spending more time than was healthy crossing the busy road surrounding the estate. His buck carried an impressive heavy, but ugly, head. Chris, alas, had so far drawn a blank.

Another report told of more success, and then three more shots punctuated the morning air. The time crept towards 8.30am as I heard a slight tapping sound below me. There was a muntjac buck nipping off the snowdrop flowers surrounding the tree in which we sat. His scimitar-shaped antlers had been knocking the lower rungs of the high-seat ladder. I nudged Chris, pointing. His eyes widened as he saw the trophy buck beneath. But suddenly the muntjac burst into life – maybe he caught our wind or somehow sensed our proximity – and crashed into a briar patch 60 yards ahead. Though dismay was written all over Chris's face, luck was with us; the buck soon reappeared looking unconcerned. He ambled back towards us, nipping snowdrops. Chris raised the rifle and leaned forward to get a steady rest on the high-seat rail. I pursed my lips, making a small mouse squeak that got the intended result: the buck froze and looked toward us. This was all that Chris needed. The .243 cracked into life, and the buck dropped into the fallen beech leaves in a heartbeat. The 100-grain Norma bullet had found its mark and the buck was dead. Climbing down, Chris was ecstatic: a finer example of a muntjac buck you could not wish for.

The antlers were long and curved with two excellent brow tines in perfect symmetry. The size and weight of this muntjac buck's crown would easily score a CIC gold medal.

Carrying the deer between us, we headed for Howe Wood to pick up our Flemish friends. The Belgians had taken six bucks between them, bringing their total to 15. Tom had also taken a superb buck that carried a thick but ugly trophy, later to be scored a bronze medal. It was cold still, but we were warmed through by the glow of a successful hunt. ⊙

## MUNTJAC FACTS

⊙ **Open season**

*Bucks & does – no close season in England & Wales. This species is not known to exist in Scotland.*

⊙ **Rifle and ammunition**

*England & Wales requires a minimum calibre of .220 with a muzzle energy of more than 1,000ft/lb.*

⊙ **Outfitters**

*Cervus UK, contact Owen Beardsmore 01283 711878 or 07968 829540 www.cervus-uk.co.uk*
*Hamptworth Estate, contact estate manager 01794 390700 enquiries@ hamptworthestate.co.uk*
*Mike Dickinson 01538 308697 or 07721 671746 michaeldickinson@ btopenworld.com*
*Steve Sweeting 07792 874511 or 07768 268410 carminnowsestate@msn. com*
*Others can be found in* Sporting Rifle *magazine   www.sporting-rifle.com*

Chapter 5: **CHINESE WATER DEER**

◑ *Chinese water
deer have spread to
populate much of the
East Midlands*

Chinese water deer (*Hydropotes inermis*) were first kept at London Zoo in 1873 and then introduced to the Duke of Bedford's estate at Woburn in 1896. After some breeding successes, 32 animals were transferred to nearby Whipsnade in 1929-1931, and later, from these collections; a number of animals were also introduced to Norfolk. Escapees from these original introductions have provided the nucleus of the populations we have in the UK today. Modern arable farmland and the fens of Cambridgeshire and the Norfolk Broads provide them with the conditions they need to thrive.

A small isolated population exists in Hampshire which probably originated from Leckford Abbas and Farleigh Wallop. But the Chinese water deer's stronghold still centres around their original escape sites in Bedfordshire, Cambridgeshire, Hertfordshire, Buckinghamshire, Northamptonshire and Norfolk. They are still spreading into surrounding areas of suitable habitat but have yet to make it across any of England's borders. However this may happen soon, as a small population in Shropshire, originating from Walcot Park, is slowly expanding west towards Wales. The Chinese water deer is found in neither Scotland nor Ireland.

Today, the British stock accounts for as much as 10% of the global population. The population of this species as a whole is spreading both in

range and numbers but this advance is still nowhere near as rapid as that of the other non-indigenous species.

The Chinese water deer is a small deer, intermediate between muntjac and roe deer. Both sexes are of similar stature, a mature animal standing 20-22in (50-55cm) at the shoulder and weighing 24-40lb (11-18kg). Unlike all other species in Britain, they do not bear antlers. Instead, mature bucks carry large tusks. Like the antlers of other species, the tusks are used as weapons during the rut and in defence against predators. These tusks indicate this species is a primitive form of deer, as in other species, tusks have evolved over thousands of years to become antlers.

The animal's ears are large and rounded, giving a 'teddy bear' like appearance. Summer pelage is a russet-red brown, moving to a pale grey-buff brown in winter. Water deer lack a white caudal patch, like that seen in roe deer.

Chinese water deer are active all day and night, with peak activity at dawn and dusk. In arable areas they may be stalked in their seats, which are usually in the open fields.

In the UK, Chinese water deer have adapted well to open arable farmland as long as there are a few woods, copses or overgrown dykes and hedgerows. In the Cambridgeshire fens and Norfolk Broads reed beds, the habitat is much more akin to their native country and not surprisingly they have thrived in this environment.

Chinese water deer are selective feeders that feed on a selection of plants – especially herbs – but may take woody browse, grasses and sedges if food is scarce. Though this deer is not thought to be a threat to trees, commercial flower crops, such as gladioli, are favoured by this species and they often browse the tops from root crops in winter when other food sources are in short supply, bringing them into conflict with farming interests. After feeding, long periods are spent lying up ruminating.

Water deer are generally solitary except when mating, but may form pairs or small groups at high density. Bucks are particularly aggressive and do not like the presence of other bucks.

Rutting begins in November and reaches its height during December. Bucks and does form pairs and defend territories, remaining together until April.

Like other deer, bucks perform parallel walks with invading rivals and resort to fighting if dominance is not established. Unlike antlered species, fighting in Chinese water deer rarely results in fatality but slashing injuries from tusks are a common occurrence.

Does give birth between May and July after a six- or seven-month gestation. Up to six fawns may be born, though between one and three is usual. Up to 40% of fawns die within the first four weeks of life. Maximum lifespan is be six years.

Both sexes give a short bark when alarmed or as a warning that danger approaches. When chasing off rivals, bucks make a rapid chattering or clicking sound called whickering. A high-pitched whistle-like squeaking is emitted by the buck as he chases a doe during courtship. Both sexes make a screaming noise when in extreme or mortal danger.

The behaviour of this species on modern arable farmland is more akin to a hare than a deer. In autumn and winter, Chinese water deer will scrape out a form or couch in the open cereal fields to rest and chew the cud. They can be difficult to stalk into in this situation and much crawling and the use of any dead ground will be essential. In a high-seat situation, however, these animals are relatively easy to bring to the book if the seat can be erected in a suitable area.

Although the law now allows the use of .22 centrefires on this species, I still prefer the use of .243 minimum, with suitable expanding ammunition.

I took Jost Arnold to stalk Chinese water deer in Bedfordshire. The pre-dawn chill gripped my joints as we climbed out of the Subaru Forester at the deer larder. Locked and loaded, Jost and I set forth, our condensed breath showing the ice-sharp wind direction: semi-favorable.

Settling into a hawthorn embankment overlooking a daffodil field, we began spying, with the rumble of the nearby M1 motorway in earshot. Focusing the Steiner 7x50 binoculars, I watched the tag-boxing of half a dozen hares competing in the mating game, while a skylark climbed ever higher, trilling its dawn song in the March morning half-light. A white ghost of a barn owl finishing the night shift beat lazily past, giving us a look of surprise, as he flitted on home to roost.

A dilute sun showed above the sycamores to banish the shadows and promised to warm our limbs. Just as I began to fear that the daffodils were devoid of deer, two young Chinese water deer bucks sped onto the scene. Frolicking in the emergent sunshine they chased each other round and round. Their play was too much for the emperor of the area: our intended quarry was indeed at home. Some 200 yards to our left, the trophy buck raised his backside above the budded daffodils, stretching to his feet to begin stamping agitatedly.

I checked his tusks through the Steiners. Both were intact, unbroken, of even length and the thickest I'd seen. But our position was unsafe to shoot, without a backstop. We'd have to crawl between the motorway embankment and daffodils to get a safe shot. Backside down and chin up, Jost was away quickly, and I followed behind.

We paused every 20 yards or so to spy the buck above the daffs. The beast was showing the two young interlopers his displeasure in a most determined manner. Time and again he charged, butting one or the other of the pair.

But we now had problems. We froze as a startled vixen, also using our trench, nearly bumped into us. The stand-off was a tense moment: bolt the wrong way and she'd scare the deer. The vixen bolted – but down the M1 embankment! A feeling of horror swept through me as I tensed in anticipation of a multi-car pile up. Fortunately for my insurance policy and the fox, the traffic rumbled on regardless.

The buck had now seen off the intruders and started to amble slowly towards us. We had 20 yards more before we would be in a safe spot to shoot. In between our intended sure spot was a deep tractor-rut flooded with water. All 6ft 6in of Jost slipped into the water as graceful as an otter on a fishing trip – that's real dedication. I saw him spy the buck one last time, and then deploy the tripod legs

*Andy Lovel
with a medal
Chinese water deer*

before fitting to the rifle. The buck advanced still – and just as I pursed my lips to whistle and halt him, he broke away from us at full gallop, charging off to sort out the two intruders who'd returned emboldened. I let out a shrill whistle in an attempt to stop the buck but to no avail. Watching him through the Steiners he eventually stopped, at some distance. My heart sank – but half a moment later he was knocked to the ground, I heard the rifle report and the delayed 'thwack' of the bullet strike in that order. Jost smiled, confident that he, the .243 and the 100-grain Norma bullet had done the job. I was a little rattled, as it was a long shot – but Jost is an experienced marksman and placed it perfectly. We returned to the larder with a trophy buck sure to make a CIC gold medal.

Another European client, Christian Herzog from Austria, returned to the English Home Counties in 2006 to hunt a medal-quality Chinese water deer after taking a superb muntjac trophy with me the previous year. But things had not been going according to plan.

We were hunting the third day of three and the scoreboard still read zero. The weather had been unkind and every other variable that Murphy's Law could possibly throw at us had been well and truly thrown.

Illegal hare coursers had ruined the first day by scattering every chink out of the parish. The second day we fared no better, as a horsey sort with a chip on her shoulder read me the riot act (while threatening me with her riding crop) for having the audacity to be 'armed and dangerous' (her words) when crossing 'her' bridleway. Normally I am adept at defusing these encounters but on this occasion all reason was falling on deaf ears. After that, Christian decided he had enough stalking for the day.

On day three, as we left the Subaru beside the embankment, I felt a stiff south-west breeze that did not bode well. The wilting sun-daffodils danced in a wind that would certainly make the deer nervous. Deer dislike the wind because their hearing is distorted by a myriad noises that could cover the sound of approaching danger.

We carefully stalked down the hawthorn hedgerow to 'Spotlight' field where I was confident we would find a suitable trophy. How wrong could I be? Where normally there would have been a dozen or more Chinese water deer, there was not one to be seen. They had obviously decided to take to the woods for shelter from the wind. We would have to go look for them in among the trees, which wasn't going to be easy because the cover would give the deer the advantage.

Chinese water deer are relatively straightforward to spot and stalk when they are lying out in a field of winter wheat but, when they are laying up in woodland, they are difficult in the extreme.

Spying slowly across the field to Will's Wood with the Steiner 8x50s, my heart jumped as I caught sight of a tremendous buck. It had Christian's name written all over it. It skipped out of the wood and cantered into the field, stopping and looking nervously around it. It carried good tusks that were clearly visible with the naked eye.

The buck was some 350 yards away and not in a safe position to shoot. We would have to get closer. That was all very well but all we had between us and the buck was 100 acres of winter wheat. The only cover was a telegraph pole.

I explained to Christian that I wanted him to walk directly behind me while I kept the telegraph pole between me and the deer, until we reached a small slope from which we could safely set up the shot. The Austrian looked at me as if I had lost my last marbles and sighed. Later, he admitted that, at that point, he was tiring of 'Carr's Comedy Tours'. However, he did as requested and followed me out into the field.

All was going well with only 10 yards to go when I spotted a slight movement in front. A hare, already squatting in its form, flattened itself a little tighter as we approached. I automatically froze which was enough for the hare to know she had been sussed. Off she went at a speed that would have left a greyhound standing – straight towards the deer. As expected, it was too much for the buck, which decided it would be better off in the woods and returned to the safety of the trees. There was nothing else for it but to follow him up.

We walked forward without much hope and entered Will's Wood through a bank of red campion that opened out on to a carpet of bluebells. I had now run out of options, we were running out of time, the sun was slipping away and would soon be in its death throes. I had no choice but to stalk the wood to the central ride where, hopefully, we might catch up with the buck yet, as this ride gets a lot of sun and consequently has a lot of quality browse growing there.

The two of us stalked forward cautiously. On reaching the ride, my confidence in the existence of the deity was restored. Our buck was right where I hoped he would be. Taking advantage of the lee from the wind that the sycamores had provided, he was browsing away unconcerned.

Despite the wind, the scene was a picture postcard, blossoming bluebells and wood anemones serenaded by a mistle thrush belting his love song out from the highest sycamore.

The buck turned broadside, offering the Austrian a shot. I raised the binoculars slowly, pinched my ears closed and waited for the shot. The .25-06 rang out to silence the thrush mid-chorus and slam the deer into the ground. It blew a great spread of loose hair towards us on the wind. The buck kicked its hind legs as life left it. The 120-grain Core-Lokt bullet had broken the shoulder blade and destroyed the main veins and arteries.

I asked Christian to make the rifle safe and slapped him on the shoulder in congratulation. The two of us moved forward together to inspect our prize. What a buck it was – easily a CIC gold medal that went on to score 13th out of the 18 shot in 2006. My clients took a total of seven of those gold medals that year. ⊙

## CHINESE WATER DEER FACTS

⊙ **Open season**
*Bucks & does, England, 1 November - 31 March*

⊙ **Areas found**
*England only –its stronghold is the Duke of Bedford's Woburn Abbey estate. It has now spread to surrounding counties, including Bedfordshire, Cambridgeshire, Hertfordshire, Buckinghamshire, Northamptonshire and Norfolk. Some reside in Shropshire too.*

⊙ **Rifle and ammunition**
*England and Wales requires a minimum calibre of .220 with a muzzle energy of more than 1,000ft/lb.*

⊙ **Stalkers/agents**
*Cervus UK, contact Owen Beardsmore 01283 711878 or 07968 829540 www.cervus-uk.co.uk*
*Steve Sweeting 07792 874511 / 07768 268410 carminnowsestate@msn.com*

*Others can be found in* Sporting Rifle *magazine  www.sporting-rifle.com*

*Chapter 6:* **FALLOW DEER**

Fossil evidence shows that fallow deer (*Dama dama*) were present in Britain prior to the last Ice Age, but became extinct during these glaciations and were subsequently reintroduced. They are, therefore, not considered as truly native to this country.

Fallow deer were later spread across central Europe by the Romans, with stock sourced from the Mediterranean basin. Until recently it was thought that the Normans introduced them to Great Britain and to Ireland for hunting in the royal forests. However, recent finds at Fishbourne Roman Palace suggest that fallow deer were introduced into southern England in the 1st Century AD. It is not known whether these escaped to form a feral colony, or whether they died out and were then reintroduced once more by the Normans.

The first written record of fallow deer is in the Domesday Book compiled in 1086 when 30 fallow deer parks were recorded. By the 17th Century more than 700 deer parks where maintained by the nobility in England alone. Ownership of a deer park was very much the status symbol of the time. Since then the number of parks has declined and by 1892 the number in England had fallen to 390. Many more parks fell into disrepair during the two world wars, resulting in escapes and deliberate release by cash-strapped lairds and landowners. This decline continued and in 1950, G Kenneth Whitehead recorded a meagre 140 parks; in 1975, D & N Chapman recorded just five in Scotland. Today, the total number is fewer than 100.

Fallow deer are now widespread on the UK mainland and are present in most of England and Wales, below a line drawn from the Wash to the Mersey, and all Northern counties in England probably now have at least some fallow present. Common in some areas, they originate no doubt from park escapees.

Longstanding wild herds have existed continuously in certain ancient hunting woodlands such as the New Forest, Epping Forest, Savernake Forest, Rockingham Forest, Cannock Chase and the Forest of Dean for many centuries. In former times, these ancient herds provided royal sport for the monarch and invited nobility and were subject to strict forest law. Vast tracks of Britain's landscape where preserved as royal forests for the king's sole use. The exceptions to forest law was when favoured nobles were granted right to a 'chase'. These in effect were large, enclosed deer parks. Landowners were allow to stock these enclosures with deer (with royal approval) to be hunted by them at leisure Fallow deer seem to have been the preferred species, no doubt due to their docility compared to red deer.

The famous black fallow of Epping Forest are rumoured to have been introduced by James I who brought them from Norway to Scotland and thence to Epping Forest for his personal hunting purposes. Fallow deer are the most commonly seen and have the longest continuous lineage of any deer species living in the New Forest National Park.

The New Forest was William the Conqueror's first hunting forest created in England. Deer were hunted with hounds until brought to bay and killed with spear or arrow.

The present New Forest feral fallow population probably owes much of its

*◑ The author with*
*a medal white*
*fallow buck*

existence to additional park escapees, which have supplemented the original surviving Norman stock. Many parks were broken up during the English Civil War in 1642.

It is a similar story for the fallow deer introduced to Cannock Chase by the Bishop of Lichfield for hunting in the early 12th Century. This Staffordshire herd now numbers nearly 1,000 head and is one of the largest in the country and certainly the largest in the Midlands. Cannock Chase has a wide range of landscapes, including coniferous plantations and open heathland, but it is the large area of natural deciduous woodland that is much favoured by the fallow.

Although the area of Rockingham Forest had been a medieval hunting forest, and was later recorded as a royal hunting preserve in the Domesday book, it wasn't until 1157 that the 'Foresta de Rockingham' is actually referred to on surviving paper. In former times, the ancient forest covered as much as two thirds of Northamptonshire. Today it is formed from a beautiful patchwork of ancient woodlands and open agricultural land, covering an area of some 200 square miles of North-East Northamptonshire. It lies between the Rivers Welland and Nene and the towns of Stamford and Kettering. Following the Normans' initial introduction of fallow deer, a deer park was later created within Rockingham Forest in 1256 and further enlarged in 1485. Many more famous parks were created in the county, such as Yardley Chase and Whittlebury deer park.

Most if not all fallow at large in Northamptonshire, Bedfordshire, Nottinghamshire and Cambridgeshire, owe their origins to these particular Parks and Forest fallow.

Management of the Forest of Dean in Gloucestershire has traditionally been associated with hunting and deer since Norman times. Since the Norman occupation, fallow deer have been the principal species. A venison record from the 13th Century shows 25 fallow, six red and one roe deer taken, but red and roe were absent by the 16th Century. The forest became a royal hunting forest by order of William the Conqueror and remained popular with the succeeding kings, although the last record of a monarch actually hunting deer in the forest was in 1256.

Nevertheless, the Dean remained an important source of venison for the royal table for centuries. There was an intricate management structure associated with the management of all royal forests and part of that lives on today in the forest of Dean through its Court of Verderers (a similar system is also still practised in the New Forest). These judicial officers dealt with poaching offences or theft of venison, the illegal cutting of wood, destruction of woodland, and encroachment through unauthorised enclosures. The earliest surviving allusion to verderers in Dean is in 1216; the earliest named are those in 1221. Today, the verderers still act in the best interest of the forest and hold office for life. There are four verderers who are aided and served by a steward.

Today, the fallow herd is carefully managed and the Forest of Dean itself is also Britain's premier oak forest, covering 35 square miles. This forest was one of the nuclei that helped establish Britain's current wild fallow deer population.

*◑ A couple of fallow bucks make their way through the snow*

Savernake Forest stands alone among the medieval forests of Wiltshire. It is one of the few with records prior to the Norman conquest, although undoubtedly it was the Normans who introduced the resident population of fallow deer. The first surviving reference to the wood, which is called 'Safernoc', occurs in a charter of 933 from the Saxon king Athelstan. Records also show a royal huntsman stationed at nearby Burbage in the 11th Century. This suggests that by the time of the Norman conquest, the forest was already fulfilling its function as a hunting preserve for the monarch. However it wasn't until 1130 that the forest was first formalised by a record such as we have today.

The forest was put into the care of one of the victorious knights – Richard Esturmy, who fought at the Battle of Hastings in 1066 – and has since passed down from father to son or daughter in an unbroken line for 31 generations. Never once has it been bought or sold in 1,000 years, and today it is the only former royal forest in Britain still in private hands.

In the 12th Century, the acreage of Savernake Forest was considerable, extending from East Kennett and Pewsey in the west, to Collingbourne in the south, the River Kennet in the north and the Hampshire and Berkshire borders in the east. This was, and still is, prime habitat for fallow deer; under protection of the foresters it isn't hard to appreciate how the species expanded.

Under forest law, the foresters, rangers, regarders and woodwards worked under the control of a warden, a hereditary office enjoyed successively by the families of Esturmy (until 1427), Seymour (until 1675) and Ailesbury, to the present day. The symbol of their authority since the 14th Century has been a magnificent hunting horn of ivory inlaid with engraved silver bands.

After the Barons' Revolt of 1173-1174 and the signing of Magna Carta in 1215 most of the medieval forests became fragmented and Savernake was no exception, with much of its former forest cleared.

Savernake fared fairly well under the hereditary wardenship of the Seymour family during the early Tudor period. Henry VIII hunted here and stayed at Savernake shortly after the execution of Queen Anne Boleyn in 1536. It was here that King Henry's eye was taken by his host Sir John Seymour's daughter, Jane. They were subsequently married and Jane Seymour was crowned Queen just months later, causing the head of the family at Savernake to suddenly find himself father-in-law to Henry VIII. Edward Seymour, Duke of Somerset and Jane's brother, went on to become Protector of the Realm during the sickly boy king Edward VI's reign following Henry VIII's death. He successfully gained Savernake as a gift from the Crown. Unfortunately for him, he fell out of favour and was executed in 1548. However his descendants managed to retain the forest.

By 1700, a series of family misfortunes had resulted in the dissolution of both the Great Park and Brimslade Park, with many deer no doubt dispersing into the welcoming woods of Savernake. After this, much of the open ground was replanted by Lord Thomas Bruce, the Earl of Ailesbury, and as was the fashion of the time, Lancelot "Capability" Brown, was brought in to landscape the unmanaged and suffering woodland. The forest extended to some 40,000 acres at this time, nearly 10 times its present size.

David Brudenell-Bruce, Earl of Cardigan, is the current and 31st warden of Savernake forest who takes an active interest in the estate. Since WWII, Savernake Forest itself has been the responsibility of the Forestry Commission, whose sympathetic management has gone a long way towards the restoration and preservation of Savernake's ancient trees and her famous fallow herd.

One particularly interesting herd of fallow deer is that in the Mortimer Forest on the Welsh Marches. Here a significant part of the fallow population has long hair with distinct ear tufts and longer body hair the like of which are found nowhere else in the world. Mortimer Forest is a remnant of the ancient Saxon hunting forests of Mocktree, Deerfold and Bringewood and, like Wyre Forest, wasn't strictly classified a royal forest in Norman times but was denoted a chase. The Mortimer family that give the forest its name arrived in England in the wake of William the Conqueror in 1066 and with them of course came fallow deer. The Mortimer family story is a colourful one of ambition, power, deceit, bitter rivalry and various attempts to claim the English throne. The Mortimers' holdings also include the Wyre Forest deer chase which would have been stocked with fallow. How far north the Mortimer family's hunting rights extended is debatable, but it may have included the whole area in south-east

*Fallow bucks on the move*

Shropshire of which they were overlords at the time of the Domesday Book. It is mainly from these two ancient hunting chases of Mortimer and Wyre, that feral fallow expanded across the march into Wales.

Fallow are the most common deer in Wales and have long established strongholds in the Wye Valley and Eastern Monmouthshire, the Twyi valley between Llandeilo and Carmarthen, the Elwy valley and the forestry adjacent to Margam Park and the Coed y Brenin forest of Gwynedd and Powys. The species also appears in smaller numbers in most of North Wales, mainly due to deer park escapes and are present all along the English border.

There are now only two areas of Wales devoid of deer. The first is the far north-west corner of Wales, although there were wild fallow on Anglesey until recently, and the second is much of the old county of South Glamorgan.

Fallow deer are not quite so widespread in Scotland as in the northern parts of England, but are present in most lowland districts. However, some Scottish populations, principally the Annandale, Galloway, the Tay Valley and Loch Lomond herds are well established and rapidly expanding. The Annandale herd especially is one of the largest unenclosed herds of fallow deer in the country. This herd was first established at Raehills, Annandale just after the death of the 3rd Marquis of Annandale in 1792. The original stock was introduced from Hopetoun House deer park, near Edinburgh by the Marquis's great nephew and heir, the 3rd Earl of Hopetoun. No trace of any enclosure has ever been discovered, either on the ground or on the old maps. There was virtually no forestry in the area at that time, with just a few old woods near to the present estate house. This lack of woodland effectively kept the newly introduced fallow close to the house. Today, with the expansion of forestry, the fallow have expanded their territory enormously and can be found from Earshaig right through to the Forest of Ae.

The fallow herd around Dunkeld in the Tay Valley has a significant number of the black variety in its number and were originally released by a former Duke of Atholl early in the 19th Century.

The Scottish Islands also hold their share of this species, with the population on Islay being the most significant. It has been argued that monks brought these deer with them in 900 AD, but historians believe they arrived in the 14th Century. Colonel Greenhill Gardyne introduced the species to Glenforsa on the Isle of Mull in 1868 where they have flourished. Just North of Jura, the Isle of Scaraba was stocked with a small number of fallow in about 1870 and some of these have swum over to the nearby Isle of Carra. On Loch Lomond, fallow deer had been introduced to the Isle of Inchlonaig in the 17th Century and some of these may have spread to inhabit other islands close by.

Dumfriesshire, Dunbartonshire, Kirkudbrightshire, Perthshire and Stirlingshire are still the strongholds of Scottish fallow and most if not all are there due to deliberate release rather than escape.

In Ireland, fallow are the most widespread deer species living wild and also the most popular park deer, with over 60 deer park herds. They are found in most woodlands with suitable habitat across the entire country and must number well over 10,000 head. Many of these fallow are descended from original Norman stock introduced soon after their arrival in 1169 and have been supplemented with deer park escapees throughout the centuries right up to the present day.

An important historical Irish herd is kept at Phoenix Park (Páirc an Fhionnuisce) in Dublin. The park is one of the largest walled parks in Europe with a 16km perimeter wall situated north of the River Liffey about 3km west of the city centre. This herd of 400-450 fallow deer descend from original animals introduced in the 1660s.

Northern Ireland fallow are found in Co Antrim, Co Armagh, Co Down and Co Tyrone. These deer became established from escapees formerly enclosed on the Baronscourt, Caledon and Shane's Castle estates. They quickly populated suitable areas of woodland close by their former parks and around the Northern end of Strangford Lough.

According to the 2007 British Deer Society survey, fallow deer have enjoyed an increase in range since the previous survey in 2000 although this increase in range is not as spectacular as for some of the other deer species.

Fallow deer are the second largest deer found in the UK. Rarely, a large buck can weigh up to 85kg (190lb), though they seldom attain over 50kg (110lb).

Only the bucks grow antlers. Bucks rarely exceed 10 years of age, but does live a couple of years longer. They are a herding species and are the most common species kept in deer parks both historically and today. The composition of the herd varies with the seasons. For much of the year it will be split into two distinct groups: one of adult females with yearlings and fawns, and a second

◑ *The author and*
*a client with a good*
*fallow head*

of bucks living together as a loose herd away from the does. Fallow deer do not establish a territory (except small rutting stands held by the buck during the rut), but inhabit a large 'home range' over which they will travel. However, favoured areas will be more frequented than others. The separate sex herds split for the rut, bucks spread out and females move between them staying relatively ungrouped compared with the rest of the year. After the rut they herd up once more into single sex herds sometimes coming together in extreme winter weather.

Fallow differ from other UK deer species in two regards: antlers and coat variations. The fallow is the only British deer with palmated antlers, making the fallow buck instantly identifiable.

Though varied, the most common fallow colouration is the familiar summer coat, which is light-tan in colour with white spots. This coat becomes longer and lighter in winter, with the spotting turning indistinct or disappearing altogether. Fallow have a distinctive white rump-patch, with a characteristic black 'M' shape similar to the McDonald's fast food sign. The menil form is paler, lacking the black 'M' on the rump though retaining its white spots all year. Melanistic fallow are almost entirely black without white coloration anywhere. Finally, the white fallow can vary from white to a light-fawn colour. Known as the white hart – incorrectly as a hart is really a red stag – it is as popular in British folklore as it is a pub name. White fallow are a true colour variety and not albinistic, although albinos do occur, they are exceptionally rare.

The tail of the fallow is the longest of all the deer species in the British Isles and is also a good recognition feature. When fallow deer are alarmed they will often move off in a distinctive manner known as pronking. Here, all four feet are brought together and leave the ground simultaneously as the animal bounds away. This characteristic behaviour is shared by sika deer, and also many antelope species.

The fallow deer are usually easily recognised by their distinctive shovel shaped or palmate antlers. Like all deer they shed their antlers every year. The young buck will grow his first antlers in his second year at the age of 14-15 months. This will be a single unbranched spike, usually 3-15cm and is called a 'pricket'; the third year, a sorrel; the fourth, a sore; the fifth, a first-head buck; and the sixth a great buck. In each succeeding year until he reaches his prime, a bucks antlers increase in size, provided that he is in good health and has not been injured. By the second or third head the buck's antlers usually show the beginnings of 'palmation', the flattening and broadening of that part furthest from the head. This palmation is usually fringed with a series of mini points called spellers. Proceeding up the antler from the coronet, the first point or tine is called the brow, the second is called the trey and then comes the flattened palmation. There is no bey tine on a fallow antler as there is on a standard red antler.

This deer is a creature of the woods and forest, preferring mature deciduous and mixed woodland, although they will colonise coniferous forestry provided these contain open areas and wide glades. Fallow deer do not inhabit the open moorland areas found in the north of England and Scotland, although they may be found in the forested valleys. Farmland is particularly favoured if there is enough woodland for daytime cover, and will feed throughout the day, but they will turn nocturnal if heavily persecuted.

Fallow deer are preferential grazers, leaving their secure woodland lying-up places to graze, and often maraud agricultural land, bringing them into conflict with farmers. These deer like to graze the grassy rides within the forest for selected shoots and herbs. They will also browse on tall herbs, heather, holly, bramble and come autumn, will switch over to beech mast, fruits, fungi and other woody browse.

Under normal circumstances, fallow feeding activity takes place around dawn and the late afternoon or early evening. Between these times, the fallow lie up in some secure undisturbed place to ruminate and chew the cud.

Before moving out into open areas to feed, the herd fragments into small groups on the woodland fringe but still stay within the wood, pacing about back and forth, until the lead doe is quite sure it is safe to venture out. When disturbed on open ground, the herd will follow the dominant doe back into cover, moving off in a distinct order of dominance. Any bucks within the herd usually make off in a different direction and usually do not follow the doe.

The browsing of tree shoots and marauding of agricultural crops by fallow deer causes conflict with farmers and foresters, due to the economic loss sustained. Fallow deer can reach high local densities which give rise to unacceptable levels of damage.

◑ *Fallow come in a range of colours from white to black*

Herd sizes, as well as mixed-sex groups, vary according to population density and habitat. Groups of adult males and females with young remain apart for most of the year in large woodlands, only coming together to breed. In more open agricultural environments, the sexes freely mix in large herds throughout the year.

The rut starts in early autumn and can last into November, this is a period of tremendous activity for the bucks, during which they mark out their territorial rutting stands. At this time, the woods echo with fallow bucks grunting a guttural, belching call to attract does and deter rivals. These stands are often in damp areas and have a strong 'rutty buck' odour. Dominant bucks frequently urinate around these stands which are topped up often. Fallow bucks are also characterised by a prominent Adam's apple at this time and a long penile sheath, known as a brush. During the rut the tip of the brush becomes a darker colour and protrudes.

The escalation of display behaviour with challenging bucks begins with parallel walking that often leads to fighting. In most populations bucks maintain a defended rutting stand, though in others a temporary rutting stand is maintained to attract sufficient does to herd them into a harem. In lower density areas, bucks simply seek out any receptive females and take their chances.

Fallow does give birth to a single fawn or occasionally twins in June after a gestation period of around 32 weeks. When the fawn is born, the doe will conceal it in undergrowth until weaned at two months.

Fallow are usually silent, with the exception of the rut. At this time bucks will issue a deep repetitive belching groan. Does and fawns will give a short bark when alarmed.

Although easily tamed in parkland, fallow deer that are regularly hunted are canny and the big bucks are normally extremely difficult to approach. Both high-seat shooting and foot stalking are regularly used methods and during the rut the 'Primos fallow grunter' call can be used to call in a buck. The fallow deer is a big animal and a .243 Winchester, although quite capable of efficiently killing a fallow with correct bullet placement, is a little light in my opinion. I would suggest a .270 Winchester as a minimum for this species.

I have taken clients fallow stalking all over the UK. On one particular morning in Scotland, dawn was bright and clear, with a welcome hard frost – a god-send that saw off the midges that had plagued my previous visit to the estate in the summer. A watery autumnal sun was a primrose blush of promise as it stained the eastern horizon. The red stags appreciated the frost too, as we could hear their roars ring out.

Andy and Bill were soon on their way, pushing through the now yellowing bracken into the mixed larch and sitka spruce forest on Carminnows hill. Close by, a blackcock croaked out his version of the stags' verse.

A wisp of snipe lifted from the frozen bog, their crops no doubt empty and their beaks bent by the unexpected freeze. Then the unmistakable grunting of a fallow buck halted the stalkers' progress. A clash of antlers from somewhere in the trees told of two bucks locked in combat. The hunters' cloudy breaths

billowed around them, showing a favourable wind, but they daren't go into the wood. All they could do was wait for events to unfold.

The duel was soon decided and the antler rattling abruptly ceased. A buck burst onto the scene to flee across the open bog. Andy quickly deployed the stalking sticks. Bill fitted his custom .275 Rigby to the centre vee of the sticks and the buck stopped briefly to stare at the two hunters.

"Shoot when you're ready," commanded Andy. Bill fitted to the rifle, ran the crosshairs up the buck's leg and squeezed off a round as the reticle came to rest on the animal's shoulder. The Rigby cracked into life and the satisfying 'thrummp' of a well-placed round hit home.

The fallow lurched forward and fell with its hind legs windmilling. Giving the buck the required five minutes before approaching, the two stalkers moved forward across the bog to inspect their deer.

Bill had come to hunt a trophy-quality fallow buck in the limited time he had available from his busy schedule as an airline pilot. Andy had been quick to take the buck and – fair play to him – he hadn't had much time to assess the trophy quality. But the antlers were inferior and the animal a young. To add insult to injury, the victor of the bout showed himself across the clearing and trotted off indignantly, showing off his huge palmated paddles. Bill put Andy out of his misery and told him he was pleased with the hunt and the result but he would be more than happy to hunt the big buck as well, if it were possible.

That evening and the following morning Andy and Bill tried for the trophy buck. The pressure was well and truly on for the final evening outing. Andy had taken some excessive ribbing about his quick decision to shoot the small buck.

True to form the fallow buck had taken up his rutting stand in the same area. Although the two stalkers heard him grunting regularly, they had seen only fallow does that were the object of his amorous intentions. The hunters decided to use the high tower that overlooks the open boggy area where they had shot the first fallow.

Taking to their vantage point in the early afternoon, the hours had clicked steadily by without a glimpse of the animal that taunted them throughout their vigil with his deep rasping grunts. At last, he decided to put in an appearance. Appearing from within the spruce trees, the trophy buck ambled on to the scene to catch some late afternoon rays from a dying sun. Thrashing some dead thistles, he stretched his neck forward and began grunting his advert to the local ladies.

Meanwhile, the buck now filled Bill's 6x42 Swarovski. He had a good lean on the tower's rail but was struggling to slow his breathing and his thumping heart. The buck returned to give the thistles another good thrashing.

Bill halted his breathing with a great effort and sent the round on its way. Exploding into a gallop, the fallow showed no other reaction to the shot and sped across the bog and out of sight into the bracken bank to the hunters' immediate left. A crestfallen Bill and Andy made for the thistles and fortunately found a heavy blood trail. As the daylight was dying Andy made the decision to call me up to bring my tracking hound to save time. It was an anxious 20 minutes for Bill until I arrived with my Bavarian mountain hound, Jaeger. I collared the dog with the tracking leash (this indicates work to the hound) and ordered her to stay while I examined the strike area which had a lot of dark arterial blood and some rib fragments. The trail looked more than promising. I called Jaeger up, commanded 'where's the buck', and let the 10-metre leash run between my fingers as Jaeger took to the trail.

The flat nylon leash pulled easily through the bracken stems, its bright orange Day-Glo colour proving easy to follow. It was an easy find, as the trophy buck had simply straightlined 120 yards with a smashed heart running on adrenaline alone, to collapse dead in the bracken. Jaeger was soon growling and tearing at the exit wound, indicating the animal's location.

Bill was a happy hunter that evening as we recovered his second fallow buck, as was Andy who was grinning his pleasure to all concerned.

My colleague and supremo stalker Mark Brackstone's passion is quality fallow trophies. He has to leave his native Wiltshire to pursue really big bucks – the following account is Mark's own successful quest to take a major gold-medal class fallow.

Typically, our mature Wiltshire bucks will have fishtailed antlers and if the palms are 4in wide it's a monster. A typical park buck with good feeding will have a comparable head at two or three years old. Most of our prickets have bumps like the top of your thumb, rather than the 6-10in spikes you might expect.

In one local area we have been selective about what we cull, in the hope of improving the quality. If I am honest about this 15-year experiment, though, we have seen little improvement. For many years before there had been no selective culling, so as a consequence the gene pool had deteriorated. It is probably beyond rescue, unless we introduce some new blood.

For years I have had a hankering to shoot a really good fallow buck trophy. in the early 1990s, my friend Robert Howat and I made contact with some super Welsh lads, who had some excellent fallow stalking around the Port Talbot area. This fallow population's origins are a direct result of escapees from nearby Margam Park, which contains superb quality fallow bucks.

As part of their cull of mature bucks we did a trade for quite a few years, swapping their fallow stalking during the autumn rut so they could shoot trophy roe bucks in the spring and summer.

As their stalking areas changed and their syndicate began to break up, the arrangement petered out. This was a great shame, as no money ever changed hands and it was always a riot with the Welsh guys. During this halcyon period, Robert and I shot some superb fallow bucks, one of which made a CIC bronze medal.

Three or four years ago I was dropping off at the taxidermist and saw a magnificent fallow buck in the process of being mounted. I asked where it had come from and was told that it hailed from the New Forest, and that the owner of this specimen was Steve Middleton. He had access to some pretty serious bucks and didn't charge the earth either. I was intrigued.

I soon gave Steve a call, introduced myself and booked an outing with him. His areas were relatively small but he had a number of them dotted around the New Forest. He explained that almost without exception, he had areas which played host to bucks and prickets, but only the odd doe.

Although we didn't have any success initially I booked a repeat outing. This time we saw bucks but again drew a blank. Steve kindly invited me again, but refused an outing fee. You can't get fairer than that.

On the third attempt we saw plenty of bucks but could not get a shot at a decent one. I shot a couple of poor cull animals that were in his management plan, but a really big buck still eluded me.

We had now become good friends and as I learned the layout I was able to join Steve in discussing approaches and ambush techniques. We humans are strange, or perhaps it's just me that's strange. The more times you try and fail the greater the need to succeed. That's all well for me, but Steve was getting frustrated indeed.

I consider myself an experienced stalker and a half-decent shot. It was about our fifth try and we approached some pony paddocks in what could only be described as poor light, and mist. Little did I realise when I got out of bed that morning that I was about to make a complete fool of myself and shake Steve's confidence in this so-called 'experienced' stalker.

The day before, Steve had seen seven big bucks and reckoned at least two were old warriors carrying huge, craggy palms that he thought may be of high medal quality. In the misty dawn we could just make out the bucks busy eating the ponies' hay. Periodically, the sound of antlers clashing reached us as the bucks sparred for position. The three resident – and now disgruntled – ponies could be seen on the bank above the mist line, having been chased away from their hay by the deer.

The fallow had moved into a tree line about 80 yards from the five-bar gate we had crawled 100 yards or so to reach. Jostling nervously, it was quite obvious they were not settled and were probably planning to beat a hasty retreat back to the safety of the forest. The light was still poor (that's my excuse) as Steve whispered, "Take the second from the left." I levelled the rifle and asked, "The black one, yeah?" "Yeah, yeah the second from the left," he confirmed.

I levelled the illuminated crosshair of my Heym .243 on his chest and sent my home-loaded bullet on its way. The herd ran 50 yards and passed us just as one of their mates keeled over. Steve and I carefully approached the dead buck.

The first words spoken after the shot were: "You shot the wrong one." I couldn't believe it. I could see the disappointment on Steve's face and knew the feeling well, having had guests and clients do the same.

On this occasion, I had actually shot a four or five year old buck with a fishtailed antler on one side and a more promising antler with a 4in palm the other. Steve took it well and I put my hand in my pocket and paid him. We had now become good mates and Steve was not comfortable taking money from me, so we agreed to trade forthwith. I would let Steve try my Devon area for a big woodland stag, and he could also come to me for a muntjac.

Two weeks later I received an excited call from Steve, just before Christmas. "I have a group of really big bucks in a beech belt and there're some masters among 'em". At 6am the next day I knocked on Steve's door and his wife answered. She invited me in and went to get him, but to my embarrassment I overheard her call to him in a quiet voice, obviously not meant for my ears: "Your blind deer stalker's here again." Steve had obviously not made much of a secret of my earlier cock-up!

This time I stalked the wood alone, to minimise noise, and soon came across an enormous fallow buck. The palm facing me must have been two feet long and at least 9in wide. Here was the buck of my dreams. I had the rifle on him in a jiffy and flicked the safety off. He turned his massive head away from me and I couldn't believe my eyes: the other antler had snapped off above the brow tine.

Deflated, I soon rejoined Steve. We stalked a few other areas and shot a couple of prickets for his butcher pal. Three days later, we were once again out stalking and full of anticipation. In the same wood I had seen the one-antlered buck we encountered eight or so big, mature males slowly ambling toward us.

Soon I soon spotted one which seemed to have exceptionally wide palms. Time was of the essence, as we were actually pinned down and directly in their path of approach, crouched down behind a small holly bush. I looked to Steve for a second opinion but he just shrugged and whispered, "Your choice."

❂ *Fallows' relative
docility make them
the natural choice
for a deer park*

It had to be the one on the left. I drew a careful bead on the beast's engine room and took up the trigger. I heard the rifle's moderated report as the big buck reared and the rest of the herd scattered. He ran a short distance before succumbing, falling to the forest floor dead. He looked good, and though not a gold he sported a super trophy. I was thrilled. Steve was pleased for me but we both knew that I was still short of my personal goal, the holy grail of a wild, gold medal fallow buck.

The buck I had grassed had a fantastic split palm, almost resembling two separate palms, and was a good buck to cull. All his teeth were worn down to the gums and he was certainly past his best. It was a superb stalk and a really interesting trophy I would always remember.

A couple of weeks passed and another call came from Steve. This time, a group of impressive bucks were launching nightly raids into an equestrian property and causing mayhem. They had attacked a 150-year-old Acer tree

and had understandably upset the owners of the property. Their nocturnal plunderings had to be stopped; we'd have to creep in during the dark hours. Steve said that he had not watched these particular bucks properly though he had been and seen some pretty serious bucks on this property earlier in the year.

We arrived in total darkness and approached the house; the marauders were walking across the patio, completely illuminated by the floodlights. They thought they were safe as they had so far been unmolested. The route of departure was pretty obvious and we soon took up an ambush position about 150 yards away on the far side of the garden.

As the Eastern sky paled into daylight we could hear the bucks approaching, their crunching footsteps unmistakable in the fragile frost.

I waited ready, with rifle resting on shooting sticks. The bucks were moving through a patch of frozen laurels and then all became still. We waited and waited, hardly daring to draw breath but still nothing moved. Had they doubled back, or simply laid up? After 20 minutes Steve said he would carefully pull back and approach from a different angle, in an attempt to locate them. I waited some time and then felt my mobile vibrate – message received. 'No sign anywhere, gone or still in bushes I will walk forward slowly be ready.' I was frozen but still ready, the minutes ticked by and then it sounded like a heard of buffalo was heading my way. The bucks burst into view at about 70 yards, trotting fast. I had about three seconds to evaluate and draw a bead on one. Number three looked good, a big common-coloured buck with a good palm facing my side. I put the crosshairs on his chest and followed him. I needed to give it 4-5in lead at that speed and distance, I reckoned. My silenced .243 spat out a Norma soft point and the buck leapt in mid-stride, disappearing from view and followed by the others.

Steve soon appeared. "Well?", he enquired. "I reckon I got him," I said. Together we approached slowly over the brow and there, in the stream before us, lay another superbly-palmated and probable bronze-medal fallow buck. I think Steve was secretly disappointed that it was not gold but I was still thrilled; we'd had good fun stalking the buck in quite a novel set of circumstances.

The owners were pleased and the nightly raids on their garden stopped. My buck measured a bronze, but the memory of that morning will always be stirred when I see the buck on my wall.

I owed Steve yet another muntjac buck or a red stag and was now so indebted that I could never hope to pay him back. Hunting is just that – hunting. We had shot some super bucks but not the gold-medal I was looking for, yet had forged a friendship which would hopefully last a lifetime.

Last year I returned to stalk with Steve, who had located the monster of all fallow bucks on a friend's ground. He didn't have the stalking but the guy would sell a buck if we were successful. This buck was indeed exceptional, and unlike all of our sorties to date it went like clockwork. After a short stalk I shot a superb one-eyed fallow buck which measured a CIC gold medal. After all the former effort and time put in, it really was a bit of an anti-climax.

I still feel that of all the UK deer, the most exciting is a crafty old fallow buck, but to get good trophies, this species needs to be managed carefully. Promising bucks need to be allowed to get to eight years plus, when they are truly mature, unlike roe which are mature at four or five years old.

Why is there not more medal-class fallow in the UK? The biggest single reason must be that they are not allowed to get old enough and, although I have shot a number of big bucks with Steve, he is selective in the numbers he shoots compared with those he could take if he had no scruples. ⊙

**A wary fallow buck**

## FALLOW DEER FACTS

⊙ **Open season**
*Bucks, England, Wales and Northern Ireland: 1 August – 30 April*
*Bucks, Scotland: 1 August – 30 April*
*Does, England, Wales and Northern Ireland: 1 November – 31 March*
*Does, Scotland: 21 October – 15 February*

⊙ **Rifle and ammunition**
*England and Wales: minimum calibre of .240, muzzle energy more than 1,700ft/lb, expanding bullet only*
*Scotland: minimum 100gn expanding bullet, muzzle energy no less than 1,750ft/lb, muzzle velocity no less than 2,450fps*
*Northern Ireland: minimum calibre of .236, bullet designed to expand in a predictable manner*

⊙ **Stalkers/agents in England**
*Cervus UK, contact Owen Beardsmore 01283 711878 or 07968 829540 www.cervus-uk.co.uk*
*Hamptworth Estate, 01794 390700 enquiries@hamptworthestate.co.uk*
*Mike Dickinson, Derbyshire, 01538 308697 or 07721 671746 michaeldickinson@btopenworld.com*

⊙ **Stalkers/agents in Scotland**
*Steve Sweeting, Galloway, 07792 874511 carminnowsestate@msn.com*

⊙ **Stalkers/agents in Northern Ireland**
*Colebrooke Park, Co Fermanagh, 028 8953 1402 www.colebrooke.info*

⊙ **Stalkers/agents in Southern Ireland**
*John Fenton, Co Wicklow +353 454 04947 Johnfenton1@eircom.net*

*Others can be found in* Sporting Rifle *magazine www.sporting-rifle.com*

⊃ *Although
dissimilar to the red
deer in looks, the
sika will hybridise
with reds*

Japanese sika deer (*Cervus nippon*) is a species native to much of East Asia, but has also been introduced to other parts of the world, including British parks. Today, its original range is heavily fragmented in all areas, except its stronghold Japan, where the species remains prolific. It is has become extinct in Vietnam and Korea and in China is limited to small wild populations in the Southern part of the country. However, there are a number of feral populations descended from park escapes across China. In Russia, the species is now only found in Primorsky Krai.

The species has been introduced to mainland Europe, the United States, New Zealand, Ireland and the United Kingdom. It has thrived in Ireland and the UK, having expanded rapidly after the two world wars, to become a significant concern to commercial forestry interests, due to tree damage caused by bole scoring and bark stripping.

One stag and three hinds were the original breeding stock for all sika in Ireland, Scotland and most English populations. These four animals were introduced by the 7th Viscount Powerscourt, a noted collector of exotic species, to his deer park at Enniskerry, on the border of County Wicklow & County Dublin in 1860. His captive sika bred well, and the Viscount moved a number of them to enclosed parks in Fermanagh, Kerry, Limerick, Down and Monaghan. He exported further surplus stock to landowners all over the British Isles.

In 1860, the first a pair of Japanese sika were presented to the Zoological Society of London and exhibited in Regent's Park. Deliberate releases and park escapees soon established them in our countryside. Today, the UK has large populations of sika deer in Northern Ireland, Scotland, England and some surrounding Islands, but is not yet established in Wales.

Ireland's present population of sika in Counties Kerry, Wicklow, Tyrone and Fermanagh is the result of escapees from numerous deer parks during the troubles in the early 20th Century and a deliberate release of a number of animals near Killarney, County Kerry in 1865 by the Earl of Kenmare, for hunting purposes. Eighty years later, the herd numbered nearly 1,000 head.

The first sika deer arrived in Northern Ireland in 1870 when a stag and five hinds were sent from Viscount Powerscourt to Viscount Colebrooke's deer park in County Fermanagh. Twenty years later, sika deer were sent from Colebrooke to Baronscourt, County Tyrone, where they thrived. In the 1920s, the entire herd escaped from the Duke of Abercorn's Baronscourt deer park and became established in the surrounding woodland.

The planting of commercial forestry in the 1940s certainly suited the free-living Irish sika and encouraged their range expansion. Further herds have since become established in Counties Dublin, Kildare, Carlow, Cork and Donegal.

Scotland's sika deer are well established on the Kintyre peninsular and most of the country north of the Great Glen, both sides of Loch Ness and in Peebleshire. The original Kintyre stock of sika deer was introduced to the Carradale Estate by Major Austin MacKenzie from a herd he owned on the family estate at Fawley Court, Buckinghamshire in 1893. Apparently, the Major shipped two stags and four hinds to Kintyre, which were landed on Carradale

Pier by the SS Davaar, along with some fallow deer. The herd was initially enclosed on Carradale Point and steadily increased until WWI, when the fence fell into disrepair and the entire collection escaped into the neighbouring woodland of the Carra Valley. This population increased dramatically until by the outbreak of WWII they had spread throughout the peninsula and into Knapdale, now numbering over 400 head.

Another notable sika release by a member of the MacKenzie family in 1900, helped to establish the species North of the Great Glen on Glenmazeran and Glenkyllachy forests. Respected railway engineer William D Mackenzie, a relation of Major Austin MacKenzie in 1900, sourced animals from the family estate at Fawley Court.

Colonel EG Frazer Tytler released eight sika deer onto his Aldourie Castle Estate at the head of Loch Ness, that he had brought up from Rosehall Park, Sutherland, also in 1900.

Other releases include that of Sir Arthur Bignold, a godson of the Duke of Wellington, who imported some sika deer from Viscount Powerscourt to his Achanalt deer forest near Garve, Rosshire in 1889. Although he initially kept them fenced, feeding restrictions forced him to release the captives into the surrounding forests in 1915. The Duke of Portland's first attempt, in 1920, to intoduce the animals to the Berriedale Castle estate in Caithness from his deer park at Welbeck in Nottinghamshire was unsuccessful, but he fared better when he tried again in 1930 and the newly established population soon spread across Caithness and into Sutherland.

There is another strong population of sika deer in Peeblesshire, originating from the famous Dawyck Park herd near Peebles. This population is rapidly expanding into Dumfries & Galloway and Ayrshire, though the M74 seems to be an effective barrier in slowing their westward advance into these counties. Again, as in Ireland, commercial spruce plantations established in the post WWII period have contributed significantly to the spread of Scottish sika.

English populations of sika deer are more patchy and scattered across England, with large densities in Dorset's Poole Basin and Hampshire's New Forest. The Dorset population has expanded from two separate introductions: the first, in 1895, at Hyde House Park north of Wareham, was relatively secure behind the park walls, until their first recorded escape in1927, when sika were reported on the neigbouring Trigan Estate. Further escapes occurred during the 1930s and the whole herd was released during WWII when the Ministry of Defence took over the running of Hyde House estate and opened the gates.

The second Dorset introduction was on Brownsea Island in Poole Harbour a year after the Hyde House imports. Apparently these animals started to swim ashore on the initial night of their release, making them the original Dorset colonizers. Numbers were swelled by further escapes and the later release of the total Hyde House stock.

New Forest sika deer largely owe their origins to a pair of animals gifted to the second Baron Montagu of Beaulieu by King Edward VII, which were penned at Thorns Beach. These soon escaped into Sowley Wood and a later

☊ *The author with client and a sika stag*

pair was also released into nearby Ashen Wood, thereby forming the nucleus of today's extensive herds of sika found in the New Forest.

Although most of the UK's sika introductions were of the smaller, Japanese variety (*Cervus nippon*), the population in the trough of Bowland in Lancashire is probably the Manchurian subspecies (*Cervus nippon manchuricus*). These sika were introduced in 1907 to Gisburn Park by Lord Ribblesdale, a former Master of Buckhounds for Queen Victoria, after the local population of fallow deer hunted by the Ribblesdale hounds had declined. The idea was to transport and plant a huntable stag onto the hunt country, where it would soon be found and pursued, captured and returned to the park. The sika stags, however did not provide good sport and after a time the Buckhounds were disbanded, the herd eventually being released to become feral in 1925 and spread across a wide area.

This species remains absent from Wales - the nearest population being introduced in 1929 from Surrenden-Dering Park in Kent to Lundy Island, situated in the Bristol Channel. The sika deer here are usually seen on the east side of the island in the rhododendron thickets and periodically have to be culled to keep numbers in check.

Japanese sika are intermediate in size between roe and fallow deer Stags stand at 27-37in (70-95cm) at the shoulder and hinds at 20-35in (50-90cm) and weigh an average 106-110lb (48-50kg). Sika have a chestnut, spotted coat in summer, turning in winter to a dark, rich brown to almost black with feint or no spots at all. They have a short fallow-like tail, white caudal and carry a small head with a pinched-faced appearance. Antlers are typically much narrower then the wider spread of a red stag and do not end in a crown, being relatively straight in comparison and normally not more than eight points in a mature stag (four on each antler). Occasionally five tines are encountered and exceptionally six may occur, though these are usually found in the Manchurian race. Bey tines are usually absent in all races. The sika is a secretive animal making it difficult to stalk. When alarmed, hinds and calves sometimes flare out their caudal patch and adopt a skipping-like movement, known as pronking. This behavior is distinctive and more akin to antelope than deer.

Sika deer tend to thrive in most habitat types with sufficient concealing cover, as they are by nature a shy species. They particularly favour pine, spruce and larch forests, with boggy ground and heath land also suiting them well.

The sika is both grazer and browser, preferring grasses, heathers, fruits, berries and tree shoots. They will browse on pine needles and ivy in hard weather. While there is no evidence that sika cause more damage to trees than other species through browsing, bark stripping and bole scoring - the gouging of trees with antlers – is specific to sika deer, and the severe damage caused seriously affects timber production. As a result, sika deer are unpopular with foresters and forestry managers. Agricultural crops are sometimes targeted and local damage may be extensive during their nocturnal depravations. Predominantly nocturnal feeders, they leave cover close to dusk and return soon after dawn.

Sika live in single sex herds for most of the year and many mature males are solitary by nature. During the rut from the end of September to November the

*♦ Sika stag in classic pose*

stag will attempt to gather and defend a harem of hinds at his rutting stand, though he often loses them and has to start over when he patrols his territory periodically. His piercing, high-pitched whistle-like call is unmistakable once heard and can be imitated with practice using an American elk (wapiti) call. Usually a single calf is born after a 32-week gestation period. Though fully weaned by ten months, the follower will remain with the hind until the following year.

Sika deer are a highly vocal species, with more than 10 individual sounds ranging from soft whistles to loud alarm screams. During the rut, stags issue a series of three high-pitched, whistle-like bugles that can be imitated by the stalker with practice.

Rutting activity starts in early September, peaking in early October but may last well into the winter months. Some stags defend a rutting territory, similar to fallow deer, but often switch to harem-holding when a suitable group of hinds has been assembled. Others simply wander throughout the hinds range in search of receptive females and rarely some stags may gather in a lek.

Sika are the most nocturnal of the UK's deer species, typically becoming active at dusk and returning to cover soon after dawn. Well-placed high seats are a good bet in suitable country if the wind is conducive. An early morning rise and a careful advance into a good ambush position often works well when

the local deer habits and preferred areas are known. Foot stalking, working into the wind, specifically along the edges of the sika's woodland or heathland sanctuaries at dawn and at dusk, is the favoured alternative to ambush.

The artificial calling of sika stags during the rut is becoming increasingly popular, as more stalkers learn the science. Proven calls are the DJ sika stag model no R-25 and the Primos 306 Jackrabbit/Sika stag rut call. American elk or wapiti calls have been used effectively to call sika stags. I remember a stag charging in through the trees to an American-manufactured Ed Sceery elk bugle call.

Sika deer are tough animals for their size and seem to absorb bullets, so I personally prefer a heavy calibre and bullet for this species. Bullet wounds seal quickly on sika, so it is prudent to widen the search when looking for a possible blood trail. It is not uncommon to find the first specks on blood 50 yards from the shot strike.

Dumfries and Galloway was the county that provided both me and my client the most memorable of sika stalks. I was with Andy Cooper, an English client from the Midlands, and we were looking to take a mature sika stag. The weather had been against us, so in desperation on the last day of our trip, we switched venues.

There was a cold and biting wind as Andy and I left the loch behind us and cut across the heather-clad hill towards the forest. The roar of the near-gale forced the sitka spruce to sway and dance alarmingly. I was not optimistic about our chances on that particular October morning. So powerful was the moist aroma of the peaty woodland understory as we entered the forest that I wondered if my sense of smell had become heightened. My hearing had been all but useless in the screaming wind outside the forest canopy.

Pushing through the sharp pine needles we were startled by an erupting blackcock, as surprised by our sudden arrival as we were by its piercing alarm. Rising almost vertically, he banked away on the wind, back across the loch like a Lancaster bomber on the dam's raid. A roe doe also crashed away at our arrival, flushing virtually at our feet. Everything was sitting tight due to the awful weather. Sika are less affected by bad weather than other deer and this fact gave us a little ray of hope amid dismal prospects.

Following the plantation rows, we headed downhill and eventually cut out into the forest road just above a steep bend that overlooked a burn. Nearby ,there was also a wallow that I knew had been popular the previous season with a stag I'd managed to bring to the book. During the rut, sika stags mark out and defend a territory rather than amass a harem like red stags. This distinction is often overlooked as occasional stags, patrolling the boundaries of their territories, seek out hinds and often try to drive them back to the rutting stand to cover them. Sika hinds still need to move out from the rutting area in the mornings and evenings to feed and the stag can often be encountered patrolling his boundaries, seeing off any interlopers and continually driving in his hinds. It was here on the high bend that we took up position, in the hope that we could ambush a patrolling stag or catch one out who came to the wallow.

*❂ A stag like this is worth shooting to prevent him causing damage to other stags with his single antler*

Making myself comfortable on the fortunately dry bank, I glassed the wallow from the previous year. The wallow was quite obviously well used, so our small ray of hope shone a little more brightly. We observed also that a stag had marked his territory by thrashing the ground cover of heather and gorse with his antlers around the wallow, leaving circular patches at intervals along the boundaries of the burn and by fraying some of the perimeter trees. This indicated an active territory. Andy deployed the legs of the bipod attached to his .243 Sako and set the rifle down within easy reach as he made himself comfortable for the wait.

The wind had eased noticeably in the time it had taken us to push through the forest. My confidence was raised further when the sun made an appearance. I knew that luck was with us today. A woodcock flitted across the glade in an erratic flight, like an owl that had had one too many. A red squirrel made an appearance in the larch stand opposite that took my attention for some time before he departed. Andy began to whisper some comment but was cut short by a sound from within the forest. It was the call of a hind in season.

The hind was bleating a protest at an interested stag that was probably attempting to force himself upon her. We listened for some time without sight of either participant, although the sounds of the stag chasing her back and forth through the trees and her squeaks seemed very close indeed. Then, from behind us, came the unmistakable sound of a rutting sika stag. A single, high-pitched whistle silenced the forest. With a noise often described as a deathly scream, it rose to a peak before tailing off and was repeated three more times. The hind became more vocal and the stag's activity became intense, but still neither of the unhappy couple showed themselves. The resident stag (for I was sure it was) let out his eerie call once more. It sounded like he was almost upon us and I feared he would wind us at any moment.

We had the arrival of another stag to thank for our opportunity. The hind broke out across the glade and disappeared as quickly as she had come, leaving behind the sounds of two stags now engaged in combat. Somehow, unseen to us, the stag had crossed or made his way around the burn to see off the interloper. Fighting between males is commonplace, as is apparent from the number of heads with damaged or missing tines and the limping stags which appear during and after the rut.

I tugged Andy's collar and motioned him to follow me a little further down the forest road, which overlooked the area where the two stags were engaged. I pointed out to Andy the spot where I thought the two stags would emerge. Andy got comfortable on the banking as we lay parallel looking toward the spruce stand, just as one of the stags made an appearance. Andy fitted to the rifle and quickly picked up the stag in the scope, before squeezing off a bullet that found its mark. The 'thwock' of the impact told of a good shot. The sika stag reared up and fell backwards, his legs thrashing for a short moment as life left him. Although I was sure he had succumbed, I covered the beast with the binoculars checking for any life signs just to be sure.

Andy was overjoyed at taking his first stag as we finally made our way to the fallen beast. This was a real beauty, marred only by one of his antlers having been broken off in the combat. But it took nothing from the trophy, as Andy decided there and then to have it shoulder mounted. I gralloched the deer, which smelled strongly of mating musk and fitted him into the new sika sack by Harlika. Heading back to the Land Rover fully laden ended a great day's stalking in the Scottish Borders for two extremely happy hunters.

If you mention Dorset to the majority of UK deer stalkers, they normally think of sika deer. The following account takes place in real sika country and is reported by my good friend and professional wildlife photographer, Brian Phipps:

In a late October downpour, I rendezvoused in the agreed Dorset layby with sporting artist and local professional stalker, Teresa Davis, who would be guiding us on what was looking to be a wet stalk.

"It's not a good start," said a voice from under a dripping bush hat, "but it's worth a go – the rut's full on and the stags are calling well. If they play ball we shouldn't have too much trouble finding them." We moved off and drove into the darkness, deep within the Poole Basin, and soon arrived at a privately managed estate covering some 1,500 acres.

After chatting for a while in the forlorn hope that the rain might ease, we bit the bullet and headed into the wind. Within seconds our waterproof gear was getting a thorough testing – I can attest that the Harkila Pro Hunter suit does what it says on the tin and Teresa's new Musto jacket, the Whisper, proved well worth the money.

Our stalker led us into the foreboding forestry as the first crack of light smeared the eastern sky. Teresa was using the estate rifle, a custom .270 made by gun and rifle-maker Mike Rainback of Owermoigne, Dorchester. It was scoped with a Schmidt & Bender 3-12x42 and the combination was completed with an SAE Utra moderator.

A high-pitched whistle erupted from the heathland beyond the trees, and within seconds a reply was heard. Our guide told us we would have to be quick on our feet, yet silent too.

The terrain we emerged upon was typical sika country: damp, acidic heath with gorse scrub. But first we had to negotiate the trees. The forest floor was littered with fallen branches and leaves from the recent rough weather and our pace soon slowed necessarily as we carefully picked our way, each groan and crack from under foot echoing through the trees. I wondered if we were already being watched.

Stopping every 30 yards to pause and listen, the eerie whistling calls were further in than we first thought. We soon ventured out on to the heather carpeted heath as the watery sun was trying its damndest to break through the low clouds. Standing on the edge of the woodland, I began scanning the heath with my Zeiss 8x42 rangefinder binoculars. These quality optics make short work of dismal light conditions and they instantly provided me with a crystal-clear sight picture.

About 200 yards away, I spied a fine sika stag starting straight back at me, watching us for a while. He was an impressive eight-pointer but he soon bounded away, taking his harem of hinds with him, to a safer place. Unperturbed, our stalking guide decided to venture further onto the heath. Distant whistles and the clash of antlers encouraged us to push through the unforgiving, head-high gorse in search of our quarry. An unseen approach proved to be less difficult this time and with the rut in full swing, the deer obviously had other things on their mind.

Four stags soon came into view, milling around a group of hinds 300 yards away. All were keen on being the dominant stag and having the privileges that went with it. Approaching to a suitable distance was almost too easy. The new morning sunlight showed the sika stags in all their magnificence, while the hinds' pelage of ashen grey stood out starkly against the black stags.

It was a fantastic experience, watching these parading stags and nervous hinds that didn't know if they were coming or going. Our guide, after careful consideration, eventually decided on taking a particular stag now 125 yards away, according to the Zeiss RF binoculars.

Teresa worked the bolt and chambered a round into the 270 Rainback, placing the rifle gently upon the shooting sticks. Stepping back slightly, the rifle was brought firmly into her right shoulder. Two fine, six-point stags walked in front of us, parallel to each other, indicating an imminent fight. Within seconds a ferocious battle commenced and the guide told Teresa to be ready. The fight only lasted for a few seconds, leaving a victor to claim his hinds. "The one on the right", whispered the stalker in Teresa's ear.

She did not need telling twice. The stag was now standing sideways on and offered her a textbook shot. A half-second later the stag reared, rushing off to collapse dead, its heart destroyed by a perfectly-placed 130-grain Norma bullet. I could detect no further movement through the binoculars, hearing a slick reload as Teresa worked the action. We waited patiently for a few more moments but there was no further movement from the stag. Approaching from the rear, Teresa touched the stag's eye with the stalking sticks. Death was confirmed by absence of retinal action and we all admired her first sika stag.

A fine six-pointer, he was maybe three years old and weighed about 80lb field dressed. He was an ideal cull stag, and juvenile stags make excellent venison. The rising autumnal sun dispersed the rain clouds as we dragged the stag back

to the vehicle. Teresa gripped the warm .270 case, all smiles once again, another deer neatly despatched and another species to notch on her stick. Only Chinese water deer and muntjac remain to complete her list of UK species; not bad for someone in their first deerstalking season. ☉

## SIKA DEER FACTS

### ☉ Open season
*Stags, England, Wales and Northern Ireland: 1 August – 30 April*
*Stags, Scotland: 1 July – 20 October*
*Hinds, England, Wales and Northern Ireland: 1 November – 31 March*
*Hinds, Scotland: 21 October – 15 February*

### ☉ Rifle and ammunition
*England and Wales: minimum calibre of .240, muzzle energy more than 1,700ft/lb, expanding bullet only*
*Scotland: minimum 100gn expanding bullet, muzzle energy no less than 1,750ft/lb, muzzle velocity no less than 2,450fps*
*Northern Ireland: minimum calibre of .236, bullet designed to expand in a predictable manner*

### ☉ Stalkers/agents in England
*Cervus UK,  contact Owen Beardsmore 01283 711878 or*
*07968 829540 www.cervus-uk.co.uk*
*Sika Deer Unit, South-West England 01963 363596 or 01747 828139 www.sikadeer.co.uk*
*Jan Andrews , Dorset, 01258 840003 www.deerdata.co.uk*
*AE Stalking, South West 07813 006929 aestalking@hotmail.com*

### ☉ Stalkers/agents in Scotland
*Steve Sweeting, Galloway, 07792 874511 carminnowsestate@msn.com*
*Ronald Rose BSc Forestry (Hons), Dumfries & Galloway 01387 373216 enquiries@eskdalewildlife.com*
*Andy Harding, Alladale Estates, Sutherland 01863 755338 www.alladale.com*
*Balnagown Estates, Ross-shire 01862 843601 www.balnagown-estates.co.uk*
*Killean Estate, Argyll & Bute, 01257 266511 or 07736 146184 www.killeanestate.com*
*Rhidorroch Estate, Wester Ross 01854 612548 www.rhidorroch.com*

### ☉ Stalkers/agents in Northern Ireland
*Colebrooke Park, Co Fermanagh, 028 8953 1402 www.colebrooke.info*
*Baronscourt & Abercorn Estate, Co Tyrone 028 8166 1683 www.barons-court.com*

### ☉ Stalkers/agents in Southern Ireland
*John Fenton, Co Wicklow +353 454 04947 Johnfenton1@eircom.net*

*Others can be found in* Sporting Rifle *magazine  www.sporting-rifle.com*

Chapter 8: **RED DEER**

The red deer (*Cervus elaphus*) is Britain's largest land mammal and one of the world's largest deer species. Red deer naturally range through most of Europe, including Sardinia and Corsica, crossing the Caucasus Mountains region into Asia Minor and parts of western and central Asia. It is also the only member of the deer species that is represented in North Africa.

In Britain there are indigenous populations in Scotland, the Lake District and the South-West of England, principally on Exmoor. Not all of these are of entirely pure bloodlines, as some of these populations have been supplemented with deliberate releases from deer parks in an attempt to increase both antler size and body weight.

Scotland's red deer adapted to a life on the open hill as the ancient Caledonian pine forests dwindled away to the remnant woodland that is left today. This was thanks to demand for timber from an expanding human population, which finally destroyed the stately Scots Pine forest of Caledonia. The clearances in the late 18th Century stripped the Highlands of its crofters, along with their sheep and cattle. This suited the hill deer and as a consequence, they have thrived up to the present day.

Unfortunately, there has been extensive hybridisation with the introduced stock and closely related sika deer in many areas. It is now thought the only truly pure forms of red deer are to be found on the Outer Hebrides and the islands of Arran, Islay, Jura and Rum. Thankfully, recent restrictions on the importation of *Cervus* species to these islands have been put in place, to safeguard the genetic integrity of these last remaining British bloodlines. It must be said however, that many Scottish deer forests on the mainland have had an influx of English park deer added to the wild herds in an attempt to increase trophy quality. The Marquis of Breadalbane for example, introduced some stags to his Black Mount estate from Taymouth and Windsor Great Park. These introductions all failed, as it is the environment, regardless of any antler enhancing genetics, that governs body weight and trophy quality of these hill deer. Other landowners imported red deer from various parks and some of these such as Woburn, may have had mixed wapiti blood in them. Therefore, the true bloodline lines of Scottish mainland red deer may have been open to question before any sika deer influence could be claimed.

Scotland's red deer carve out a harsh existence in her hills and islands, foraging on stunted heather and grass in a windswept and inclement landscape. Little wonder then, that they sport lesser headgear and lighter body weights than their English woodland counterparts and continental cousins.

All the red deer of Great Britain and Ireland are classified as the subspecies *Cervus elaphus scoticus*, literally meaning 'Scottish red deer'. I do not know who makes up the rules, but the English and Irish representatives of this species are more akin to the European subspecies (*Cervus elaphus hippelaphus*) and really ought to be classified as such, or else as another separate subspecies.

In England, Exmoor is the home to the largest concentration of red deer in the country. Historically, Exmoor's red deer are unique, living in the only place where they have roamed truly wild since prehistoric times. They have survived

*⋂ The author with Balmoral stag, flanked by Private Turnbull and Sergeant Davis from the on-site security team*

through the ages under Crown protection as 'Royal Beasts of the Chase' on Exmoor Forest. The writer and Naturalist Richard Jeffries wrote in his book, *Red Deer*, published in 1884, a fitting tribute to the Exmoor stags: 'There is no more beautiful creature than a stag in his pride of antler, his coat of ruddy gold, his grace of form and motion... The branching antlers accord so well with the deep shadowy boughs and the broad fronds of the brake; the golden red of his coat fits to the foxglove, the purple heather, and later on to the orange and red of the beech; his easy bounding motion springs from the elastic sward; his limbs climb the steep hill as if it were level; his speed covers the distances, and he goes from place to place as the wind. He not only lives in the wild, wild woods and moors – he grows out of them, as the oak grows from the ground. The noble stag in his pride of antler is lord and monarch of all the creatures left to us in English forests and on English hills.'

I couldn't have put it better. Even in modern times, hunting in one form or another has been the main reason red deer have survived and indeed flourished across Exmoor's moorland majesty. This single fact was conveniently overlooked by those politicians who were instrumental in banning the hunting of hare, fox and deer with hounds.

Other than Exmoor, the Lake District probably held the only other true herd of original English red deer. However, the red deer of Cumbria have had new bloodlines introduced from deer parks and other sources. Historically, an upland herd of red deer have occupied the Martindale Estate between Ullswater and Haweswater, for more than 300 years. Dalemain Estate, at the head of the ancient Martindale deer forest, once hosted many foreign dignitaries for deer hunting. In 1910, the then Earl of Lonsdale (from Lowther Castle) received as his guest Kaiser Wilhelm II, to hunt on the Martindale deer shoot. Four years later, the Earl formed a Border Battalion to fight his former guest's German army in the trenches during WWI.

Managed by subsequent landowners, the herd at Martindale has grown and over-spilled into neighbouring Mardale, Kentmere, Thirlmere and Armboth Fell.

Separate woodland herds are also based in Grizedale Forest, the Rusland Valley and at the head of Morecambe Bay. These woodland red stags are better nourished and generally stand taller and weigh heavier than their closely related, fell-living counterparts.

Elsewhere in England, there are several other red deer populations, most of which have originated at the hands of man. Historically, carted deer kept for stag hunts were often left out at the end of the chase. In Victorian times many stags were imported from various deer parks (often containing wapiti blood), to a number of stalking estates in an attempt to 'improve' the resident stock. Carted deer were normally kept by those stag hunts that had no wild red deer in their locality and were normally recaptured after the hunt, to be used again. The red deer of Thetford Forest in Norfolk were probably accidentally established in this manner when the Norwich Staghounds (which actually only hunted hinds) failed to recapture their quarry (some of which may have been in calf) on a number of occasions and over many years.

*A hill stag*

The New Forest has a rich royal hunting heritage but hasn't always gone the hunter's way, as Richard, Duke of Bernay, found out to his cost. The elder brother of King William II, he met his fate on the tines of a New Forest stag that gored him to death after being brought to bay.

Introductions from Warnham and other deer parks to the New Forest probably re-established the present New Forest red deer. Other red deer populations likely to originate from escapes or deliberate releases in England and Wales, include the Peak District, Suffolk, Brecon Beacons and West Yorkshire herds, as well as other, smaller populations scattered throughout the woods of England and to a much lesser extent Wales. Most of these are increasing in numbers and range. More recent escapes from deer farms and other deliberate release have aided their expansion. A recent census of deer populations co-ordinated by the British Deer Society records red deer as having expanded their range in England and Wales since the start of the new millennium. The most notable increase has been in the Midlands and across East Anglia.

In Ireland, the only truly native wild red deer that exist today can be found on the Torc, Cores and Mangerton mountains, with other herds in the lowlands of the national park in Killarney, County Kerry. The species nearly became extinct after the great famine and numbered as few as 60 animals. Today there are more than 1,000 and numbers are expanding. However, as in Scotland, sika deer are a potential threat to the genetic integrity of Irish red deer through interbreeding. This has already happened in County Wicklow, but so far no cases of crossbreeding have been recorded in Killarney. A high priority is attached to maintaining the genetic purity of Ireland's native herd and the situation is being closely monitored.

Introductions from Scotland, England and France in the early 19th Century formed the nucleus of the red deer herds now found in the Glendalough Valley and Turlough Hills of Co Wicklow, Glenveagh, Co Donegal, Connemara, Co Galway and areas of Co Mayo. Northern Ireland's wild red herds are all descended from reintroduced stock. Free roaming red deer are found in Co Tyrone, Co Fermanagh and Co Down. Several enclosed herds live on private and Forest Service estates such as Gosford Forest Park.

British red deer have been exported to the former Empires colonies and thrived. The first red deer to reach Australia were probably the six that Prince Albert sent in 1860 from Windsor Great Park to Thomas Chirnside who was starting a herd at Werribee Park, south west of Melbourne in Victora. Further introductions were made in New South Wales, Queensland, South Australia and Western Australia.

New Zealand's first red deer were a pair sent by Lord Petre in 1851 from his herd at Thorndon Park, Essex, to the South Island. Sir Frederick Weld was responsible for the first release of red deer on North Island with animals sourced from Windsor Great Park. These initial introductions were followed by a further 220 releases. Many of these originated from the Earl of Dalhousie's Scottish estate Invermark or one of the major English deer parks, principally Warham, Woburn Abbey or Windsor Great Park. There has also been some hybridisation with the closely related wapiti or American elk (*Cervus canadensis nelsoni*) introduced in Fiordland in the early 1920. New Zealand red deer have thrived to such an extent that they are officially regarded as a serious pest and heavily culled using professional teams of hunters working with helicopters. New Zealand red deer produce large antlers and are regarded as the best in the world by trophy hunters. This proves the point that habitat conditions often outweigh genetic make up in trophy quality, as much of the New Zealand bloodline is of Scottish hill stag origin.

Summer pelage is reddish brown, while in winter this changes to a brown or grey with a yellowish rump patch, many animals also have a dark dorsal stripe but not all. There are no spots present in the adult coat. Prior to the rut stags develop a rough mane. Adult red stags weigh 300-400lb (130-200kg) and stand up to 50in (130cm) at the shoulder, hill stags weigh up to 210lb (95kg) and measure up to 40-44in (101-112cm). They rarely live past 12 years but a few, noteable examples are known to live as long as 18 years.

Stags carry large, wide, highly-branched antlers. The number of branches increases with age until the animal passes its prime and starts to go back. Native woodland living animals have up to 16 points, although park stags can have considerably more. Hill living stags carry fewer points, with a 12-point head or Royal head considered a top trophy and a 14-point or so-called Imperial head, considered to be exceptional. An antler-less stag or 'hummel' is occasionally encountered in Scotland but these are extremely rare in other races of European red deer. Hummel's are not impotent and will compete for hinds and produce normal offspring. Red hinds are antlerless.

Forest dwellers at heart, red deer in Scotland have adapted to the harsh open hills of the Highlands, as has the population in England's Lake District. Hill red deer unsurprisingly, have lower body weights, with the stags carrying lighter antlers with fewer branches than their lowland counterparts, due to poorer feeding and more exposure to the elements.

Stags and hinds are typically segregated for most of the year. The different sexes traditionally occupy separate areas of their range, and generally interact only during the rut. Many Highland estates are referred to as either stag forests or hind forests, to indicate which sex favours that area. However there are quite

a number of estates with vast acreages that carry both sexes in separate glens throughout the year.

Female groups tend to be matriarchal, led by a dominant female. The lead hind becomes obvious when the group is disturbed and moving. Young hinds usually remain with their mother's group; young stags disperse to join other bachelor males.

Further south, the species is found in traditional woodland and forestry, where better natural shelter and higher quality feed increases both body weights and antler growth. The species is widespread in Scotland and locally common in some English counties.

Red deer are active over 24 hours but make more use of open spaces at night in areas of frequent disturbance. However, woodland-living red deer activity normally peaks at dawn and dusk if the animals are undisturbed.

Red deer are predominantly grass grazers, and browsers of low shrubs such as heather and bilberry. Woody browse such as tree shoots and bark-stripping occurs when other food is limited during harsh winters. The grazing of tree shoots and agricultural crops often puts red deer in conflict with farmers and foresters. Worryingly, highland red deer are increasingly being blamed for heather loss on Scottish grouse moors, where some owners are now fencing their boundaries and shooting out the red deer contained. Whether in conflict or managed as a resource, red deer populations require careful management to maintain health and quality and ensure a sustainable balance with their environment.

Woodland red deer are generally crepuscular, feeding mostly at dawn and dusk. In the Scottish Highlands, hill red deer often show diurnal movement patterns, descending from the high to low ground at dusk and returning at dawn. Feeding normally occurs in bouts and at intervals of three hours or so, after which the deer 'lie up' to ruminate.

You will hear a deep, low drawn out bellow or roar during the rut. When alarmed, hinds may issue a harsh bark and often moo when locating their calf.

The rut on the hill occurs from the end of September to November, when the single-sex groups begin to mix. Stags 'break out' of their bachelor groups to find and claim groups of hinds in September as the females come into oestrus. There is no finer sound to be heard than the roar of red stags and the clash of antlers throughout the Scottish glens in autumn. Stags return to the hind's home ranges and compete for access to them by engaging in elaborate displays of dominance including roaring, parallel walks and fighting with rivals. Serious injury and death can result, though fighting only occurs between stags of similar size that cannot assert dominance by any of the non-contact means. A stag's dominance ensures exclusive sexual access to the hinds. Winning stags gather a harem of hinds around them and continually herd them together, attempting to add more hinds as and when opportunity arises. Normally, only stags over five years old that tend to achieve mating access, despite being sexually mature far earlier.

Woodland-living red stags gather a smaller parcel of hinds together than hill stags do. Some woodland stags live a more nomadic lifestyle during

the rut, stealing a sly mating with any receptive hind encountered during his wanderings. Woodland hinds over a year old give birth to a single calf after an eight-month gestation, between mid-May and mid-July each year. However, puberty may be delayed until three years old in hill hinds, which may give birth only once every two or three years. Heavy infant mortality occurs at and shortly after birth and during the first winter, especially among Scottish hill populations.

For hill stalking, fitness is essential. Stag stalking is often a full day's undertaking in mountainous ground, with more than a fair chance of bad weather. Strong, worn-in boots and gaiters with adequate clothing for hard walking in inclement conditions are a must. Most stalkers will be guests on the hill (whether they have paid for the experience or not), and a professional stalker will guide you onto a suitable beast. The actual hunt will involve spying for a shootable stag and then trying to get into a shooting position to take him. This usually entails a long detour to work the wind into the stag using dead ground and often one will be shooting down from above the beast. Old stags past their prime and switch heads (antlers carrying no tines) are the objects of the exercise when hill stalking.

Woodland-living red deer are generally taken from high-seats or stalked in the early or late hours of the day. Heavier heads, carrying more points, can be expected from woodland or forest stags and are a better proposition for the trophy collector. During the rut, stags may be called out of their woodland sanctuary by mimicking the rutting roar. Stag calling is common practice on the continent and is catching on fast in the UK. The most commonly used call that is easy to use is the Faulhaber Stag/Elk call.

Red deer are a large animal and require a suitable calibre with a heavy bullet. Although many are shot with a .243 Winchester, I would recommend a minimum of .270 Winchester.

It was certainly Highland weather, complete with horizontal rain as ghillie Sean Kennerly and I left the great grey castle of Balmoral behind us and headed out onto the hill in the Land Rover. The previous night I had enjoyed the hospitality of the Scots Guards and ghillie Sean into the wee hours and was feeling a little the worse for wear.

However, the hangover was soon dispelled by fear as the ground became a good deal steeper and the Land Rover struggled for grip on the gravel incline above Loch Muick. Far below us, Queen Victoria's picture-postcard Highland Lodge Glas-allt-Shiel towered gracefully on the North West shores of the Loch. It was here that the widowed Queen spent much of her time in mourning after losing her beloved Prince Albert, with faithful servant and famous ghillie John Brown in attendance. I mentioned to Sean that he was actually Brown's modern-day counterpart. The comment was met with much humour and took my mind off our precarious pace up the mountainside. History in the Highlands has often been turbulent and Balmoral is no exception. The road we were travelling on was used by the young pretender – Charles Edward Stuart, better known as Bonnie Prince Charlie – in 1745 en-route to his disaster at Culloden.

*◑ The author heading up the hill at Glen Etive, Argyllshire*

*◒ A well-fed southern red stag*

⊃ *If you have never seen it, the red deer rut is one of the great spectacles of British nature*

Eventually and with great relief, we rolled to a halt beside Alan's hut, which was where the Highland ponies or garrons are stabled during the stag stalking season. We were met by Sergeant Davis and Private Turnbull, leading a couple of fine garrons. The two Scots Guardsmen tended the ponies and assisted in ghilling for the Castle guests as part of their main posting duty, providing protection for the royal household.

Fortunately the rain stopped as abruptly as it had started; the fresh washed Highland heather stood out in all its autumn splendour, shadowed by the impressive peaks of Broad Cairn and Loch Nagar. Sean led the way with my TC Icon rifle in canvas slip slung over his shoulder as tradition demands. I strode on after him with the guardsmen and ponies following on close behind. Our stalking party zig-zagged down the old drovers path, past the picturesque waterfalls on the River South Esk and up into the blaeberry-carpeted woods of Bachnagairn. The gentle ascent became steeper as we left the forest and once more padded onto the peat and heather of the open hillside. Heading up the Glittering Skellies, we were met at the summit by our stalker Stuart Donald.

After exchanging pleasantries and a good spy across the landscape, Stuart decided on Glen Doll as our best destination to get to grips with a suitable stag. Descent soon turned to ascent as we wound our way up and along the Altduthrie Burn and onto the open flats of the peat hags. It was here that we saw our first group of stags. We were caught out half-way across the flats when the beasts trotted into view exiting Glen Doll. Our present position was hardly tenable, but for now the deep peat hag hid our stalking party well. Telescopes were deployed and both Stuart and I picked out a huge, banana-shaped switch head. There couldn't have been a more suitable stag to shoot on the hill that day but the problem was how to get into him. Moments turned into minutes, that turned into two hours and still we remained marooned. Eventually, it was decided to move the stags. In an attempt to do so, the pony-men made their way out of the peat hags as we watched. The ruse worked to a degree, as the distant stags did not immediately burst into flight at this disturbance to their browsing, but turned around to head back into Glen Doll.

This pleased Stuart, who was happy with the result because he thought there was a good chance that we could catch up with them again in the Doll. Half an hour later we crested the summit of Cairn Damff and spied across the corrie to find there wasn't a stag to be seen. Pressing on, we carefully traversed the steep hillside and approached the edge of the precipitous cliffs of Glen Doll. Again after much glassing, the beasts appeared absent but Stuart felt that they would be hidden somewhere in the dead ground out of sight.

However, Sean soon spotted a lone stag to our right about 150 yards away, working his way through the boulder-strewn, dead ground. He was an ageing, big-bodied animal but with a poor head so Stuart gave the go-ahead to shoot when a suitable shot was offered. Annoyingly the beast moved and remained hidden behind a big brute of a boulder. Although the red rut hadn't yet broken out, Stuart attempted a roar and the elusive beast stepped out to the challenge. The stag filled the Zeiss scope, I held my breath, aimed and winged a bullet on its

*Stalking is fun for the whole family. Here the Simes triplets from Leicestershire pose in front of a stag shot by their dad Mark at Tulchan*

way – but completely missed. Realising it wasn't such a great place to be around, the beast changed ends and dashed downhill. I instantly changed position and followed the stag in the scope, he paused mid-flight, looking back unsure. I took a careful bead up the beast's front leg to the heart and lung region and squeezed off another round. This time the bullet ran true and the stag tumbled spectacularly head-over-heels down the Glen toward the White Water Burn. "Aye your second shot was better than your first one laddie,'"murmured Stuart, his eye still transfixed on the Swarovski telescope trained on the now still stag. I couldn't offer an excuse for the first miss; I felt I hadn't pulled the shot but who knows. Maybe it was my precarious position, on the precipitous edge of a 200ft plus drop that had held my attention more than I had thought. The main thing was the second shot had counted and more than made up for the first.

Stuart dispatched the pony men, who had a long walk around the corrie to drop into Glen Doll and onto Jocks Road, to eventually follow the burn down directly below the fallen stag. Sean made ready to descend to the stag when another beast trotted into view. I deployed the rifle once more onto the Harris bipod and adjusted the magnification on the 2.5 – 10 x 50 Zeiss Victory scope. Stuart confirmed that the stag was an old beast carrying a good head that was going back, at about 250 yards range. The TC Icon .243 was zeroed 1in high at a hundred yards so I held true onto the beast's heart, held a half-breath and fired. My majestic monarch of the glen absorbed the bullet; clinically dead on his hooves he stood stock still for a moment, before beginning to sway alarmingly and eventually tumbling forwards toward the first stag shot in a similar fashion. "Aye, your shooting is improving and twa stags is a good day," murmured Stuart, still with the Swarofski scope glued to his eye, like Nelson approaching the French fleet at Trafalgar.

Sean skipped away down the sheer slopes, to bleed and drag the beasts downhill to a suitable place for recovery by the ponies. Stuart and I picked our way down to eventually meet both Sean and the soliders on Jocks road, where we all admired my two trophies. Both beasts were old animals with well-worn teeth, but the second stag had a wonderful dark, antlered head of 12 points, making him a royal. It had been one of the best stalking days I have ever had and to shoot a royal head on the royal estate in such good company was a fantastic result.

Two more guardsmen joined us – Silva, a Fijian, and Van, a South African, and after strapping the stags onto the ponies, we began the long hike back to the castle. A celebratory dram was enjoyed en-route as we passed Stuart Donald's estate cottage, Moulzie. More of the same hospitality and further Highland nectar (single malt) was offered and enjoyed back at the larder by manager Mike Muir and head 'keeper Gary Coutes. All deer are skinned on arrival, as Balmoral venison is, as is to be expected, aimed at the top end of the market. I marvelled as the other stalkers returned from their respective beats and processed the beasts of the day. Casting a glance at the skull mounts adorning the wall, it was hard to ignore the sense of history. For the past 150 years, kings, princes and leading aristocrats of their time had all sampled the same sport I had enjoyed that day. I had been introduced to Balmoral nearly a decade before by then head keeper Ben Fearny. Sadly he has since passed away but his two sons Phillip and Arthur are still carrying on the family tradition as stalkers for the Windsors.

Balmoral is a founder member of the East Grampian Deer Management Group and has taken a lead in the contentious management of deer by establishing a deer model. Game and all wildlife are well managed by an efficient team of stalkers, gamekeepers and ghillies, under the expert guidance of head keeper Gary Coutes. The estate also produces excellent grouse driving for the Duke of Edinburgh and his guests, as well as some productive salmon pools on the river Dee. Balmoral is the epitome of the Scottish sporting week and hill stag stalking was practically invented there. In former times, many heads of state enjoyed the stag stalking here. Prime Minister Disraeli loved both the place and the sport and often joined the royal stalking parties at the castle. Tony Blair has been a guest here, but I cannot imagine he donned the tweeds and tested the wind for a stag. Whereas David Cameron – now there's a thought: as he now has the top job at Westminster, I am sure he will be happy to sample some royal stalking. He has felt the tug of Nimrod before and I believe he has been a keen stalker and also enjoyed riding to hounds.

Highland hill stags are almost a sub-species of red deer. They are smaller both in body weight and antler than their southern England or mainland Europe counterparts. However, the pursuit of them on the open hill is as challenging a sport as one could wish for. This is not an out-and-out trophy hunt by any means: indeed, it is just the opposite, as switch heads and poor confirmation or aged stags are the priority.

That said, one may be lucky, as I was, to take an impressive trophy head from an ageing animal. Either way, switch head or multiple points, any stag taken through fair chase on the hill is well-earned and deserves its place above the fireplace, regardless of trophy quality.

Balmoral is mostly private shooting but there are many Highland estates offering sport on weekly lets that include lodge accommodation, stag stalking, salmon fishing and grouse shooting. It is a sporting pastime unique to the Highlands that has changed little since Victorian times and is none the worse for that. As a pursuit of wild game in a true wilderness it cannot be bettered.

Many dead deer are carried off the hill in Scotland by garrons. Also known as a Highland pony, this is the native horse breed of Scotland's mountainous regions. It is not known whether these wild horses first spread into Scotland when the last glaciers receded some 10,000 years ago, or whether they were introduced by early prehistoric settlers. What is known is that by the 8th Century, horses were in Scotland, and by 800 AD their images were appearing on carved Pictish stones. In one of Scottish history's most noted incidents, Robert the Bruce, King of Scots, was most likely mounted on a sturdy Scottish Highland Pony when he fought and killed Sir Henry de Bohun with his battle-axe at Bannockburn in 1314. Highland ponies became the workhorse of the Highland croft and estate. During the heyday of stalking in the late 19th Century, they served as the most efficient way to transport deer and other moor game from the hill to the larder, with special saddles and panniers being used. Today the Highland Pony continues to be used in this role. They are ideally suited to work on the hill because of their strength and agility, even over the roughest and steepest ground, or for forestry work where mechanised access is difficult. Many other modern-day estates have reverted back to the ponies, since they are both more environmentally friendly and cost-effective than 4x4 vehicles. In WWI, the Lovat Scouts used Highlands as army mounts and they were also used by the military in the Boer War. With the advent of pony trekking in Scotland in 1955, the Highland came into its own and the breed became more widely known. ⊙

---

## RED DEER FACTS

### ⊙ Open season

*Stags, England, Wales and Northern Ireland: 1 August – 30 April*
*Stags, Scotland: 1 July – 20 October*
*Hinds, England, Wales and Northern Ireland: 1 November – 31 March*
*Hinds, Scotland: 21 October – 15 February*

### ⊙ Rifle and ammunition

*England and Wales: minimum calibre of .240, muzzle energy more than 1,700ft/lb, expanding bullet only*
*Scotland: minimum 100gn expanding bullet, muzzle energy no less than 1,750ft/lb, muzzle velocity no less than 2,450fps*
*Northern Ireland: minimum calibre of .236, bullet designed to expand in a predictable manner*

### ⊙ Stalkers/agents in England

*Cervus UK, Owen Beardsmore 01283 711878 or 07968 829540 www.cervus-uk.co.uk*
*Nigel Milsom, Tufton Arms Hotel, Cumbria 01768 351593 www.tuftonarmshotel.co.uk*
*Mike Dickinson, Derbyshire 01538 308697 or 07721 671746 michaeldickinson@btopenworld.com*

### ⊙ Stalkers/agents in Scotland

*Steve Sweeting, Galloway, 07792 874511 carminnowsestate@msn.com*
*Peter Swales, Inverness-shire, 01463 741894 or 07703 594462 www.kiltarlity.com*
*Mark Piper, Isle of Islay 01496 850120 or 07786 906472 www.thegearach.co.uk*

### ⊙ Stalkers/agents in Southern Ireland

*Tailormade Ireland, Co Carlow + 35 359 9161473 www.tailormade-ireland.com*

*Others can be found in* Sporting Rifle *magazine   www.sporting-rifle.com*

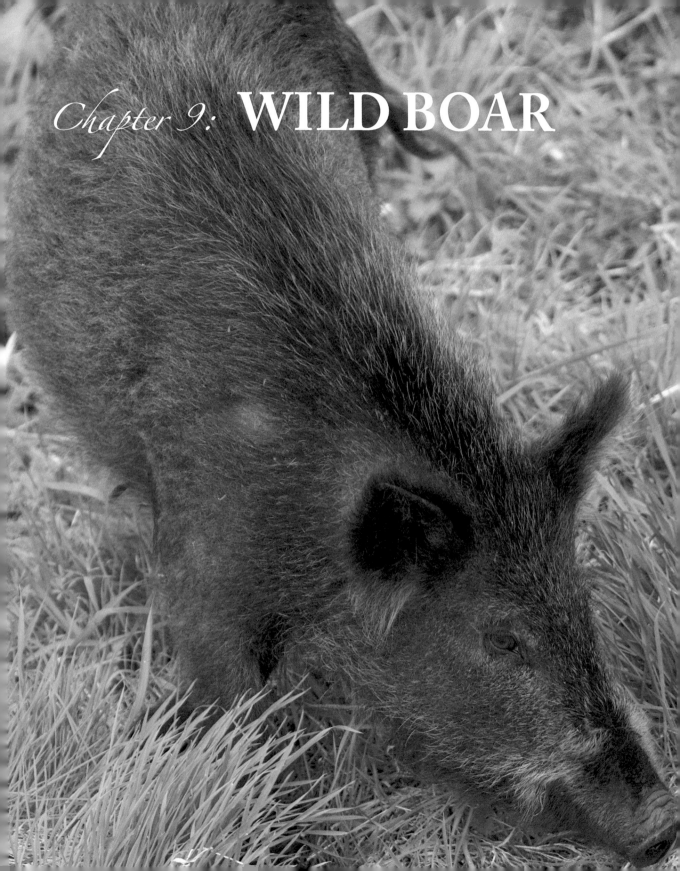

# Chapter 9: WILD BOAR

*⊙ Boar form family groups*

The wild boar (*Sus scrofa*), ancestor of the domestic pig, is native to much of central Europe, the Mediterranean region (including North Africa's Atlas Mountains) and parts of Asia.

Although the wild boar was extinct in Great Britain by the 17th Century, wild breeding populations have recently become re-established, following escapes from boar farms and are a continuing worry to DEFRA, as it is believed total eradication of the species in Britain will be virtually impossible.

Internationally, the wild boar is recognised as an extremely invasive species, with numbers been increasing in many European countries. The typical pattern for a population increase sees feral populations appearing to remain low for a number of years before a sudden explosion in numbers. In the UK, wild boar populations may still be in this initial phase.

In Denmark, the last boar was shot at the beginning of the 19th Century. Today the Danish government is making great effort, at considerable expense, to stop the return of the boar as they are considered to be a threat to the bacon industry. Wild boar are vectors of serious pig diseases such as swine fever and tuberculosis.

In the 1970s the species was recorded in Sweden, where captive animals had escaped and become established in the wild. The population in Sweden rose to a staggering 80,000 in 2006 and is now estimated to be more than 100,000. In 2006, Swedish hunters killed 25,000 wild boar.

If Sweden is an indication, British hunters can anticipate plenty of sport in the near future, but it must not be forgotten that this animal can cause massive damage to agriculture and possibly to gamekeeping interests.

In France and Germany, wild boar are the mainstay quarry species for hunters. The boar population in Germany has seen a massive surge with a reported 320 per cent growth in 2007 alone. This has had a significant financial impact on

farmers' incomes. Wounded boar and sows with piglets can be aggressive and in Germany, attacks on people – even fatal attacks – are becoming more frequent. Increasingly, conflict between boar and man, is becoming inevitable.

Captive wild boar in Britain have been kept since the 1970s, to provide exotic meat and have gained poularity throughout the 1980s, up to the present day. A number of other animals were kept in private or public wildlife collections, in zoos and on tourist-orientated farms. The main laws pertaining to keeping wild boar, and to the protection of the environment from invasive species, are the Wildlife & Countryside Act 1981, the Dangerous Animals Act 1976 and the Zoo Licensing Act 1981.

The original wild boar farm stock was of mainly French origin, but as the industry rapidly expanded from 1987 onwards, farmers added to the original stock with animals sourced from both western European and eastern European origins. There are now about 100 wild boar farms in the UK, including 30 or so in Scotland, with approximately 2,000 breeding sows.

Sporadic escapes of captive wild boar from wildlife parks since the 1970s and the severe gales of the late 1980s, bringing down livestock fencing, led to a significant number of animals being freed. Further escapes have occurred and also some, posssibly deliberate, releases from farms or private collections during the 1990s, which resulted in rumours of breeding populations being established in southern England at this time.

On 21 October 1998, the Ministry for Agriculture and Fisheries confirmed the presence of two populations of free-roaming wild boar living in Britain. The wild boar had returned after more than 300 years.

In England, feral wild boar are now present in a number of public forests in Kent, Sussex, Gloucestershire, Herefordshire, Devon and Dorset.

It is estimated that there are no more than 1,000 wild boar roaming free in England, but this number could be as high as 5,000. Boar have been spotted during pheasant drives in Nottinghamshire, Leicestershire and East Somerset - areas supposedly clear of boar.

The Forest of Dean and the New Forest populations have received a great deal of media attention over the last few years and it remains to be seen whether these populations will be allowed to prosper.

Several other substantial escapes have been reported and many of these may have resulted in boar breeding in the wild. These include 27 animals close to Catterick North Yorkshire in 1993, 10 near York in 2003 and a small number in the Bodmin area in Cornwall in 2002.

Scotland has a rich hunting history. One of the most famous boar-hunting stories comes from the dark ages and is centred around Glenshee, where I too have pursued stag, grouse and ptarmigan on many occasions over the past three decades. The earliest recorded reference to Glenshee concerns the legend of Dermid and the wild boar. In the Dark Ages, Glenshee was renowned for its hunting and the hunting forest belonged to a local noble named Fingal. Grainne, the wife of the noble Fingal, became infatuated with her nephew Dermid, who was a famed warrior.

When Fingal learned of his wife's infidelity, he ordered Dermid to track and kill a huge wild boar which had been terrorising Glenshee.

Dermid did so and survived the encounter, but the jealous and enraged Fingal demanded a careful measurement of the huge animal. Dermid walked along the beast's back, but in doing so, was fatally poisoned by one of the sharp bristles of the razorback's dorsal mane that pierced his foot.

Grainne begged her husband to send his personal physician to Dermid's aid, but he refused. Dermid, the great warrior, passed on to the happy hunting grounds in the sky, closely followed by his lover, who flung herself on to an arrow in her grief. Local legend claims that a large elevated barrow, close by the Spittal of Glenshee with four standing stones on top, is the final resting place of the two lovers.

It is likely that wild boar originally occurred throughout most of Scotland, wherever there was suitable forest for them to live in. Fossil and archaeological remains have been found in Caithness and Sutherland, Perthshire, Fife, Berwickshire, Wigtownshire and the islands of Colonsay and Orkney. Wild boar numbers dwindled over the centuries, as the forest cover shrank, and excessive hunting for both meat and sport accelerated the species' disappearance. An exact date for the wild boar's extinction in Scotland is unknown, but it is generally considered to have been in the late 16th Century.

A number of wild boar farms exist in Scotland, and animals that have escaped must account for the boar that was photographed roaming wild near Fort William in September 2006. This animal was said to be the first evidence in at least 400 years that there have been free-living wild boar in Scotland.

There are presently two thriving colonies in Dumfries and Galloway – one in forestry north of Dumfries and the other in forestry to the south-east of Carsphairn. These populations must soon meet if they haven't already. Wild boar can disperse long distances from their birth area.

Recent introductions include the Glen Affric National Nature Reserve which has introduced a small, free ranging, fenced population to determine whether boar can fulfil their ecological role of ground disturbance and bracken control in native woodland. Landowner Paul Lister introduced 17 wild boar and two European elk onto his estate near Ardgay in Sutherland into fenced enclosures.

Much of Scotland from the Borders to the Highlands and from Fife to Galloway has extensive acres of forestry that may prove to be habitable to boar, if we use the Dumfries and Galloway populations as a yard stick - and history does show us that boar are bloody good escapers.

Wales also has its boar hunting legends and none is more famous than the tale of the hunt for a particular large and fearsome boar named Twrch Trwyth by King Arthur.

It is not clear when wild boar finally became extinct in Wales, but what is certain is they are now back. It seems that boar have crossed the Welsh Marches and begun to colonise Wales. Animals from the Forest of Dean also appear to have crossed the River Wye into Monmouthshire.

⋒ *A wild boar shot in south-west Scotland*

*⟳ Retreating
backsides is a typical
view of British wild
boar*

There have been further sightings in Staunton, Monmouthshire, where one sounder apparently chased a woman on horseback, and another when a wild boar was run over at Trellech. Others reports cite boar spotted at Cledon Bog and Peckett Stone, on the Welsh side of the border.

Wild boar became extinct in Ireland in prehistoric times. These animals would of course have been a prime food source for Ireland's first people, the Mesolithic hunters.

The UCC mammalogist Paddy Sleeman has calculated that, based on densities of wild pigs in modern day New Zealand, there might have been 844,210 of them on Ireland.

On present evidence, it appears the boar became extinct in neolithic times. They were no doubt harried relentlessly by hunters, but the loss of habitat as neolithic farmers cleared the forest was probably the most significant factor.

In modern day Ireland, there have been a number of reported sightings in varied locations locations across Ireland.

The most startling of these was a reported 396lb boar, shot near a school playground in south Tipperary.

Coillte's game and wildlife manager, Barry Coad, was reported saying he had dealt with a number of wild boar over the past year and described wild boar as "quite widespread throughout the country". Mr Coad has been directly involved in removing nine animals from Piltown in County Kilkenny and Glenealy in County Wicklow.

Chairman of the Wild Deer Association of Ireland Pat Scully reported one of his members shot a wild boar in Clogheen near Cahir in Co Tipperary earlier in 2010.

Other recent sightings and shootings have confirmed a quite widespread presence of wild boar in Leinster and elsewhere. These populations began as escapes from farms, or perhaps by deliberate release.

Regular reported sightings of sows, boars and piglets keep coming in from

Counties Kilkenny and Wicklow, so it appears this species has certainly got a foot in the door in Ireland.

The body of the wild boar is compact, with a large head and short legs. The coat consists of stiff bristles with finer fur underneath. The colour varies from dark grey to black or brown, but there are great regional differences in colour. In western Europe, boar generally have brown coats, while in eastern Europe black coats are more common and as the present British feral stock is of mixed origin any colour could be encountered. During winter the fur is much denser and depending on the area, much of this hair is lost during the summer months.

An adult boar's average weight is 120–200lb, though there is a great deal of variation between different areas. A French boar shot in the Ardennes in 1999 weighed 550lb. But Romanian and Russian boars are the biggest, reaching weights of over 650lb.

When a sounder of boar arrives at the high seat, the largest pig is usually the mother. Mature males usually arrive alone but often they will come to a feeding sounder and their presence is usually shown by the uneasiness of the feeding pigs. He may be wary and circle the area before making an approach; the smaller boar will then keep their distance. Apart from bulk, male boar have a thicker-set neck and shoulders than sows and a wide dorsal stripe of bristles may be evident.

Thick forestry with areas of dense undergrowth for daytime resting, adjacent to rich feeding and a water source is prime habitat for boar. This animal is adaptable and opportunistic, which often brings it into conflict with farming interests as wild boar respect no boundaries when it comes to monopolizing food sources.

However, wild boar will utilise a mosaic of habitats, which most of rural Great Britian now is. Agricultural land, with some deciduous, coniferous, or mixed woodland with some undergrowth, will support a wild boar population. Even scrubland or heathland may be populated if there is sufficient forage and cover. The assumption that wild boar are dependent on single large blocks of woodland is incorrect, as these animals have become adaptable.

Wild boar are nocturnal creatures. They are also certainly not fussy eaters and will eat just about anything they can get hold of, from tubers, root crops, fruit and nuts to invertebrates, amphibians, carrion and deer fawns. Beech mast and acorns are an autumn favourite and maize is the most popular bait food on the continent to draw this animal into shooting range of high-seats. Plant material forms about 90 per cent of their diet.

Damage can be severe, not just to standing crops but to grazing pastures where the animal turns over turf when rooting for invertebrates.

Wild boars live in groups called sounders, containing around 20 animals. A typical sounder would be two or three sows together with their offspring. Adult males are generally not part of the sounder unless following an in-season sow, and are usually found alone.

Breeding usually occurs in the autumn, in October and November, and the females have a 21-day oestrus cycle. Successful males mate with many females

a number of times during the mating season. Gestation is an average of 115 days, and farrowing happens in the spring. The sow leaves the sounder 2 or 3 days before farrowing and builds a special farrowing nest. This takes the form of a mound made from twigs and other vegetation, built over a hollow scrape.

Farrowing takes place in a secluded area away from the sounder and up to 12 piglets can be born, although between five and eight is more usual. Piglets have a characteristic striped pattern on their coats, with longitudinal bands of light brown and cream. This gives way to a solid ginger colour before full adult colouration is achieved at about six months.

The female wild boar, or sow, reaches sexual maturity at 18 months of age, on average. A male may reach sexual maturity as young as 10 months old, but it is generally not until they are fully grown at about five years that they compete for females.

This animal is extremely vocal in company of its own, and feeding sounders may be heard from a great distance. Snorts, grunts and squeals generally signify different age groups and sizes attempting to assert dominance during feeding. A low snuffling sound is produced when foraging or rooting, but wary boar can be quiet.

Shooting boar in the UK is hard work. I recall an occasion in Scotland, when the eastern sky began to pale into the ashen grey shade of the pre-dawn. Somewhere among the foliage of a stately spruce, an insomniac cock pheasant's 'kok kok' heralded the approaching new day.

I was sharing the rather spacious high tower with my client Bill Kinsley and estate stalker Gavin Mcghie. It had been an interesting night's vigil.

Frustratingly, we had heard the squeals and grunts of feeding pigs from near and far throughout the dark hours. The boar had even hit the barrel of feed that was anchored by rope in the centre of the open glade that our shooting platform overlooked. The problem had been the cloud cover.

The previous evening's dismal, overcast sky didn't look at all promising as we had climbed the ladder into our lofty perch. Bill, however, had made the valid point: "We won't shoot a boar in the pub." Gavin and I both nodded sagely at his remark.

The three-quarter full Galloway moon had shown itself infrequently between the clouds, but the boar, tantalisingly close, chose to remain in the shadows during these brief periods of illumination.

As the watery autumnal sun lazily rose above the forest canopy, my aching muscles had about had enough. I was just going to sound the retreat when an agonised squeal echoed around the glade.

The sound was repeated and followed by what can only be described as the 'expressive pig vernacular' of two wild boar engaged in combat.

Our options were limited to say the least. We would have to attempt to stalk the two combatants that were, by the sound of them, further down the glen where the forestry opens up into a marshy area of reeds and peat bog. After discussing our intended approach, we decided that the three of us would have to make a short detour and re-enter the forestry below the clashing boar and hopefully stalk up the burn to the scene of the combat.

*The author and a big keiler*

It has to be said that Gavin is a lot younger than me and keener than a cutthroat's razor. The idea of wading up a burn that had only yesterday been in full spate was not as appealing to me as it was to him. Furthermore I knew that Bill had previously served in the Parachute Regiment and 21 SAS, so it was safe to assume a little dampness would not deter my client in the least.

Assuming a willing expression, I enthusiastically led the way down the ladder in anticipation of an interesting stalk towards the still-vocal pigs.

Heading downhill, the woodland ride soon met with the burn which had fortunately receded enough to allow us carefully to stalk along the watercourse towards our objective. It was about this time that the rain started with a vengeance. The noise of it and the babbling burn drowned out the gruff grunts and squeals of the fighting boar and I became concerned that the bout was over and the pigs had departed.

The three of us made good time and soon followed the burn into the depths of the forestry. The going then became more difficult, as anyone who has crawled under the cover of sitka spruce will understand. We were forced by the canopy to make our way on all fours. I endured the questionable pleasure of fallen pin-sharp spruce needles embedded in the palms of my hands, not to mention those that fell from above and made it down my collar. Sitka spruce needles have a habit of working their way into everywhere, especially down your shirt and into the valley of your derrière. Reminds me of the Johnny Cash song *Ring of Fire*.

The incessant rain had by now beaten its way through the Gore-Tex and I was wet. However, the three of us had made it to the marsh. Leaving the liquid burbles of the burn behind we could hear the warring boar once more.

Gavin and Bill bellied through the mire like two otters, followed by your reluctant scribe. I noted that Bill did not need reminding to beware of fouling the muzzle of his rifle or to keep his backside down. In my experience ex-military types generally make good stalkers, but when it comes to taking the shot they often prefer, let's say, 'extreme range attempts'. Maybe on target paper that's OK, or when shooting at an insurgent who is chucking mortar rounds at you, but my rules are a maximum of 150 yards on the low-ground or 200 yards on the hill.

I hate the wounding of any animal, as all ethical guides should. The suspense and most of the fun is during the stalk and the shot just concludes (we hope) events. I have a damn good bloodhound that excels in tracking wounded game but I prefer not to have to use her.

Reaching firmer ground, the three of us carefully edged forward to the top of the small brae (hill), which was the last obstacle between us and our quarry.

The argumentative boars were running parallel to each other, venting their displeasure vocally and with occasional bites and swipes as they turned to repeat the manoeuvre. They were lit up by a thin patch of moonlight.

The approach had taken us the best part of an hour, but the bout between these two denizens of the forest showed no sign of abating. Bill deployed the tripod attached to his .308 Steyr Mannlicher and joined Gavin and I spying the two boar through his Leica range-finder binoculars.

I was surprised to see that one of the boar was in fact a big, old, dry sow who was getting the upper hand of the duel against an ancient male who had broken off both of his tusks. The old sow was inflicting some fearsome bites on her adversary. I wanted to shoot both animals if at all possible. The problem was that neither one would stay still, even for a moment.

Finally, the male admitted defeat and backed away defiantly into the forest. The victorious sow stood exhausted as her condensed breath billowed from her in great clouds in the cold air.

"Now's your chance," whispered a kneeling Gavin, as Bill fitted to the rifle. The dull 'bufft' of the .308 report, instantly followed by the 'thwok' of a bullet striking true, poleaxed the immense sow who frantically kicked her last.

On this occasion there was no cause for my usual worries over client accuracy. Bill is both an experienced stalker and an expert marksman.

Giving the sow the customary 10 minutes, we walked over to inspect our quarry. Bill had taken a real old timer that later weighed out at 96 kilos. She had put up a good fight and had died clean. The three of us were all smiles in the pouring rain, content with the satisfaction of a perfectly executed stalk, in adverse conditions, finished by a well-placed strike on an impressive animal, in a wonderful part of Scotland. ⊙

---

# WILD BOAR AGENTS

⊙ **Galloway**

*Steve Sweeting*
*07792 874511*
*carminnowsestate@msn.com*

⊙ **South-West Scotland**

*Peter Kingsley*
*01387 850234*
*kinharvie@tiscali.co.uk*

⊙ **England**

*Pete Law*
*07836 249807*
*petelaw@ukonline.co.uk*

*Others can be found in* Sporting Rifle *magazine   www.sporting-rifle.com*

*Chapter 10:* **FERAL GOATS**

➲ *As with any stalking, there is no shortage of walking when you are out after goats*

The goat was one of the first animals to be domesticated by man. It was originally introduced to Britain by neolithic farmers for milk, meat, horns and skin over 3,000 years ago. Although most of these goats would have remained hefted to a particular area, occasional animals would no doubt disperse to form feral herds. It is possible that other stock were also introduced during the Roman colonisation. A number of wild herds descended form these neolithic and possible Roman animals and were later recorded in the Domesday Book.

England's current wild goat population is of questionable origin with perhaps only the Cheviot herd being of neolithic provenance. Northumberland has three distinct wild goat populations, which in the past may have intermingled. Besides the largest group in Kielder Forest, managed by the Forestry Commission, other herds populate the Cheviot hills and Coquetdale. These goats have roamed the remote border fells of Northumberland, for centuries. There is some debate as to the origins of these animals; some say they are descended from domestic stock, which were taken to the hills by farmers centuries ago. Questionable evidence has since surfaced saying the goats were rounded up and taken to market on the Scottish side of the border in the distant past. Other experts believe the goats were are descended from farm animals that escaped earlier still in medieval times. A third camp maintains these goats hark back to the original neolithic settlers. Whatever their origin, they have taken on the markings of feral animals, and have been a rich part of border wildlife and culture for hundreds of years.

Wild goats have certainly roamed the Valley of Rocks near Lynmouth, north Devon, for 1,000 years. The herd today numbers around 100.

In 1970, it was thought the herd had died out and the council introduced a small number of goats of British Saanen type. Numbers increased, both by breeding and additional dumping of unwanted stock of questionable breeding into the valley. By the mid-1970s there were about a dozen mongrel ragged looking types roaming the area causing visitors to complain about their state. This herd was led by an infamous Billy that attacked picnickers and raided gardens. Lynton council replaced this rag tag herd with genuine feral goats, the reasoning being a truly 'wild' herd would confine their activities to the valley.

With the help of the Rare Breeds Survival Trust, three genuine British primitive goats, one male and two females, were introduced into the valley in December 1976 from the College Valley in Northumberland. However two or three crossbreed goats remained at large in the area and as can be expected they covered the introduced nannies.

The Bagot feral goat issue is clouded by the status of this animal as a rare breed. Many questions remain unresolved, but whether this animal is a true feral fragment of neolithic stock that has become isolated and bred true to type, or descends from stock gifted by Richard the Lionheart, will no doubt never be confirmed.

What is known, is that the Bagot breed of feral goat has, for several centuries, lived a semi-wild existence at Blithfield Hall, Staffordshire, England. Local legend claims the Bagot goats were introduced to England at Blithfield

*The author with a feral goat in south-west Scotland*

in the 1380s for hunting purposes. These goats were supposedly brought back to England by returning Crusaders, possibly from the Rhone Valley, and given to John Bagot of Blithfield by King Richard II to commemorate good hunting the monarch had previously enjoyed at Blithfield.

Sir John Bagot released these goats into 2,000 acres of woodland known as Bagots Wood, with a few also liberated in the estate's 1,000-acre park and were hunted just like deer. The herd prospered through time and on a number of occasions had to be culled back to more manageable numbers. Documentation shows that this happened in 1710, in the interests of agriculture and again in 1938. An extermination order for the entire herd was placed by the War Agriculture Executive a year later, due to the damage sustained to agricultural crops, badly needed for the war effort. Fortunately, the then Lord Bagot successfully appealed against this order, but agreed to keep the herd below 60 animals. Post WWII, the Bagot herd increased again and a further cull was initiated bringing the numbers back down to 60. In 1954 more Blithfield stock were sent to some other large country estate parks and a number were released in the Welsh mountains.

In 1957, the fifth Lord Bagot sold the Blithfield part of his estate and the remaining goats were dispersed to parks, zoos and private enthusiasts. However, Lady Bagot bought back 20 of the surviving goats in 1962 and returned them to the Hall at Blithfield. These animals never prospered and Lady Bagot eventually entrusted their care to the Rare Breeds Survival Trust.

The Bagot goat is impressive to look at: a small goat, with a black head and white body. It has the longest-recorded history of any British goat.

Wild goats are present across Scotland in various local populations, some of them isolated, from the Shetland Islands to strongholds in Galloway. However, the greatest numbers are to be found in the Highlands and along the west coast and the offshore isles. Goats were still popular domestic animals in Scotland up until the 1700s, when more profitable sheep farming took over. Then, the infamous Highland clearances forced most of the crofters off the hills and many goats where abandoned through necessity by the departing Highlanders. These goats would have joined the existing wild goats of neolithic descent.

Another interesting theory was related to me many years ago by Islay stalker John Law, concerning the possible origins of the west coast goat populations. John believed that their establishment is directly due to surviving goats from wrecked ships belonging to the Spanish Armada. After suffering defeat at the hands of the English Navy, the Armada attempted to sail back to Spain in a circuitous route, along England's East coast and around Scotland into the Atlantic, before eventually changing course southwards towards Spain, to sail past Ireland. Severe storms disrupted the fleet's course and countless vessels were wrecked on the unforgiving coastlines of Ireland and Scotland. Some of the goats, which were carried on board the ships as a source of fresh milk and meat, must have scrambled ashore to safety.

The wild goats of the Trossachs and Loch Lomond have three separate populations, although some previous authors have regarded these three herds as a fragmented, extended, colony. The hills and forests of Ben Venue and nearby Loch Achray, Ben Lomond and Inversnaid had historically held goats for centuries.

The population as a whole was once referred to as the Stirling population and has been heavily culled in the past, due to forestry concerns. During the 1960s, as many as 350 of the Stirling goats were culled by the commission.

Trophy records show that the Trossach and Lomond side goats were highly prized by hunters in history and none no more so than the Ben Venue and Loch Achray herd. Three fine rams were shot from this flock on Achray, Callander, by the then shooting tenant, Captain RT Hinckes of Foxley, Hereford, in 1922. Another exceptional Achray goat head is recorded in Rowland Ward's *Records of Big Game* in 1928. Furthermore, copies of *The Field* magazine contain a number of excellent goat heads shot on Ben Venue in the 1920s and 1930s.

Ben Venue's wild goats' fortunes have fluctuated through the years, there were around 50 in 1898, 30 in 1913 and as many as 100 by the late 1930s. Considerable culling of these goats during WWII reduced the herd to thirty by 1945. The population dwindled over the next 15 years and G. Kenneth Whitehead recorded only one nanny and her kid in 1959. By the start of 1970, this population had improved but was decimated once more when the Forestry Commission implemented a cull of both these and the Ben Lomond goats during the 1960s. Today there is a healthy number of feral goats living on the slopes of Ben Venue and the surrounding area.

Ben Lomond formerly had a resident herd of feral goats of probable ancient origin, but these were virtually wiped out at the turn of the last Century. It seems that some remained however and a herd was re-established by local domestic goats, which either went wild or were deliberately liberated. G. Kenneth Whitehead tells a similar story, stating that the few goats in the area were descended from domestic goats originally kept at Inversnaid and French. The goat population of Ben Lomond had risen to more than 300 by the end of the 1930s, but both during and after the war, the Forestry Commission considerably reduced their numbers. By 1952, Whitehead recorded the total between 70 and 100.

There is no doubt that this herd has domestic origins and indeed some locals refer to domestic billies being liberated to improve the blood from time to time. It has also been said that milking goats were released from the disbanded WWI army camp near to Loch Ard to join the Ben Lomond goats. That said this population is certainly now feral and deserves inclusion. By the mid 1990s the Ben Lomond population stood at around around 200 and remains strong today. The fortunes of the feral goat population of Loch Lomond undoubtedly have an interesting place in local legend, but none more so than the Inversnaid goat herd. These are said to possess the longest pedigree of any feral goats in Scotland, and are sometimes termed a royal herd. Legend asserts that Robert the Bruce was evading English soldiers, on the eastern banks of Loch Lomond and tired of fleeing, he attempted to throw off his pursuers by hiding in a cave used by goats. Like sheep, feral goats defecate in favoured resting and shelter sites that can have deep accumulations of dung, due to years of repeated use. The English soldiers, seeing a herd of goats browsing by the mouth of the cave and on smelling the goat guano therein could not believe that the Bruce would hole up in such a place and passed him by – hence the Royal decree that King Robert later passed, protecting these goats from further molestation.

Inversnaid Royal goats have remained relatively sedentary. The Arklet Water ravine, combined with a later deer fence and other stock fences to the north have kept this herd relatively confined.

Unfortunately, the alleged pedigree of the Inversnaid herd has been diluted by at least three domestic goats introduced into the population in the 1980s. In the mid 1990s the Inversnaid herd consisted of nearly 90 animals. Interestingly the Inversnaid goats of the 14th Century are the earliest ever to have been recorded as feral in Scotland.

Populations appear more sporadic on Scotland's North East coast, but historical herds cling on today around Loch Fleet and Reay Forrest and other isolated locations in Caithness, Sutherland, Invernesshire and Morayshire.

There were goats on the slopes and summit of Brin Rock Strathnairn near Inverness, that probably owed their origins to the aftermath of the last battle fought on British soil on nearby Culloden Moor during the Jacobite uprising in 1746. Local families fled from their scorched hovels, burnt out by the victorious English troops the day after the battle. Most of their livestock was either confiscated or driven away and many goats must have escaped to the hills of Nairnside to form the nucleus of the Brin Rock colony that survived until recent times. The area was left de-populated after the battle and many locals that survived the bullet and bayonet succumbed to starvation. Although these feral goats prospered for some time, I am informed by my good friend Hamish Cromarty, that the Brin Rock feral goats have now become extinct.

One of the finest Scottish wild goat heads was credited to the renowned big game hunter, Roualeyn Gordon Cumming (who famously hunted elephant in a kilt). This trophy was held at the family estate at Altyre Morayshire in the late 1800s. However, it appears that this trophy wasn't shot, or if it was, it certainly wasn't hunted and must have been a mercy killing, as the goat in question was a tame goat and actually the great white hunter's mascot. Roualeyn George Gordon Cumming was born in 1820 the son of Lt Colonel Sir William Gordon Gordon Cumming, 4th Bt of Altyre and Gordonstoun. After Cumming finished his education at Eton, he embarked on a military career and was commissioned Cornet in the Madras Cavalry in India. However, the climate did not suit him, so he sold his commission and started off on a series of hunting expeditions. After five years of adventure, Cumming returned home and toured the United Kingdom, exhibiting his hunting trophies, eventually settling at Fort Augustus. Here he exhibited his collection to travellers that used the steamers on the Caledonian Canal. Cumming greeted the visitors in full Highland dress, leading a large tame Billy goat that sported huge horns. The price of admission to his trophy collection was one shilling and appeared to keep Cumming and his goat in a reasonable living. However he died a relatively

*The author and Tommie Hynes with trophy billy goats in Ireland*

young man at 46 and it is not clear if his goat outlived him, but the horns certainly ended up on display at Altyre House.

Probably the most historic of Scotland's feral goats are those living in the Moffat Hills around Loch Skene. This herd has had little human interference and shows phenotypic characteristics, typical of ancient populations. The Moffat herd numbers around 250 animals and is one of the best examples of primitive goats to be found in Great Britain.

Today most Scottish wild goats will be hunted in the Highlands, Galloway, the Cheviots, or on one of the many west coast islands, where they are often found in great numbers. Other than on the mainland I have either seen or hunted wild goats on the Islands of Arran, Islay, Jura, Mull, Eigg, Muck, Rhum, and Skye, but they are present on many more. Taking to the islands to hunt a trophy billy is an exciting undertaking and here they are a truly sporting species to stalk in such wild and wonderful surroundings, mostly untouched by humans.

Snowdonia National park is the stronghold of the wild Welsh goat and these are thought to be descendants of neolithic stock. However it seems likely that all herds of feral goats in North Wales have undergone some crossbreeding with modern breeds in the last 200 years and for several of these herds, this may have occurred in the last five decades.

In Eryri there are three main areas populated with wild goats. These are the Rhinogydd uplands above Harlech, the Nant Gwynant area beneath Snowdon, and the Glyderau mountain range from Capel Curig to Llanberis. Outside the

National Park, there are also herds near Nefyn, Stackpole and a historically famous population of Kasmir goats on the Great Orme near Llandudno.

In the Harlech area there has been more than a 50% increase in recent years. This population explosion had to be reduced and a closely monitored cull recently reduced this herd to an estimated 500 goats.

In the Nant Gwynant and Beddgelert area, there has been little or no culling, but the high density of garden-raiding goats has angered many local residents, who are bitter towards the authorities due to the damage done by the animals and have called for a cull.

Tryfan is part of the Glyderau group of Mountains in Snowdonia and is also home to a well established population of feral goats. These animals spend some of their time around the lower slopes such as those near Tryfan Bach, Bochlwyd Buttress, and within Cwm Tryfan. Wild goats are also fairly abundant above the Llanberris quarries in the Northern Glyders.

The famous Great Orme cashmere goats owe most of their origin to Major General Sir Savage Mostyn, who introduced the original pair from Windsor to the grounds of Gloddaeth Hall in 1897. However, it is thought that they proved unsuitable as park animals. There is an old Welsh farming practice, known as 'Llwgu'r defaid' or 'starving the sheep.' This was a method whereby goats were run with the sheep, in the hope of precluding the latter from straying onto cliffs and other dangerous places. Goats are more surefooted than sheep and would find forage on the cliff faces, keeping the sheep away. Perhaps this may have been the reason why the goats were transferred to the Great Orme, Llandudno, and released to run wild in North Wales. Certainly, they are frequently to be seen browsing on extremely narrow ledges, and they climb the steep precarious cliffs with amazing agility.

The liberated herd did extremely well in the wild and the Mostyn Estate keepers occasional have had to cull their numbers. In 1990, due to excessive numbers, a goat capture exercise was carried out on the Orme, and 26 goats were re-located to Hereford and the Island of Flatholm. This resulted in a public outcry and Aberconwy Borough Council was criticised over their handling of the exercise.

The great Orme herd remained mostly pure until three goats were introduced into the herd from Whipsnade Zoo. One soon succumbed to the Welsh weather, another fell off a cliff and was killed, but the third goat survived, and eventually became accepted by the herd. Interestingly, this introduction formed a link between the Great Orme goats, Lynton's feral goats in England and the Royal Welch Fusiliers. The Royal Welch Fusiliers have obtained most of their regimental goat mascots from Whipsnade stock and the Lynton goats owe at least some of their origins to stock sourced from Sandringham via Windsor, where of course the initial Great Orme goats came from.

The Orme goats today are of a far heavier build than their Windsor counterparts. Their coats are shorter and less shaggy, with longer and more massive horns. No doubt, these differences have come about, due to these animals existing in virtual isolation for more than a hundred years, evolving into the unique breed they now are. Some of the goats however have dark, facial

*The author and a French client with a trophy Billy*

marks and it is possible that these are a result of the possible release of domestic goats into the herd, despite the rigid management policy of Mostyn Estate, which tries try to maintain a pure strain.

Feral goats occur on many of the Welsh mountains. They are also used for conservation grazing in a number of places, such as at Stackpole Estate, once owned by the Earls Cawdor in Pembrokeshire in south Wales. This herd is of mixed domestic descent and comprises 20 nannies and one Billy and was recently introduced to graze clematis, brambles, sea buckthorn etc, in an effort improve the habitat for lichens. In winter months, these goats retreat into local woodland until the springtime.

Most Irish wild goats are descendants of livestock abandoned during the land evictions and act as a living reminder of a turbulent past. Many more goats have been both intentionally and accidentally released into the wild in Ireland since the great famine and become part of Irelands wildlife heritage. Small groups are found across Northern Ireland in isolated hilly and mountainous areas and on the coastal cliffs of north and east Antrim. In County Fermanagh they occur mainly in woodland and on some islands in Lough Erne.

In Southern Ireland, wild goats are found in isolated areas mainly in the western counties and are locally common. The Burren National Park, County Clare has quite a number of large herds. The species is plentiful in County Galway and are common in many areas of the Irish west coast including Counties Mayo, Donegal and Kerry and populate many islands off the west coast.

A unique herd of feral goats habit Bilberry Rock in Waterford City and have been there for hundreds of years. The Bilberry Herd is probably related to Pashmina, Maltese or Cashmere goats and is thought to have arrived with the Huguenots fleeing France some 300 years ago. They have lived on Bilberry Rock ever since. These goats came close to extinction in the year 2000, the population numbering only seven and rising to 21 in 2005. However, the herd's fortunes have since been reversed and they now number around 40 animals.

Wild goats, to be technically correct, are actually feral goats, but are usually referred to by English stalkers as wild goats. However international hunters always refer to our British wild goats as feral goats and they are listed as such with all major trophy measuring organisations.

Feral goats are smaller than most modern domestic goats, with adults weighing between 35-75kg. Males or billies are heavier than females or nannies. They have long shaggy coats that vary in colour from white, through dark brown, to black, grey and piebald. The tail is long and flat with no hair on the underside.

Both sexes usually have backward sweeping horns that grow continuously; some males may grow horns more than a metre long. A thickened pad of skin called a callus is present on the knees of the front legs. Both sexes sport bearded tufts but these beards are much more pronounced in the males.

Billie's have a strong, offensive body odour which is at its worst during the rut and difficult to remove during trophy preparation – a fact worth noting if you intend to hang your trophy in the house. I have been told by one leading taxidermist that if the cape is soaked in vinegar, it will remove the odour, but I have as yet not tested this.

Goats like to live together in family groups, but will often make loose herds with other same sex groups. Males and females with followers usually form separate groups, generally staying apart until mating time.

In Britain, they are usually found in isolated mountainous moorland areas of Scotland, northern and western England and Wales. Some forest-living populations have been recorded, but most are adjacent to moorland or rugged coastline. They also occur on many offshore islands and sea cliffs.

Goats are browsers and eat whatever is available from grasses, heather and

sedges in summer, to gorse and heather in winter. It is fair to say that their plant diet is extremely varied, and includes some species which are otherwise toxic to many other animals.

Feral goats are sometimes used for 'conservation grazing', to control the spread of undesirable scrub or weeds in open natural habitats, such as chalk grassland and heathland. However, goat eating habits can have both positive and negative effects on the environment. By browsing on unwanted woody plants, they can help maintain plant diversity in grassland and control invasive scrub species. But if herds are not managed properly they can become too large and may over-browse sensitive areas. Bark stripping can also be a problem in some places.

In the autumn rutting season, billies fight with each other to gain access to females that are ready to breed. Male goats smell strongly, due to special musk glands becoming more active. Goats become sexually mature within their first year. Nannies and kids stay in separate herds away from the billies until the breeding season, when male groups join with the matriarchal social groups. Rutting takes place from September to October, with one to two kids born per year between January and March.

Their extended breeding seasons allow them to have up to two litters a year and nannies can conceive while still lactating. Gestation period is approximately 150 days. Twins are the usual result per pregnancy, though triplet births are also common. Most young goats, known as kids, are born in late winter or early spring. Kids are often born in extreme weather conditions and mortality may be high in some seasons. For the first few days the kids are left in a sheltered hiding place; when they are stronger they join their mother and the rest of the group.

Wild goats are extremely resilient animals and seem to absorb a bullet. I recommend a minimum calibre of .270 Winchester with a suitable expanding bullet for this species.

I accepted a kind invitation from my Irish client and friend Tommie Hynes to visit the Emerald Isle and hunt *gabbhar fia* (Gaelic for wild goat). I have hunted *capra hircus* on the cliffs and beaches of the Western Isles, in the Galloway hills of Scotland and also in England's Kielder Forest. However, this would be my first bash at an Irish billy.

St Patrick himself must have been looking down on us as the sun came out to show off the splendour of the Irish countryside. Boatman Liam opened up the outboard and the little skiff skipped over the rippled water. A half-hour later, Liam expertly steered us into a narrow cutting and silenced the engine. The boat smoothly scraped to a halt on the gravel bottom.

I surveyed the island as we disembarked. It was about 10 acres in extent and a mixture of rough grass, heather and blackthorn thicket. Liam informed me that it was formerly populated, including a school of about 20 pupils, but the islanders had deserted it during WWII.

Our plan was simple: we would stalk into the wind until we spied a suitable goat or reached the other side of the island.

I had dressed for the worst that the weather could offer and as the wind had fallen away and the sun was now beating down, I was sweating like a Scotsman in a distillery. We passed by the old school house standing mute and forlorn, surrounded by thorns and being invaded by creeping ivy. I glanced above the door way and noticed it was built in 1908, a full Century ago.

Liam froze as he stepped into an open gateway. I raised the 8x50 Steiners and followed the direction of his gaze. About 20 goats were nipping off the first buds of the blackthorn. Among them were two fine billies.

Tommie had already deployed the shooting sticks and slipped the rifle out of the slip. It was a heavy piece of kit. However, the weight was not a problem when I placed it in the crook of the sticks, chambered a round and drew a bead on the left-hand Billy.

Tommie whispered: "Wait until the nannies move away, shoot in your own time and take both if you can."

The nannies duly moved and I put the reticle on to the goat's shoulder, holding my breath as I squeezed off the 168-grain round. The moderator suppressed all the recoil and there was no muzzle flip to speak of, enabling me to see that the bullet strike was straight and true – further confirmed by the thwack of lead and copper hitting home. I instantly chambered a second round and swung on to the other billy, who stood broadside, alert, but due to the moderator, unsure where the danger lay. I drew a bead on a goat's shoulder for the second time that morning and sent another round on its way, just as the herd started to flee.

The second billy stumbled, but regained its feet in an instant and made for the safety of the thicket. I bolted down a third round and picked it up once more in the scope just as it was disappearing into the thorns. The shot was good and the Lapua round went through the body, destroying most of its vitals. The goat fell dead, half in and half out of the thorn thicket. ⊙

---

**WILD GOAT AGENTS**

⊙ **Cheviot Hills**

*David Virtue*
*07866 901019*
*info@dvsporting.co.uk*

⊙ **Galloway**

*Steve Sweeting*
*07792 874511*
*carminnowsestate@msn.com*

*Others can be found in* Sporting Rifle *magazine  www.sporting-rifle.com*

---

*Chapter 11:* **SOAY SHEEP**

The Soay sheep (*Ovis aries*) is unique in being Britain's only wild sheep species. It shares a similar set of historical events as its cousin, the mouflon, but on a significantly smaller scale. Soays originally developed on an island and were then introduced elsewhere. The same happened with the mouflon, which originated on the island of Corsica. The mouflon has prospered well in Hungary, Germany, Austria and elsewhere since being introduced and is certainly regarded as much a German species now, as the fallow deer is regarded here as a British species.

The diminutive Soay sheep comes from the St Kilda Archipelago, 110 miles west of the Scottish mainland - specifically from the isle that bears its name. A primitive sheep breed compared to modern farm stock, it is said to be a species suspended in time, thanks to its isolation on St Kilda.

No one really knows for certain, but most experts agree that this primitive sheep species arrived in the St Kildas around 5,000 years ago, roughly concurrent with the Bronze Age culture in the British Isles.

Soays have been introduced in more modern times to other areas of the UK, mainly in small numbers. The biggest flock today is at Woburn Abbey where it was first introduced in 1910 by the 11th Duke of Bedford and the noted zoologist HA Russell.

A decade earlier, Lt General Henry Pitt-Rivers introduced a flock to his ancient hunting forest in Dorset.

This adaptable little sheep has proved popular for keeping down excessive vegetation growth in sensitive areas, such as Cheddar Gorge in Somerset. It has also been introduced for similar reasons, to a number of islands: Lundy off the Devon Coast in 1944, Cardigan Island off the western shores of Wales and Hirta, a neighbouring island to Soay, by the Marquess of Bute in 1930.

Other small flocks have prospered on certain estates across Great Britain and Ireland, but the species is still considered threatened.

Soay sheep are usually dark brown or black, but occasionally light brown or grey with white underparts, and naturally shed their wool in spring and early summer. The tails are short and both sexes are horned. The ram grows up to 55cm (22in) in height at the shoulder and weighs from 26-30kg (57-66lb). The ewe can grow up to 45cm (18in) and can weigh from 20-25kg (44-55lb). They are distinguished from domestic sheep by a number of physical features such as their shorter tail and white belly wool.

The Soay is a grazer and is normally found in areas of poorer quality grassland such as offshore islands and coastlines. Today, a number of Soay flocks are kept in large parkland environments. Other populations have been introduced as free ranging or feral flocks in sensitive areas to keep vegetation under control.

Soay is a grazing species but will occasionally browse on other available forage. Being a wild species they are nervous and vigilant feeders, but in time will tame to a certain extent in close proximity to humans. Soays spend more time grazing than domestic breeds, however this is probably due to poorer quality grazing. The original Soay population on St Kilda is directly linked to the

*The author poses with a medal-class Soay ram*

*A good head on a Soay ram*

grazing pastures and cannot achieve equilibrium, instead rising to unsustainable numbers before crashing drastically and rapidly reproducing again.

Soay sheep start rutting in autumn and are normally finished by the onset of winter. Most ewe lambs tend to come into heat (oestrus) in November, while older ewes might come into estrus in October. Gestation in Soay sheep can range from 147 to 155 days, with an average of 150 days and usually one or two lambs are born.

Soay have an average life span of eight to 10 years. One interesting point is that the breed also lacks the flocking instinct of many breeds. Attempts to work them with sheep dogs result in a scattering of the group.

If a ewe and her lamb are separated, both 'baa' repeatedly. Older sheep do this if separated from the flock. Rams make a grumbling sound during the mating season and ewes have a specific parturition call.

This is a small animal and although woolly, a .243 Winchester is the suggested minimum calibre.

I shot my first soay ram in Galloway. We were looking for a particular ram that had gone lame and was now living a solitary existence away from the flock. Peering over the rocky ridge, the pair of us scanned the small gully before us. I noticed a small movement down to our right and trained the 7x50 Steiner binoculars on the area. Sure enough, there was the back-end of a black sheep protruding out from behind the granite outcrop. I nudged the stalker Gavin and pointed out the sheep some 80 yards away. The young Scot soon had him in the glass and we waited patiently for the sheep to show itself. I was starting to feel discomfort from the sharp edges of the stone scree digging into my elbows and knees, but the sheep eventually backed out from behind the rock, which took my mind off the discomfort. I could see clearly that it was a ram with a definite limp. Gavin confirmed that it was our intended quarry. The ram wasn't carrying a great head, but he was a mature representative with an obvious disability. Soay sheep are nervous in the wild state and flee at the slightest hint of danger, so we waited a while until the ram began feeding once more. Gavin asked if I was happy to shoot the beast from our present position, which I affirmed with a definite nod. We backed away from the ridge and un-slipped the Tikka .25-06. I pressed home the clip and chambered a round with an oily double click, applied the safety and bellied forward once more.

The ram had lain down, facing almost directly toward us, between two boulders with some smaller rocks in front of him that covered his chest area. Normally I am not happy to take head shots unless the animal is facing away and I have a steady mark at the back of the head. But the ram was injured in some way and would probably disappear into the next county if we tried to move him; the midges had found us again so I wasn't keen to wait out the stand off. All things considered, I elected to attempt a head shot if Gavin was in agreement. He was, and the Tikka 25.06 came up to fit my shoulder; I picked up the resting ram in the Meopta 7x50 scope. I shuffled a little and spread my legs to get a comfortable steady rest off my elbows in the prone position. Catching my breath as the crosshairs rested between the ram's eyes I squeezed off the shot. The ram's head just slumped forward, no kicking, and no rolling – just brained. ⊙

---

## SOAY SHEEP AGENTS
⊙ **England**
*Mike McCrave*
*01573 470 771*
*mike@cms-hunting.co.uk*

⊙ **Galloway**
*Steve Sweeting*
*07792 874511*
*carminnowsestate@msn.com*

*Others can be found in* Sporting Rifle *magazine   www.sporting-rifle.com*

---

*Chapter 12:* **FOXES**

The ancestors of this species were certainly smaller than the red fox (*Vulpes vulpes*) we have today and are of Eurasian origin. The earliest red fox fossils date back to the mid-Pleistocene and confirm that these foxes were indeed smaller than their modern counterparts. These fossils seem to be among the refuse of early human settlements, showing that the fox was probably exploited by primitive humans as both a source of food and for pelts.

British red foxes have crossbred extensively with foxes imported from Germany, France, Belgium, Sardinia, and Siberia over the last 200 years. During colonial times, the British exported this species to the Americas, where it has interbred with the North American species.

Introductions to Australia for hunting purposes have proved disastrous for native wildlife. The first introduction occurred in 1845 near Keilor, Victoria. The introduction of a further two male foxes was reported in the *Sydney Echo* in 1855. One male and two females were released in 1864 by the Melbourne Hunt Club. Another pair was released some 20 km from Ballarat in 1871 and several more animals on Point Cook. By 1880, these populations had spread and linked up. Less than a decade later, foxes had colonized most of Victoria and by 1911 they had become established in southern Queensland. Australian red foxes now occur throughout mainland Australia, save for northern Queensland and the Northern Territory. Many of Australia's ground living animals have disappeared in the foxes' wake and many of these species are only to be found on fox-free islands.

The UK fox population is estimated to be some 240,000 (pre-breeding) of which 14 per cent is in urban locations. Some 425,000 cubs are born each year and clearly unless the population is to increase, a similar number of foxes must die each year.

The red fox is a small canid, native to much of Eurasia and North America, as well as northern Africa. It is the most recognisable species of fox and in Great Britain it is referred to simply as the fox. This is the largest species within the genus Vulpes and the largest of the true foxes, as well as being the only representative of the genus in Britain. Adult red foxes range in weight from 3.6 to 7.6kg (7.9 to 17lb) depending on region, with those living in higher latitudes being larger. Sexual dimorphism is noticeable and males are typically 15% heavier than females.

The red fox is most commonly a rusty red, with white underbelly, black ear tips and legs, and a bushy tail, usually with a distinctive white tip. This red tone can vary from dark chestnut to golden and almost black, leucistic variants have also been recorded in the wild.

The fox can live in areas which are diverse in terms of natural conditions and the animal is both a natural survivor and an adaptable predator. Foxes can be found in farmland, moorland, heathland, urban and mountainous or afforested areas. This animal has a series of dens that it uses within its range throughout the year. These are usually rock crevices or enlarged rabbit holes. However the fox will utilize land drains, straw stacks, compost heaps, the list is endless.

*⌒ Another fox caught out on a lamping expedition*

When raising a litter, the vixen chooses a den, known as an earth, to have her offspring. This is usually in a well-drained site and may be a commandeered badger sett or enlarged rabbit burrow.

Although classified as carnivores, red foxes are omnivorous and are highly opportunistic. Prey can range in size from insects to deer fawns. The majority of their diet consists of invertebrates, such as insects, molluscs, earthworms and some shellfish in costal regions. They also eat plant material, especially blackberries, apples, plums, sunflower seeds and other fruit. Common vertebrate prey includes rodents, rabbits, birds, eggs, amphibians, small reptiles and fish. Foxes kill deer fawns and in Scandinavia, predation by red fox is the most important mortality cause for neonatal roe deer. They will scavenge carrion and other edible material they find – and in urban areas, they will take human refuse, often eating from pet food bowls left outside. Analysis of country and urban fox diets show that urban foxes consume a higher proportion of scavenged food than country foxes.

The red fox breeding period varies widely but is usually from December to February. Females have an annual oestrous period of between one and three weeks; ovulation is spontaneous. Copulation is accompanied by a tie similar to domestic dogs that may last for more than an hour. Although a female may mate repeatedly with several males, she will eventually settle with only one to rear her litter. Gestation lasts between 49 and 56 days, but is most typically from 51 to 53 days.

Average litter sizes consist of four to six cubs, which are born blind, deaf and toothless, with dark brown fur. Vixens remain with the cubs for the first two to three weeks of their lives; she is fed by the dog fox during this time. Lactation lasts for seven weeks. The cubs' eyes open after two weeks and are initially blue, but change to amber by one month. At this time, white patches appear on their faces, their ears become erect and their muzzles elongate. Cubs begin to leave their dens and experiment with solid food brought by their parents at the age of three to four weeks. If the mother dies before the cubs are independent, the father takes over as their provider. By the age of four months, the cubs are long-legged, narrow-chested and inquisitve. They reach adult proportions at the age of six to seven months.

While foxes do not howl or socially vocalize the way coyotes and wolves do, they still have a limited range of vocal communication. Family members will occasionally use these calls, chuckling, 'gekkering' noises, whining, whimpering, shrieking, to keep track of one another when separated. A short sharp alarm bark is often issued by both adults to silence the cubs in time of danger.

The mating scream is a long, drawn-out, monosyllabic, and rather eerie wail most commonly heard during the breeding season; it is widely thought that it is made by a vixen in heat summoning dog-foxes. Contrary to common belief, however, it is also made by the males, evidently serving some other purpose in the courtship ritual.

There is a legion of sportsmen and women who solely target this species in Britain and set out in pursuit of this species in the dark hours with an array of calls and high power spotlights. In America, this kind of shooting is known as varminting and the term seems to be catching on over this side of the Atlantic pond. Lamping, as it is more commonly known, is for the specialist fox shooter. The fox is included in this book as it is commonly taken as an incidental while out deer stalking. Many stalking leases have an associated proviso that entails the culling of foxes. It as well to take a fox in these situations as stalking permission is easily lost, especially in areas of game preservation where the presence of a fox is of serious concern.

Any of the .22 centrefire calibres are suitable for fox shooting but be sure you have a variation on your FAC to shoot foxes before doing so with the larger calibres, such as the .308 Winchester or .30-06 Springfield.

I spent a number of mostly happy years 'keepering on both the lowground and on the moor. Arch-enemy number one was, of course, the fox, and most suitable nights were spent in pursuit of Charlie with a lamp. Obviously this wasn't the only method employed in the fox offensive, but it provided a significant back-up to the snaring programme. Occasionally, I would encounter an extremely difficult vulpine adversary that had probably been educated by a long range raking shot from some numpty with a lamp. I used to groan inwardly when we encountered a lamp-shy fox because it would often take many man

hours to bring Charlie to book – unless we were lucky with the wires, of course, and found him ensnared. However, I had never run into such a cunning fox as I did in the spring of 2009.

At home on the Yorkshire coast I am fortunate enough to rent a superb roe shoot that produces some respectable bucks every season. In addition to the dozen bucks or so that I take annually, I normally add half-a-dozen foxes to the bag. These incidentals are usually taken from a high-seat when waiting for roe. The farm is a fantastic wild bird shoot, mainly for woodcock and various duck, with a good stock of wild pheasant, so vermin control is a high priority.

Last spring, I joined forces with the landowner in pursuit of a particularly difficult fox marauder. I first noticed Charlie's depravations at the beginning of April. Old habits die hard and I am always subconsciously on the look-out for signs of predation when out stalking. This particular predator had developed a regular habit of chopping laying hen pheasants on the nest. I started to regularly pick up pairs of wings with the tell-tale snail-trail-type mark of dried fox saliva. Every loss of a laying bird is serious on a wild bird shoot, as it equates to losing a full brood. After liaising with the farmer, I found out that he had been having a great deal of trouble in coming to terms with a lamp-shy fox and he asked for my assistance. I was only too willing to help, having experienced such a worrying scenario in my previous career.

Snaring wasn't an option, due to the high public access, mostly of dog walkers and equestrian hobbyists, who I try to avoid during my stalking forays. My only real option was to spend time in the field at dawn and dusk and try to catch the marauder out. This can be a soul-destroying pastime, as to be successful, one has to pass other quarry up in favour of a meeting with Mr Fox.

I had checked all known earths to no avail, and had also looked in any likely spots for fresh digging or drawn-out rabbit warrens without result. Days passed and the fox seemed to be taunting me as I found fresh evidence of his activities daily. On one occasion he had insultingly defecated on the feathers of his last victim – it felt like a goad. I suspected that this vulpine was a dog fox and was tending to a new breed in an old wood that was off-limits, adjacent to my southern shoot boundary.

Sure enough, after setting up in a strategic position that overlooked this no-man's-land woodland I spied a big dog fox slinking out of the trees. Observing him through the superb lens of my Swarovski three-draw scope, I watched him work away along the hedgerows, obviously scenting out any squatting hens. Unfortunately, he headed away from my position, mobbed by an angry crow. Paying the corvid no heed, Charlie disappeared to continue his depravations out of sight.

Rather than change position and give the game away, I sat tight and hoped Charlie would return via a different route than he had departed from. However, the hour hand worked its way to 10 bells with no further sighting. Returning early that same evening, I set up in a small plantation that had a commanding view of the fox's former exit point and waited. One's worst enemy in an ambush situation is boredom. Improvised hides are the worst, as there is often

➲ *A Pere David
deer – among the
exotic deer species in
parks in England*

insufficient cover to begin with and any movement is easily visible. It is hard to sit still for long periods at a time, by way of human nature. The trick is to get into a comfortable position to begin with and totally relax.

Anyway, I began another vigil and actually nodded off, which was slightly counter-productive. The early evening chill woke me from my slumber and I cursed myself for my tardiness. However, not long afterwards, my feathered friends of the forest alerted me to the fox's presence. First a wren began its kricck, kricck scolding, which was soon taken up by a blackbird's plup, plup, plup as she followed the as-yet-unseen pest. The wind was good and Charlie must have passed within 10 yards of my position – exiting the wood at the expected place but, unfortunately, on the west side of the hedge away from me. Charlie's decision was no doubt due to the last warming rays of the setting sun. I benignly watched him disappear into the distance for a second time as darkness descended, but I remained determined to take him the following day.

Arriving well before dawn and topped up with cappuccino to stave off any further snoozing, I soon settled down in the same place to ambush Charlie. The breeze was hardly evident, but what wind there was seemed favourable. My caffeine hit was subsiding as dawn smeared into life across the eastern horizon. Yawning like I hadn't slept for a millennium I began to regret the copious amounts of coffee I'd taken earlier, as my bladder now felt like it was about to burst.

My morale began to fade as the sun rose higher and my discomfort increased. Then, without warning, a pair of blackbirds set up an almighty ruckus in the hedgerow some 200 yards away. Deploying the Swarovski draw scope once again, I was just in time to see Charlie trot onto the scene, fortunately at the right side of the hawthorn hedge this time.

Quickly switching the draw scope for my Sako 75, I picked him up in the Zeiss Davari. The fox was now no more than 80 yards away. I pursed my lips and forced a mouse squeak through my front teeth. The effect was instant - Charlie's neck snapped back toward me as he halted mid-step. The pause was enough to send the 125-grain Nosler into his vitals. The fox spun round in spectacular fashion, as the bullet did its work and delivered an instant death.

After admiring my adversary, I realised it had been more than 10 years since I had last targeted a fox in the daytime, other than as an incidental. It reminded me of the hard work and dedication put in by 'keepers across the country in the name of game and wildlife preservation. The landowner was overjoyed at the result, but I knew that somewhere out there would be a vixen with a breed of cubs that would have to be dealt with sooner rather than later. But that would be another foray for another day. ⊙

## FOX SHOOTING
### ⊙ Outfitters

*Pat Carey, The Warrener
05601 714580 (office hours
only)
sales@thewarrenersden.co.uk
for information on fox-
shooting courses*

*Others can be found in*
Sporting Rifle *magazine*
*www.sporting-rifle.com*

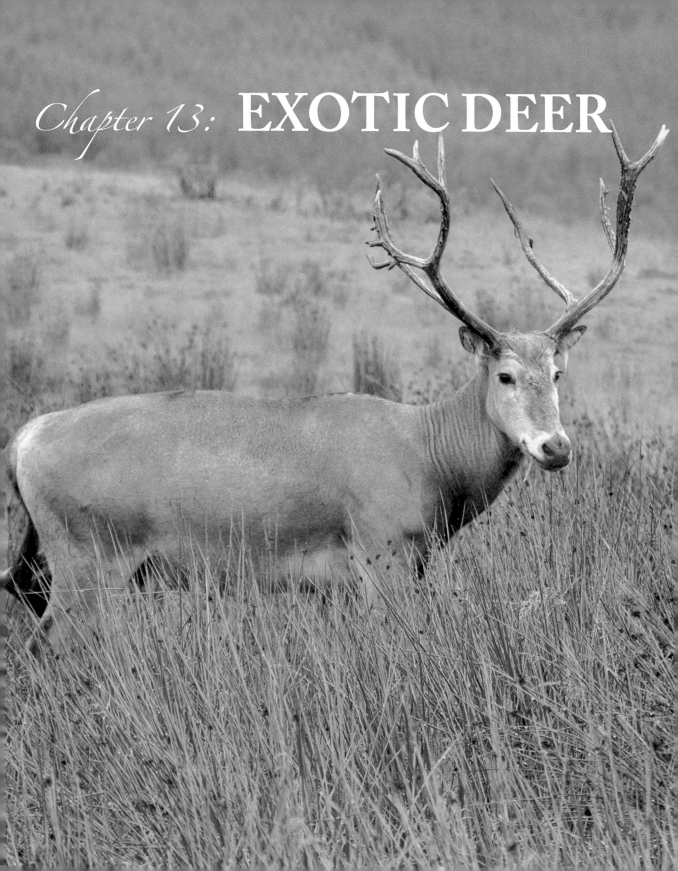

Chapter 13: **EXOTIC DEER**

There has been much misunderstanding and misrepresentation about hunting exotic game species in Great Britain. Some animals have escaped or deliberately been released to become established in the wild and become naturalised, the muntjac and Chinese water deer for example. In other parts of the world it is a similar story. Blackbuck in Texas and axis deer in Australia are both good examples. However, most exotics are hunted in game fenced areas and this is where the controversy lies. In Texas it is big business conducted on huge ranges and although there is a perimeter fence, on some ranches one could walk a day before hitting the opposite fence. In the UK we have many walled or fenced deer parks and the animals within must be managed. Nevertheless, the idea of pursuing game in an enclosure is repugnant to many. Each to their own I say and before one can really condemn another, all aspects must be looked at.

The term 'canned hunting' was first used regarding the repugnant release of a lion into a small enclosure for a hunting (using the term loosely) client to follow up and shoot. This, in anyone's book, is morally about as wrong as it gets. Quite rightly, this has been banned in Africa and now strict guidelines have to be followed. The question is, what is classed as an enclosure? Using southern Africa again as an example, nearly all of it is fenced to some degree. The Kruger National Park is totally fenced and the acreage confined is bigger than the country of Swaziland. The question of how big an area needs to be in order to be an acceptable hunting ground, is difficult to answer, due to the many variables encountered. A 200-acre enclosed park, deliberately overpopulated with put-and-take animals is a disgrace. However, a self-perpetuating population of blackbuck antelope living in a large enclosure on a Texas ranch is a whole different ball game. Indeed there are some ancient hunting chases in England that still have walled parks, many some thousands of acres in extent, dotted around the country. These deer parks have healthy populations of well-managed deer and their numbers quite rightly are kept within correct stocking densities. Of course, culling the excess animals is the only practical way of keeping these populations in check. This in turn creates a by-product of venison. Additional and often substantial revenue can also be generated from the sale of trophy-class animals to trophy collecting hunters.

In the UK, we are primarily a nation of bird hunters, with an antiquated set of Victorian values which we bring to our other ancient sport of deer stalking. Don't get me wrong, I am a traditionalist at heart and welcome the adherence to the traditional values of our hunting heritage. However, we must look at the practicalities involved in managing a deer park. If there is both supply and demand and all safety and ethical considerations are in place and being adhered to, then I can see nothing wrong in a visiting sportsman wanting to shoot an exotic deer in an enclosed reserve or park, although I agree that the pursuit of such animals can hardly be called hunting - in truth it's more the collection of a valued trophy. That, said some of the most challenging fallow buck hunting I have done was inside a 5,000-acre deer park, with lots of cover and trees.

*⌒ A Pere David deer – unusually, this cervid produces two sets of antlers each year*

I have guided clients in these places, whether it be a prestigious park, owned by the aristocracy or a privately owned estate, bordered by a high fence. Herd numbers have to be kept in check and paying clients provide much needed currency to maintain the upkeep of the estate and animals. Many of these parks are heavily wooded and their inhabitants are as close as they can get to being totally wild, without actually removing the fence. Culling is certainly not a matter of going into an open field and pulling the trigger from the Land Rover window. As is true in the wild, on a days hunting the odds are often in favour of the quarry. With the exception of the Pere David deer, which even in its previous wild state was about as tame as an armchair pooch, most deer if culled regularly become pretty damn wild and are difficult to approach.

Of course, many exotic species are closed for hunting in their remaining wild populations and some are even extinct in the wild, with captive collections being the last link between existence and extinction of a species.

Deer species are the most commonly collected exotic trophies with Pere David, barashinga, hog, axis, rusa and sambar being the most sought after.

Exotic antelope species normally hunted are the scimitar-horned oryx, addax and the beautiful blackbuck. The Safari Club International (SCI) has a list of exotic species taken in its record book of big game. The SCI book also differentiates between wild stalked game and fenced game within a particular species. Park-shot red deer trophies are recorded in a separate list under the heading Estate Red Deer and the book needs to be commended for doing so. One can hardly compare a supplement-fed park red stag to a free roaming forest red subjected to the rigors of nature, in a wild state.

Hunting of exotic species may not appeal to all, but there can be no getting away from the fact that without these enthusiasts it would be the species concerned whose survival would suffer. Whether we like it or not, we need their currency to support conservation efforts in this country and abroad.

Everything in the modern world is a commodity, whether we like it or not. Game and all wildlife must be looked upon as a commodity to ensure its survival. If something doesn't have value, it will be quickly swallowed up or lost forever in the modern dog-eat-dog world. That value may be secondary to the stalker, such as currency gained from tourists in big game parks but it is value nevertheless. ⊙

---

# COMMON EXOTICS
## ⊙ Pere David
*For trophy collectors, the only real possibility of securing the unusual trophy from this deer (*Elaphurus davidianus*) is to harvest one from a deer park. There are number of extensive parks in Great Britain that have a herd of PDs. However, it has to be said that these deer are easily tamed and it is, in reality, a cull situation, with little or no actual hunting involved. Even in their former wild state in China, these deer were so tame, it led to their eventual downfall.*

## ⊙ Hog deer
*There are two sub-species of axis deer, which are of the same genus: hog deer and chital deer (*axis porcinus *and* axis axis*). The former is found in Northern India and Burma, whilst the latter is from Thailand Vietnam and Indo-China. There are a number of these animals kept in a variety of British deer parks.*

## ⊙ Blackbuck
*This antelope has been introduced from India to Texas and Argentina in the Americas and also to private collections in Britain and elsewhere in Europe. It is these closely controlled captive populations where the trophy collector will have the occasional opportunity to harvest one of these stunning antelope. Fortunately, the blackbuck population is stable with 50,000 native Indian individuals, plus an additional 43,000 descended from individuals introduced to Texas and Argentina.*

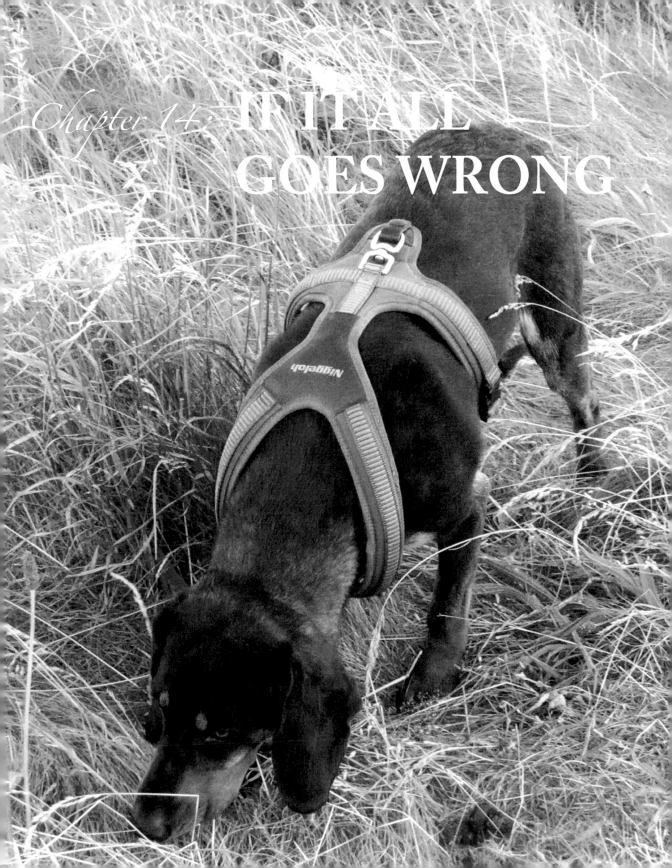

Chapter 14: IF IT ALL GOES WRONG

The Bavarian mountain hound is a specialist hound that was developed in the Bavarian and Austrian Alps, by selectively breeding small, lighter pups from the larger Hanoverian hound and out-crossing to – among other breeds – the Tyrol bracke, a lighter boned black and tan hound. The result is the small red/chestnut hound with a dark face and ears that we have today.

The breed is legendary for its nose and is used extensively in Europe as a specialist tracking dog for wounded game, as it has proved capable at tracking cold trails two or three days old. Its only drawback is obtaining one, as ownership is jealously guarded by professional foresters.

A few UK stalkers, notably Jan Andrews in Dorset, persevered and a number of imported bloodlines are now in the country.

The Bavarian is generally taken to the shot strike and clipped on to a 10-metre tracking leash which signals 'work' to the dog. The dog then (hopefully) leads the handler to the wounded game. The hound is only slipped if a wounded animal is flushed from its wound bed, then (hopefully again) the hound will bring it to bay where it can be stalked and despatched by the handler or (hunting within the law), in the case of smaller game such as roe, dragged down.

There are many advantages to working the hound on the leash. The dog must work at your pace. It is also easier to read the dog's reactions as it often goes up a gear when the scent gets 'hot'. This then enables you to build up a picture of the animal's injuries, as you read the spoor pointed by the dog that would otherwise be missed.

It is not the only breed available, but I believe the Bavarian to be the ideal dog for the UK stalker. The hound is a great companion dog, good with children, easily trained and eager to please. It is big enough to bring down a wounded roe buck (roe will not stand at bay) and brave enough to bring stags and boar to bay.

A tracking hound is a ground-scenting dog, with the dog's nose firmly fixed on the ground when working, as opposed to air-scenting dogs such as pointers. Air-scenting breeds do find deer and they will certainly excel at pointing unseen deer upwind of the rifleman when stalking, but the specialist breeds of bloodhound all hunt by ground scent. Nevertheless, scent hounds will also air-scent when accompanying the rifleman stalking but they will not indicate the presence of living deer as well as the pointing breeds. My own Bavarian hound's body language tells me if there is a deer nearby and if close she half sneezes with anticipation. This isn't a trait that I can claim to have been instilled by me; no, this came with experience and her confidence in me – and mine in her. This is a partnership that is cemented by stalking together over a period of time. Stalking is a lonely sport and the participation of a well trained dog is not only ethical, but enjoyable to.

Our continental cousins have been using these specialist bloodhounds for generations for finding lost and wounded big game. Back here, in Blighty, we have been slow to catch on to to the use of specialist hounds for this type of work. Let's not forget that stalking is a relatively new sport to this country (hill stag stalking being the exception), but fortunately for the sport, many enthusiasts are now actively seeking a specialist tracking dog to accompany them.

◐ *The author's Bavarian mountain hound, Jaeger, finds a lost Chinese water deer*

A tracking dog is expected to be able to indicate the shot strike area or injury to an animal and then, primarily by the use of ground scent, follow that particular animal's individual track, ignoring all other distractions including living deer, until the target animal is recovered. This is normally done on an extended tracking leash, but occasionally the hound is released, for instance if the wounded animal bolts from its wound bed or heavy cover forces the handler to release the dog.

In this instance, the hound must be able to report the find to the handler. This was done in former times by the hound baying dead at the carcase. Today this is still an advantage, as with modern day telemetry and GPS locators, it is enough that the hound stays with the find until the handler arrives.

The training of a deer tracking hound starts early. Puppies must be conditioned to deer from day one, as soon as their eyes are open, and sometimes before this. Many enthusiasts smear blood upon their hands prior to feeding their young charges and most will let the young pups play with discarded deer hocks or cleaves from freshly shot deer or boar.

It is not rocket-science to train a tracking hound, indeed it is much easier to train such a hound than it is to train a lab or spaniel for game shooting. A bond with the handler must be developed throughout puppyhood. Above all, training must be fun for both dog and handler, otherwise adverse effects may be encountered.

The first short tracks start at six weeks of age and are done by dragging a lung, beside the handler, preferably a few feet away using a broomshaft handle. This is essential, so that the pup is not hunting the handlers foot scent. The object of this exercise is to encourage the dog's desire to track. The trial doesn't have to be long and always ensure there is lavish praise and a treat at the end of the line. Short tracks in the garden are gradually lengthened to 100 yards or so, as and when the dog gets stronger and keener.

This is enough and must not be overdone. It is important to add variation i.e. change locations etc but always ensure the dog has success. A word of caution - do not over do this, as once or twice a week is enough, dropping in frequency as the dog gets older.

General basic training must have priority as the tracking side of things is the easiest to apply. Sit, stay, heel and the recall are absolute musts to be instilled in the hound. After this has been done, all other work is just an extension of the dog's work.

When the hound is broken to the lead, a separate tracking leash and collar must be added to the training sessions and this is when the real work begins. It is important that the tracking leash is used every time the hound is set on a trail and the particular collar and leash must be used for this purpose only. In that way, the hound knows that the leash means work and work to the hound must always mean fun.

Working a tracking hound on a long leash the German way is far more efficient than using a free-running dog. Firstly, the hound will mark out interesting developments such as bits of bone, or where the animal may have

○ *The author's*
*talented deer dog,*
*Jaeger*

stood and moved on, or point out a vacated wound bed. This all helps to build a picture in the handler's mind on how badly or indeed where injured, the missing animal is. Secondly, it helps bond the dog to the handler and vice versa.

The handler increases the length of the blood trail and now uses a broom shaft handle with a small square sponge attached to dab a bloodline and then preferably offers a deerskin and head as the prize at the end. As a general guide a six-month old dog should be capable of working a 500-yard trail 24 hours old. When the dog reaches the skin, it is a good idea to encourage the hound to rag the skin and always give him a treat and lavish praise at the end. By this stage, running an artifical bloodline should only be attempted once a week at the most. Continue with this work, but gradually increase the distance and add a couple of right angles and a ditch crossing etc, just to make it more interesting.

The use of coloured clothes pegs are ideal for marking out the trail, so that the handler knows were the actual trail is and can guide the dog back onto the line in the case of a bad check, or if the hound goes off the scent onto something more interesting. Laying blood trails in areas with a high population of deer is perfect as the hound is easily trained to ignore the more interesting fresh scent of healthy deer. When the handler is sure that his hound is wedded to blood work, then the track can be increased in distance,

less blood used and made a great deal more difficult in slow stages but again, do not over do it.

One excellent way of introducing realism into the equation is the use of scent shoes. These are simply a platform, strapped to one's boots, with the cleaves of a deer or boar attached. A small amount of blood is added to the cleaves and a trail is set by use of the scent shoes alone. Any manner of obstacles may be introduced, but as long as the dog gets success at the end and the training is not overdone, all will be well and the handler can take his dog to the field. An extension of training the dog in the field is to hunt up heart-shot deer that have run into cover and died. This is as realistic as it gets and opening up the found deer to give the hound a fresh, warm treat of heart, is real encouragement. The rest comes with work and experience gained in the field. Remember always to trust the dog and give them the benefit of doubt, as their noses are far better than ours will ever be. If your hound is regularly completing a 48-hour old, 100-yard false trail made with scent shoes, involving two right-angle turns and a ditch crossing, it's certainly capble of finding a wounded deer at three times that distance. Don't worry if your dog doesn't bay dead at a skin or carcase, this trait often manifests itself after the hound has run down its first wounded animal and if it never develops into a vocal marker, do not despair as modern GPS and telemetry collars negate the need for a vocal dog. For example, my bitch Jaeger, who has more than 70 true finds to her credit, does not bay dead at roe, muntjac or Chinese water deer, but she barks like crazy at red, fallow and boar.

On the whole, we UK stalkers are far behind our continental cousins regarding the use of deer dogs. Fortunately more and more of us, professional and amateur alike, are realising the benefits of working a dog on deer. Ethical considerations aside, a well-trained dog equates to more beasts in the larder, and an accompanying Fido can be a great companion during what is often a solitary pastime.

Deer dogs come in all shapes and sizes and elsewhere in the world many are bred for specific tasks when deer hunting. During their work many are often away from their handlers for quite considerable periods of time. In Sweden, hunters use a single elk hound for hunting moose. The hound, which is similar to a small husky-type sled dog, is cast off into the wind to locate and hold at bay a moose, enabling the hunter to stalk in to the bayed animal. In times gone by, the hunter was limited to the use of his ears to locate his baying hound, which had obvious limitations. Technological advances initially used in falconry telemetry were adapted to dog collars and quickly caught on. Improvements were made and soon radio-wave localising collars were also able to indicate if the dog was actually barking or, in the case of pointing dogs, a further refinement was the ability to indicate if the dog was motionless.

Another Swedish hunting hound, called a drever, is a roe-hunting specialist. This hound looks like a shorter-eared lemon and white bi-colour basset and is used singularly to move roe around their territories, until eventually a suitable animal passes by one of a number of hunters strategically placed in high-seats. The drever is a short-legged hound and relatively slow compared to much faster beagles and other higher standing hounds. Therefore, the drever tends to be more of an annoyance to the roe, who simply circle a figure of eight around their home turf, reluctant to leave their territory, which is covered by the waiting hunters. A taller, faster hound would be useless in this situation as the roe would just straight-line it into the next county. The advantage of a locator collar for the later recovery of the dog in this kind of hunting is invaluable.

The Germans were soon to catch on, and as they were world leaders in the field of bloodhounds for deer recovery, the localizing collar became popular very quickly indeed. Formerly, a bloodhound was trained as a *totverbeller,* which basically means to bark at the found game until the handler arrives. This is in comparison to the HPRs and retrievers, which were trained as a *verweiser,* which means to return to the handler and lead him to the fallen game. A further refinement of this was the *bringsel* method, whereby the animal is trained to return with a leather strap (bringsel) that hangs loose from the collar. This strip is then taken in the mouth when the game is located and the dog returns to the handler to confirm a find before leading him back to the game. This method was originally developed in the Great War for locating wounded German soldiers lost on the battlefield.

More recently, GPS technology has come into the equation and overcome some of the failings of radio transmitting collars. The main problem with the radio devices was topography. Radio waves, in layman's terms, are straight pulses that cannot go through hills, which has obvious consequences if Fido is on the other side of a mountain to the handler. But GPS is accurate and as it works by the collar signal being bounced back down to earth to the receiver held by the handler, topography is much less of a problem. It also reduces other problems, such as false signals – echoes and interference from electrical pylons and the like.

Unfortunately, localising collars have been difficult to source in the UK. Stalkers have had to look to Europe or the USA to obtain this essential equipment. But as more and more enthusiasts are taking up deer stalking and realising the advantages of a deer dog, it can only be a matter of time before we have a UK distributor for this type of equipment. I believe manufacturers have, until quite recently, overlooked the possibilities of the UK market. Although we have been one of the leading pack hound hunting nations for centuries, our formal packs have hunted over vast acreages of hunt country and have had professional huntsmen and whippers-in to drive wayward hounds back into the pack. In mainland Europe and the United States, there are many small packs hunting areas of limited acreage, where the rapid recovery of rioting hounds is essential. It is these sportsmen who have shown the demand for localising collars. Many small shooting packs that have sprung up around the UK, since a number of formal foxhound packs dissolved as a consequence of the ill-conceived hunt ban, could take advantage of this technology. ⊙

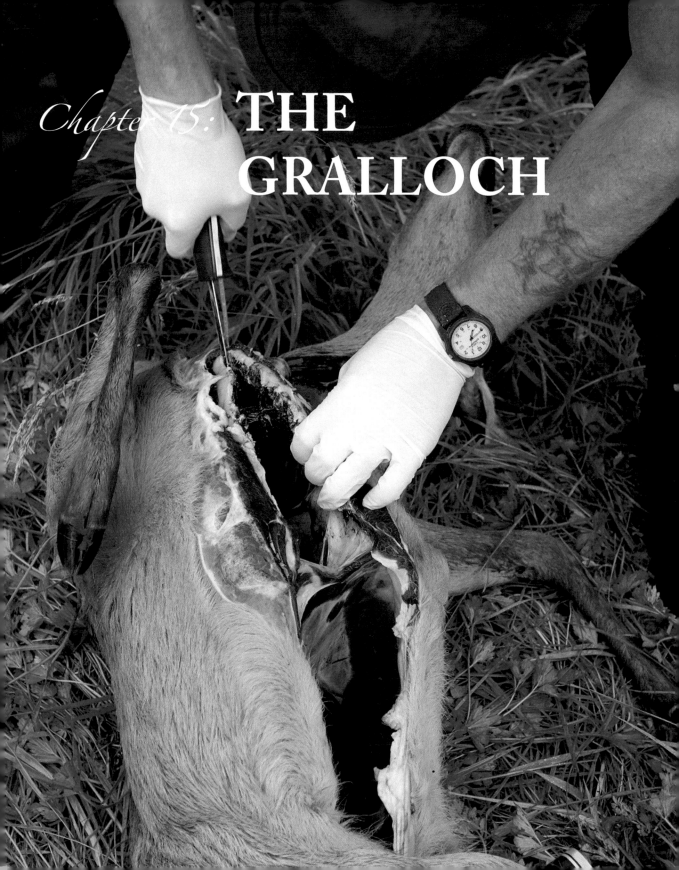

*Chapter 15:* **THE GRALLOCH**

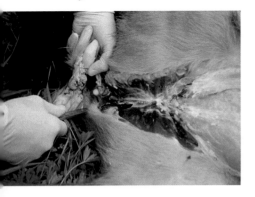

lways ensure your hands are clean - preferably use disposable surgical gloves and a knife that is easily cleaned. Cleanse the knife prior to performing the gralloch with a surgical wet wipe. If the gut contents have spilled into the stomach cavity, remove them as quickly as possible by wiping out the worst of the contamination with disposable paper towels.

**Bleed the carcase**. Once you have established that the deer is definitely dead by the lack of any eye response when touched with the stalking sticks, the animal should be bled without delay.

To bleed the animal, face it downhill if possible, bend back the uppermost foreleg against the upper leg, flat against the body and find the upper point of the breast bone. This is closest to the neck and easily found by probing with the finger. Insert the knife at this point towards the heart, working the blade until you find the aorta. The effect can be quite dramatic if the animal bleeds out well.

**Tie off the food pipe**. From the initial bleeding incision, cut up the centre of the neck, exposing the trachea or wind pipe. Close to and behind this is the oesophagus or foodpipe. Locate and separate the oesophagus from the trachea and cut it as high up the neck as possible, allowing enough length to tie a knot. Scrape the flesh downwards so the knot won't slip and tie off or use a cable tie. This prevents leakage of the stomach contents into the chest cavity. Using thumb and fore-finger, work down along the outside of the oesophagus, to the chest hole made when bleeding, to free the connective tissue without breaking the oesophagus.

**Open up the stomach cavity**. Turn the deer on its back, but keeping the legs apart by using your right leg, and make an incision with the knife, taking care not to puncture the stomach, running forward from the udder or to the side of the penis, up to the breast bone. Avoid cutting into the udder or the urethra behind the penis as this can contaminate the venison.

**Remove the stomach and intestines**. Turn the deer on to its side with the aid of a back leg, shake out the stomach bag and remove from the cavity. Carefully sever the connective tissue between the spleen and the diaphragm using your fingers. Leaving the spleen attached to the stomach, remove all the intestines, leaving behind the liver, kidneys, diaphragm, lungs and heart. Sever the connective tissue using fingers, to free the knotted oesophagus where it passes through the diaphragm. Grip the oesophagus and steadily draw the knot through into the stomach cavity and remove from the carcase with the gralloch.

**Free the rectum**. Gently squeeze any pellets in the rectum back toward the stomach and pinching close to the anus, break it free, keeping the rectum pinched closed. Remove from the cavity and bury the gralloch.

**Inspection of the carcase**. This should be carried out during and after the gralloching process. Any unusual behaviour in the field would have been noted before the shot. A cursory check over the animal during bleeding and in preparation of the gralloch is good practice; heavy lice infestation is often a sign that all is not well. The carcase and gralloch should be given a thorough inspection in the field prior to removal, paying particular attention to the lymph nodes for any signs of disease. The head and hooves should also be carefully

*◗ Cut carefully
and you can tease
the skin away from
the flesh*

*⟲ Locate and separate the foodpipe (oesophagus) from the windpipe (trachea)*

checked over at this stage. The pluck may be removed at this stage if preferred, but the carcase will be kept cleaner if this is done at the larder during the final lardering process.

Bury all traces of the gralloch in the field. If the pluck, head and legs are removed in the field, these are best taken away with the carcase, as a member of the public's dog digging up a deer head could cause a sequence of events that is best avoided.

Now you have to consider lardering:

**Removing the legs**. Locate the flat joint on the leg, cut the outer skin across and around the joint, crack the joint by twisting and sever the remaining connective tissue with the knife. Repeat on all legs.

**Opening up the chest cavity**. Score along the sternum with the knife and then invert the blade, cutting upwards alongside the sternum and cut along the score line, taking care not to let any hair come into contact with the exposed meat. Carefully saw along the sternum cut from bottom to top, using your thumb inserted into the bleed hole as a guide. Cut open the skin along the neck from the top of the sternum, all the way up to the upper throat.

**Opening up the pelvis**. (Hind or doe): remove the udder by cutting carefully around it, gripping firmly, and using a sharp knife, taking care not to burst the udder. (Stag or buck): cut down to pelvic bone either side of the pizzle, using angled cuts, as for hinds above, and taking extreme care not to cut the haunches. Saw through pelvis using two parallel cuts to isolate a small area of bone. (Hind or doe): using a knife, cut round rectum and vagina at base of tail and free from

the inside of the pelvis, gently pulling forward into the pelvic area. The whole anal passage, vagina and urinary tract can now be removed

**Removing the pluck**. After inserting chest-spreader between breastbones, carefully cut away the diaphragm, keeping close to the rib cage. Run the knife behind the pluck to cut the connective tissue close to the spine and cut through the aorta. Work down around the oesophagus, pulling steadily upwards and freeing it by cutting off at the neck. Pull the oesophagus down and away with the pluck, through chest cavity. Remove the kidneys and trim away any contaminated meat with a clean sharp knife.

**Removing the rectum and urinary tract**. Using a sharp knife cut down and round the rectum at base of tail and by cutting and careful manipulation with fingers, the whole anal passage and urinary tract can be drawn through and removed. The pluck should be carefully inspected for signs of disease at this point.

**Removing the head**. I prefer to hang the carcase overnight to let the neck stiffen and remove the head the next day, when hanging. If the head is removed during the initial larder, the neck curls back at an unnatural angle. Leaving head removal until the next day makes a neater carcase for the game dealer.

To remove the head, bend it head slightly back. Using the knife, make a horizontal cut across the back of the neck just below a line drawn between the ears and cut round either side. This should expose the atlas joint. Twist the head back against the joint to achieve dislocation of the joint. Trim away any tissue to free the head, cut back the jaw skin and make inspection of the lymph nodes associated with the head. ⊙

# Acknowledgements

There are many people to whom I owe a great debt of gratitude for their wisdom, experience and company over many years, but I would particularly like to thank the following:

The late James Thompson, a unique grandfather, Joe Stadler, Gordon Smith and Stephen Needler, for introducing me to shooting and the countryside.

John Waller, a school master in a million, for letting me skip class to go shooting.

Robin Fisher, Richard Crawforth, Dick Beadle, David Long, and Sir Lawrence Barratt, for their faith in me as a gamekeeper.

Melvyn Thompson, David Lloyd, François Croft, George Thompson, Tony Megson and Steve Kershaw, for sharing their skills and guiding me on a 'keepering career.

Neil Robson, Pete Law, Peter Kenworthy and Pete Lincoln, for their support and for backing me as a sporting agent.

Stuart Donald and Anthony 'Selwyn' Morris for teaching me how to stalk.

The 'two Tommies', Tommie Hynes and Tom Black from Ireland, for entertainment value alone.

Matt Brammer for his basic ballistics wisdom, to whom most of chapter three is credited, and Robin Horsfall, for his formidable sniping skills.

Mike Powell for his guidance through out, and his unfathomable knowledge on foxes, to whom most of chapter three is credited.

All the staff of *Sporting Rifle* magazine, with particular reference to Colin Fallon, Lynne Stephens, Kirsty Poole, and contributor Byron Pace.

Thanks also go to Mark Brackstone and Brian Phipps, for the use of their photographs and anecdotes.

James Marchington, without whom I would have never taken the path of a writer.

Wesley Stanton, Ruth Burgess, James Folkard and Nigel Allen, for their faith in me as an editor.

Charlie Jacoby, for his guidance and faith in me as a writer, editor, presenter and stalker, and for always being at the end of a phone when the shit hits the fan.

Ma and Pa Carr, for indulging a wayward son's interest in all things shooting.

Extra special thanks to 'Debs' for her patience, understanding and support during the long absences when her other half (Me), was away stalking something, somewhere, and for enduring countless episodes of her kitchen being commandeered as a butcher's shop prep room.

Dedication to 'hunters all':
Steve Sweeting, Jost Arnold,
Stuart Donald, Mark Brackstone,
Geoff Garrod, Paul Childerley,
Tommie Hynes, Wesley Stanton
and Charlie Jacoby,
without whom
none of this would have been possible.

*◑ The author,
stalking at Balmoral*